ADVANCE PRAISE FOR NEIL MILLER'S
SEX-CRIME PANIC

"Part Theodore Dreiser, part William Burroughs, Neil Miller's *Sex-Crime Panic* devastatingly mixes mordant sexual vaudeville and inspired, crusading reportage. Ward 15 East of Mount Pleasant Mental Health Institute *is* the American heartland, and Miller revisits its horrors and wonders with singular tenacity, verve, and tenderness. Novelists will envy Miller his gallery of vivid players, and historians marvel at his judicious narrative of official stupidity and violence."
—Robert Polito, author of *Savage Art: A Biography of Jim Thompson*

"*Sex-Crime Panic* is a powerful, well-written, moving story from our extraordinary history. Miller takes us back to 1950s Iowa, and we watch in disbelief for page after page the witch hunt for gay men in middle America. A must-read, especially for our young who need to be reminded of our tribal courage."
—David Mixner, author of *Stranger Among Friends*

"Miller brings a journalist's eye for telling detail and a playwright's ear for dramatic pacing to this chilling history of what happened to 20 gay men who were caught up in one of the sex-crime panics that swept the nation in the 1950s. The history told here has more than local significance because it was no anomaly: The Sioux City story was repeated around the nation."
—George Chauncey, author of *Gay New York*

"Through the lens of McCarthyism and the sexual hysteria of America in the 1950s, Neil Miller has masterfully re-created one of the most harrowing and shameful antigay episodes in American history, one that haunts us to this day. Part political exposé, part historical narrative, part true crime thriller, *Sex-Crime Panic* deserves a place on every bookshelf of journalistic classics."
—Chris Bull, Washington correspondent for *The Advocate*

SEX-CRIME PANIC

SEX-CRIME PANIC

A JOURNEY TO THE PARANOID HEART OF THE 1950s

NEIL MILLER

alyson books
los angeles | new york

MANUFACTURED IN THE UNITED STATES OF AMERICA.

THIS TRADE PAPERBACK ORIGINAL IS PUBLISHED BY
ALYSON PUBLICATIONS, P.O. BOX 4371, LOS ANGELES, CA 90078-4371.
DISTRIBUTION IN THE UNITED KINGDOM BY
TURNAROUND PUBLISHER SERVICES LTD.,
UNIT 3, OLYMPIA TRADING ESTATE, COBURG ROAD, WOOD GREEN,
LONDON N22 6TZ ENGLAND.

FIRST EDITION: JANUARY 2002

02 03 04 05 06 a 10 9 8 7 6 5 4 3 2 1

ISBN 1-55583-659-3

LIBRARY OF CONGRESS CATALOGING-IN-PUBLICATION DATA
   MILLER, NEIL, 1945–
      SEX-CRIME PANIC : A JOURNEY TO THE PARANOID HEART OF THE
   1950s / NEIL MILLER.
      ISBN 1-55583-659-3
         1. MURDER—IOWA—SIOUX CITY—CASE STUDIES. 2. MURDER—
   INVESTIGATION—IOWA—SIOUX CITY—CASE STUDIES.
   3. HOMOSEXUALS—IOWA—SIOUX CITY. 4 SIOUX CITY (IOWA)—
   SOCIAL CONDITIONS. I. TITLE.
   HV6534.S53 M55 2002
   364.15'23'0977741—DC21   2001045807

COVER DESIGN BY LOUIS MANDRAPILIAS.

For Tim Orwig and Alan Hesse

Contents

Acknowledgments xi

Author's Note on Names...xiii

Prologue xv

PART 1: TWO MURDERS

Chapter 1: A Boy Is Missing 3

Chapter 2: Enter Ernest Triplett................................12

Chapter 3: Truth Serum 26

Chapter 4: "A Lover of Liberace" on Trial 38

Chapter 5: The Body in the Cornfield 62

Chapter 6: Needed: 25 Sexual Psychopaths 76

PART 2: THE ROUNDUP

Chapter 7: Pinched...93

Chapter 8: Enemies Within 105

Chapter 9: Naming Names....................................112

Chapter 10: Morals Crusader................................124

PART 3: THE SEXUAL PSYCHOPATH WARD

Chapter 11: The Arrival.......................................141

Chapter 12: The Men in the Pink Shirts.................153

Chapter 13: Dancing With Greta Garbo 160

Chapter 14: Therapy 176

Chapter 15: Matters of the Heart..........................184

Chapter 16: The Power and The Glory 189

Chapter 17: Christmas in Sioux City 192

Chapter 18: Cured 193

Chapter 19: Closing the Books..............................205

PART 4: THE SECOND ROUNDUP
Chapter 20: Fighting Back 209

PART 5: THE RECKONING
Chapter 21: Crimes of the Past 1 237
Chapter 22: Crimes of the Past 2 248

PART 6: SEX-CRIME PANIC: LEGACY OF A TROUBLED PAST
Chapter 23: Sex-Crime Panic 259

Sex-Crime Panic Timeline.....................295
People Interviewed 296
Bibliography......................................297
Source Notes 299

Acknowledgments

Because it concerns itself with events that took place almost 50 years ago—events that many people wanted to forget—researching *Sex-Crime Panic* more often resembled detective work than conventional historical research. I am grateful to many individuals who made it possible to write the book. I am especially indebted to Tim Orwig, who shared his extensive knowledge of Sioux City and Iowa history and aided in crucial aspects of the research. His assistance was absolutely invaluable. Alan Hesse provided a home away from home as well as perspective and encouragement. Aleta Fenceroy and Jean Mayberry introduced me to Sioux City's lesbian and gay community and enabled me to make important contacts. Connie Jones and Brenda Collins provided me with hospitality and many helpful suggestions. Jackie Yamahiro offered vital information about Mount Pleasant Hospital and the sexual psychopath ward that truly made it possible to illuminate that part of the story.

Robert Bartels's book *Benefit of Law* was important in helping to frame my narrative of the arrest and trial of Ernest Triplett and the aftermath, and it provided crucial details. The book is essential to any understanding of the complexities of the Triplett aspect of this story. Essays by Estelle Freedman and George Chauncey enabled me to put the Sioux City events in the context of 20th-century sex-crime panics.

Jonathan Strong, Steve McCauley, Sebastian Stuart, Ken Rabb, Morgan Mead, Scott Elledge, David Gilbert, Michael Bronski, and Paul Brouillette all read portions of the manuscript and offered helpful suggestions. Ann Godoff made it possible for me to undertake this project. Scott Brassart nourished it, and Angela Brown provided a sharp editorial eye. My thanks to Eileen Ahearn for her assistance in many aspects of publication. My parents, Selma and Leon Miller, were supportive as ever. And I'd like to express special appreciation to my mainstay, Paul Brouillette.

I would also like to thank: Dick Bell, Mike Blim, Chris Bull, the Des Moines Public Library, Sarah D'Imperio, Arlene Donovan, the Elledge and Jackson families, John Gallagher, Helen Keefe, the Le Mars Historical Society, Karen Mackey, Jim Marko, Justin Richardson, Linda Santi, Ira Silverberg, the Sioux City Public Library, the State Historical Society of Iowa, Bill Sturges, Julie Swalve, Three Cheers, and Jerry Wyant.

There are also many people in Sioux City and the surrounding towns who spoke to me in confidentiality and whose contributions to the book were extremely important. I am very grateful to them.

Above all, I want to thank those men arrested in the 1955 and 1958 roundups who shared their experiences with me after so many years. I could not have written this book without them. More than anything, this is their story.

Author's Note on Names

I have changed the names of all the men brought in during the 1955 roundup as well as others who were patients in the sexual psychopath ward at Mount Pleasant—living or dead. I did this in some cases at the request of the men I interviewed, and in cases where I was unable to interview them, out of respect for them and their families. I also employed pseudonyms for the men arrested in the 1958 roundup, with two exceptions. One exception was Peirce D. Knott, because as a pediatrician he was well-known in Sioux City, and his arrest was prominently covered in the newspapers at the time; his case reached the Iowa Supreme Court. (I did, however, change the name of Dr. Knott's 16-year-old accuser.) The other was the teacher, J.B. Kuhler, who was also a public figure and whose conviction on charges of embezzlement made front-page headlines in *The Sioux City Journal*. Beyond those mentioned above, all names in the book are real.

One further comment on names regards the murdered boy Jimmy Bremmers and his family. Although newspaper articles and Robert Bartels's book about the legal case, *Benefit of Law*, all spell the name Bremmers without a final s, the correct spelling of the name is Bremmers; in fact, Mrs. Bremmers was asked about confusion over spelling of the family name when she took the witness stand during the Triplett trial. I have used the correct spelling throughout the book, except when quoting from other sources.

Prologue

Mount Pleasant, Iowa, September 29, 1955

This is how they remembered the day they got there:

It was late in the afternoon on the last Thursday in September, 1955. The sedan in which they were passengers turned off a two-lane highway outside a small town in the hilly country of southeast Iowa near Burlington. The automobile continued down a drive lined with shade trees. For a moment it had seemed as if it were the approach to an English country house, one like they had seen in the movies—the gracious avenue, the well-tended lawns, the benches dotting the grounds. But that was not the case. Instead the car halted in front of a stark four-story concrete structure whose institutional wings twisted behind in either direction.

Doug Thorson and Duane Wheeler emerged from the rear of the automobile and were led through an inconspicuous side entrance into the main building of the Mount Pleasant State Mental Hospital.

The men had been traveling all day from Sioux City. They hadn't eaten throughout the entire 10-hour journey, permitted to stop only to go to the bathroom. Doug and Duane carried no suitcases. They were dressed in the same clothes they had been wearing the day they had been arrested three weeks before and charged with conspiracy to commit a felony.

In Sioux City, Doug had been a management trainee at S.S. Kresge, the five-and-10-cent store downtown on Fourth Street, and Duane had been a student at Marie Ellis's School of Cosmetology. But that counted for little now. In the admissions area on the first floor of the hospital, a doctor was asking them the standard series of questions that was asked of all incoming mental patients.

"Do you know what your name is?"

"Do you know where you are?"

"Do you know what the date is?"

"Do you hear voices?"

He spoke in a Slavic-sounding accent so thick that the young men could barely make out a word.

The doctor seemed satisfied with their answers and scribbled down the same diagnosis for both of them: "Sociopathic personality disturbance. Sexual deviation (Homosexuality)."

Doug and Duane were outfitted with the state-issue clothing worn by all male mental patients: blue jeans and blue work shirts. An attendant dressed in white, except for black shoes, a black belt, and a black bow tie, ordered them to come with him. A large key ring jangled as he walked.

They went by elevator to the third floor. The attendant unlocked a heavy wooden door. He led the two men down a long corridor where they were surrounded by patients in various stages of undress who looked as if they'd been there forever. The walls were smeared with excrement. The smell was ghastly—a combination of urine and feces and disinfectant. It was the "untidy ward," where psychotic men who had regressed to a near infantile state were housed.

At the end of the corridor, they halted at another door. The attendant fumbled with the keys, unlocked it, and they found themselves in a second ward that was similar in layout to the first. Again, men crowded around them. But this time they were men whom Doug and Duane knew or had seen before. There was a man who owned the House of Beauty in Kingsley, Iowa, and another who ran a hair salon in Sioux Falls, South Dakota. There was a dance teacher at Arthur Murray's in Sioux City and a salesman who worked at the Younker-Davidson department store, next door to Kresge's. For a moment it seemed as if all the hairdressers and window dressers from northwest Iowa were there to welcome them. Doug and Duane had reached their final destination—15 East, the sexual psychopath ward.

They were there because they were homosexuals, "sexual deviates" in the popular language of the time. They were among 20 men from Sioux City and the surrounding towns who had been rounded up and declared to be criminal sexual psychopaths and sentenced to the state mental hospital at Mount Pleasant for an indefinite period of time—until they were "cured." They were there because in Sioux City, a little boy named Jimmy Bremmers and a little girl named Donna Sue Davis were dead, victims of two terrible sex crimes. These men had nothing to do with those crimes; the authorities never claimed they did. In Sioux City, indeed in the entire state of Iowa, however, the public was clamoring for action. Something had to be done. So Doug and Duane and the other men were arrested and put in a locked ward in a mental hospital far from Sioux City. They were scapegoats in a sex-crime panic.

PART 1: TWO MURDERS

SIOUX CITY, IOWA, AUGUST 31, 1954 AND
JULY 10, 1955

"Sioux City must be made the most
feared town in America for the sex deviate."
—*The Sioux City Journal*, July 12, 1955

A Boy Is Missing

When Jimmy Bremmers disappeared the year before, on the last day in August 1954, Doug Thorson was far away. He was in the service then, working air-to-ground on the president's plane at Andrews Air Force base. Duane Wheeler was in Sioux City starting cosmetology school. Of course, Duane read about the missing boy in the papers. Everyone did, you couldn't avoid it. But Duane was too absorbed with learning about hair color and the roller set and mastering the intricate art of the permanent wave. What did it have to do with him, after all? As for Jimmy's parents—they were building their dream house.

The afternoon of the day it happened, Joseph and Dorothy Bremmers were laying brick for the basement. Mr. Bremmers had taken a week off from his job. It was the Tuesday before Labor Day, and he had a seemingly uninterrupted stretch of time ahead of him. He hoped to make some progress on the house while the weather stayed warm and the days were still long.

The house was in a new subdivision, just across the road from the bluffs of the Loess Hills. At this time of year the bluffs were covered with tall prairie grasses and plants with names like wild rose and yucca and blazing star. The sumac that climbed the crest of the hills would soon change color, turning the landscape into a brilliant, heart-piercing red, if only for a moment. Today, a 13-foot-high steel statue of War Eagle, the Santee chief who befriended the first white men to come to northwest Iowa, looked out from one of the high bluffs across the Missouri River into the open country of Nebraska and

South Dakota. But in 1954 the War Eagle memorial was just a slab of stone, frequently vandalized, and the silty bluffs were mainly a place for beer parties and stolen kisses.

The Bremmerses were building their new house out of reddish concrete block, almost as handsome as brick but cheaper and easier to construct. The house would be solid, modern—ranch style, with a roomy garage and even a picture window. There would be plenty of space for the family's three children—Karen, 14; Patricia, 12; and Jimmy, who had just turned 8. There was no doubt about it: The Bremmerses were moving up in the world.

Mr. and Mrs. Bremmers were doing most of the work on the house themselves; the family income was modest, and contractors were expensive. Mr. Bremmers had been employed by the Metz Baking Company in Sioux City since the end of the war. He had risen through the ranks to his current position as stock clerk, checking the trucks as they left to deliver bread and other baked goods. At 35, he was a rough-looking but handsome man, with dark hair and large working-man's hands. He had labored steadily on the basement that entire afternoon. Mrs. Bremmers had gone home to fix dinner, returning at about 5:30 to drive him home.

While the new house was under construction, home was still the one-story bungalow at 2701 Cottage Avenue in a lower-middle-class neighborhood on the fringes of Sioux City's west side, where the Bremmerses had lived since 1944. The area was sparsely populated and almost rural in character: Cottage Avenue and most of the streets around it were little more than dirt lanes shaded by cottonwood and walnut trees. Across the street from the Bremmers's property was a hay field; there was a cornfield next door, and behind the house was rolling pasture. The nearby houses all had large vegetable gardens.

At dinner Mr. Bremmers joked with his son, Jimmy. A friend had asked Jimmy for their address, and as Mr. Bremmers later recalled, Jimmy had confused the numbers.

"Well, Jimmy, you gave him the wrong address," his father remonstrated gently.

"Huh, I did, huh?" Jimmy stammered.

Jimmy had a slight speech impediment; in the slang of the day, he was a little "dutch" or "dutchy." He was a quiet and obedient boy who never gave his parents a moment of worry; he never stayed out after dark, and if he and the boys he played with were planning to do anything beyond their usual routine, he always told his mother. Jimmy was beginning second grade at Emerson School the following Tuesday. His closest companion was his black-and-white dog, Specks, who was devoted to Jimmy and slept curled up beside him every night. Before Jimmy, Mrs. Bremmers had miscarried six sons; after all that pain and loss, he was particularly precious, the baby of the family.

After dinner, Mr. and Mrs. Bremmers returned to the new house to do some more work. It was a perfect late summer evening, cloudless and still warm, with one of those heavenly breezes that sweep across the Great Plains, full of fragrance and possibility. At the Capitol Theater on Nebraska Street, *Seven Brides for Seven Brothers* was playing. The Turin Inn at 11th and Steuben was offering a special on steak dinners, starting at $1. In the American League, the Cleveland Indians were five and a half games ahead of the Yankees, on their way to a first-place finish that they wouldn't repeat for 41 years. That day in Washington, D.C., the Senate committee investigating Wisconsin senator Joseph McCarthy's tactics in ferreting out alleged Communists in the U.S. Army was issuing a report critical of McCarthy; the full

Senate would censure him two months later. The Red scare that had gripped the country almost since the end of the war was finally starting to wind down.

Most nights, Jimmy went along with his parents to help with the house, but tonight he was going to visit his friend Joey Hamel, two doors away on Prescott Street. Mrs. Bremmers didn't give Jimmy's plans much thought; Jimmy's oldest sister Karen would be playing baseball with some girl-friends in the side yard and promised to keep an eye on him. Anyway, it was the kind of neighborhood where everyone looked after everyone else's kids. During the day, when their husbands were off at work, the women—none of whom worked outside the home—would stop by each other's hous-es for coffee and gossip. No one locked houses or cars. There was little coming and going or foot or automobile traffic. If there was a stranger in the neighborhood, everyone knew it immediately.

At the Hamels', a group of boys were gathered in front of a television set. Television was new in Sioux City in 1954 and still the object of much excitement. The Sioux City station was presenting *Make Room for Daddy*, an early version of the *Danny Thomas Show*; the Omaha channel, the only other one you could pick up in Sioux City, offered *Juvenile Jury*, in which a panel of five children solved real-life problems. Among the boys watching TV that night was Steve Counterman, Joey Hamel's cousin. He was 13, older than Jimmy, but he and Jimmy and Joey Hamel would still play together—"cowboys and Indians" and "trucks." Jimmy joined the group for a while, but he seemed restless. He kept wan-dering in and out of the house.

At 8 P.M., just as *Life with Father* came on, the phone rang. It was Steve Counterman's mother. The family was going visiting in Morningside, a neighborhood on the other side of town, and Mrs. Counterman wanted Steve to come along.

It was growing dark, and in the surrounding houses, lights had started to come on. As Steve was leaving, he saw Jimmy standing all alone by a fir tree in front of the Hamel's porch. Jimmy was wearing blue jeans, a gray gabardine belt, and a pair of high-topped shoes that his mother had bought him the Friday before; he didn't have a shirt on—it was that warm. Steve ran up the hill toward home, but something made him stop for a moment and look back. In the waning light he could still make out Jimmy standing next to the tree. He was just standing there, Steve would repeat later with disbelief. That was all he was doing, just standing there. They called good night to each other, and Steve continued on his way.

No one who knew him ever saw Jimmy Bremmers alive again.

After the war and into the early '50s, a lot of things went wrong in Sioux City. Just before Christmas 1949, a gas explosion at the Swift packing plant in the stockyards killed 20 people and injured close to 100. To this day, old-timers say that some of the survivors are still at Cherokee, the state mental hospital, somewhere between the living and the dead. In 1952 came the Missouri River flood, one of the worst in the city's history. And then in '53 the Floyd River overwhelmed its banks, advancing right to Fourth and Nebraska streets in the heart of downtown; 14 people drowned. The polio epidemic hit Sioux City very hard as well—almost 1,000 cases in Woodbury County in 1952, the peak year of the epidemic nationwide. Summer, so beautiful in northwest Iowa and so easy and carefree, became a season of dread because of polio.

In those days Sioux City was an important metropolis—the second biggest city in Iowa, with 83,991 people, according to the 1950 census. Established in 1854 as a frontier settlement along the Missouri, Sioux City owed its early prosperity mostly to the real estate and railroad boom of the 1880s and 1890s; within a decade its population had soared from 19,000 to near 50,000. During this period, the city's extravagant and now-legendary corn palaces were built. Great things were expected of Sioux City. It was going to be the next major metropolis of the Plains, "Little Chicago." Then came the panic of 1893, and the dreams were shattered. But if Sioux City's phenomenal growth came to an end, the stockyards and livestock markets established during this period continued to flourish for most of the next century.

Through it all, a feeling of safety and security persisted. This is the middle of the country, after all, where trouble always seems far away, on the East or West coasts—never here where fields of corn and soybeans extend almost to the horizon. Sioux City was a working man's town, a family town, where church and high school sports were the major recreational activities. People could leave their doors unlocked and their windows open. Everyone seemed to know everyone else; everyone was, above all, "nice." There was a veneer of culture: a symphony orchestra, community theater, band concerts at Grandview Park in summer, right out of a Midwestern dream; and two colleges—Morningside and Briar Cliff. The town had just celebrated its centennial the month before. It was filled with many young families like the Bremmerses—war vets and their wives and children—looking hopefully toward the future.

This was the 1950s, a decade of optimism. The interstate highway system was on its way, replacing Iowa's infamous "concrete cow paths." Sioux Cityans would soon be able to drive to Omaha—the nearest large city—in an hour and a half and to Des Moines in a little more than three. Problems could be fixed: Engineers dammed and rechanneled the volatile Floyd River; Woodbury County was one of the first places in the United States chosen to test the Salk polio vaccine. Eisenhower was president; he was a reassuring figure—he hadn't suffered his heart attacks yet.

But the sense of safety and security began to break down that late summer evening in 1954, when Jimmy Bremmers didn't return home. Things like that weren't supposed to happen in Sioux City in those days. Some will tell you that's when the town first really came face-to-face with the ugliness and unpredictability of the modern world.

Jimmy Bremmers was the object of the biggest search in Sioux City history. Beginning on Wednesday, the day after he had disappeared, hundreds of national guardsmen and troops from the nearby Air Force base combed the landscape a mile in every direction from the Cottage Street house. Sometimes they searched with their hands joined together, as if to ward off some unknown evil. An Iowa Army National Guard helicopter—with Mr. Bremmers as a passenger—buzzed overhead. On Friday, guardsmen patrolled all the highways leading out of Sioux City. The head of the National Guard search team declared that they had checked every cave, cistern, well, garage, barn, shed, and brush pile in the area. But they found nothing.

As the days passed without any sign of Jimmy, Mrs. Bremmers became increasingly convinced her son had been the victim of foul play. "I know somebody took him," she told *The Sioux City Journal*. "I don't think they'll find him anywhere around. Down in my heart I know Jimmy's been kidnapped." Her son had been so well behaved and obedient that there could be no other rational explanation. He had always obeyed her instructions never to take rides with strangers. "So I know that whoever took him had a struggle," she said. "A stranger would have to knock him on the head to get him into a car."

On Thursday evening, two nights after Jimmy's disappearance, two of Mr. Bremmers's brothers stood vigil the entire night at the Bremmers's home with the lights out. Their hope was that someone with knowledge of the boy's whereabouts might leave a note or come to the door. This did not occur.

Jimmy's friend Steve Counterman, who had seen him standing beside the fir tree in the waning August light, was particularly affected by Jimmy's disappearance. "It made me awful nervous when I found out he was gone," he said. "I wish I knew what happened. I pray for him to come back. Everybody's praying around here. I can't understand why he was just standing there."

Meanwhile, reports of sightings of Jimmy began to filter in. Detectives in Omaha received a tip from a certain T.A. Cooper of Woodward, Iowa, near Des Moines, who told them he thought he had seen the boy at a café in Cedar Rapids three days after his disappearance. A boy whose description matched that of Jimmy Bremmers had entered the café with a middle-aged man who was dressed in a worn brown suit and had a disfigured left hand. Cooper said the man ordered a dish of ice cream for the boy, and the boy refused to eat it. The man told the boy, "Eat what your daddy tells you." The boy replied sharply, "You are not my father!" In the end nothing came of the report.

In Friday's edition, three days following Jimmy's disappearance, *The Sioux City Journal* reported that the police were checking on the city's known morals offenders. There was a possibility, the newspaper wrote, that a "sex fiend" might have abducted the boy.

CHAPTER 2

Enter Ernest Triplett

That Tuesday, the day Jimmy vanished, Ernest James Triplett Jr. awoke at 8 A.M. at the Bus Hotel at Fourth and Douglas streets, as he had every morning since he had landed in Sioux City three weeks before. Triplett was employed as a door-to-door salesman selling music lessons and musical instruments for the Flood Music Company, so he didn't have to get up too early. The music store, located around the corner from his hotel, didn't open until 9, and anyway, a salesman didn't want to start knocking on doors any earlier. That day Triplett dressed in a pair of brown Oxford shoes, casual gray wash trousers purchased at the Salvation Army store in St. Joseph, Missouri, a mustard-colored shirt, and—the final touch—a Stetson hat. In his right pants pocket was a pocketknife and a dollar in change, all the money he had in the world. Triplett didn't have many possessions: two or three shirts, a set of underwear, and the pair of trousers he was wearing that day. He carried everything he owned in a shopping bag.

Triplett headed over to the Katz Drugstore on Fourth Street for breakfast, where he sat at the end of the counter and traded jokes with the cook, a Bohemian woman. He had his usual, the Four Star breakfast (eggs, bacon, toast, and coffee) for 29 cents. Then he walked around to kill some time until the Flood Music Company opened.

There were already people on the streets. Sioux City was bustling in those days, functioning as a regional hub for the hundreds of small towns and farming communities in northwest Iowa, Nebraska, and South Dakota known as Siouxland.

The commercial district was dominated by six- and seven-story office blocks—large, handsome sandstone and brown brick buildings, with an occasional ornamental frill and names like Davidson and Benson and Badgerow. There were 800 hotel rooms downtown, seven movie houses, and a county courthouse—an architectural jewel crowned by a leaded glass dome—that was the largest Prairie-style building in the country. Just a few blocks away, the stockyards and the packing-houses spread out along the Missouri River. At the beginning of each week, as farmers brought in their hogs and steers for market, the streets surrounding the stockyards were blocked by trucks; the area became virtually impassable. Sioux City was the fifth largest livestock market in the country; only Chicago, Omaha, Kansas City, and St. Paul were more important. By this hour of the morning, the city was already beginning to smell like a barnyard—pungent and oppressive but somehow familiar and comforting.

Triplett wanted to ask Mr. Flood for some lunch money. He wasn't earning very much at his job. He'd visit 20 or 30 homes a day, but he'd enrolled only 18 new students for Flood's music courses during his two and a half weeks at work. It should have been a busy time of year: School was set to open the following week, and parents and their children had their eyes on lessons. Triplett was working on commission: $5 for every student he obtained. The day before, he hadn't made anything at all.

Ernest Triplett was tall, with dull black hair that had no sheen to it. His skin was pale and unhealthy looking. He was suffering from an untreated case of syphilis. To those who met him, he was "strange," "flaky," "not real bright," and "unaware of what was going on around him." A man who had a couple of conversations with him at the time said, "If you had a scale of one to 10 he would be number one at the bottom in

13

terms of aptitude and intelligence." To another Sioux Cityan, he was "the creepiest person I ever laid eyes on."

Still, he was extremely gregarious, with an original sense of humor and a homespun way of describing things. In Triplett-speak, the Depression was "Hoover's time," a lawyer was a "good front," the police were "them boys," and the police station was simply "headquarters." He'd never gone beyond eighth grade in school; his spelling was abominable, and he could barely write a coherent sentence. Triplett relied on cunning for his survival. He would try to put something over on someone he was talking to, but it was so obvious what he was doing—obvious both to himself and to others—that there was a certain charm to it. He also loved to be the center of attention. That characteristic, above all, may have been his undoing.

Ernest Triplett was born 50 years before on a farm in Woodbine, Iowa, near the town of Missouri Valley, south of Sioux City. At 16, he began living on his own in Council Bluffs, Iowa, and Omaha, where he worked as an apprentice painter. After someone gave him a shot of morphine, he woke up in the army training post at Fort Mead, South Dakota. He went AWOL, spent four months in a military stockade, and returned to Omaha where he married a prostitute named Doris Spencer. There he worked at a carnival, a pool hall, and as a poker shill at a saloon. Doris continued to carry on her trade, sometimes giving the proceeds to her husband, sometimes keeping them for herself. Triplett didn't seem to mind. In fact, he was doing some of the same, hanging around an Omaha park where "fairies" would give you a dollar if you let them "suck your peter," as he later told an interviewer. A dollar would buy "10 sticks of hay (marijuana)," he said, which could "really knock you out."

When the Depression arrived, he and Doris hitchhiked

across Nebraska, learning to "eat off every sheriff from Omaha to the Colorado state line." They'd tell the sheriff they had no money and no work, and the sheriff would give them a meal and a ticket to spend the night at a hotel. Along the way, Triplett served a number of jail sentences for offenses ranging from vagrancy to pimping. Eventually, he and Doris went their separate ways.

After Pearl Harbor, he found himself in Portland, Oregon, painting battleships in the Navy yards, and he married again. He and his new wife bought a house, and he helped her to raise her three children. After the war, he found a job in Portland selling guitar lessons and second-hand musical instruments. It was the closest Ernest Triplett ever came to the settled, bourgeois life. Eventually, when his wife threw him out of the house, he went "on the bum," hitchhiking and taking freight trains as far east as Providence, Rhode Island, and working at odd jobs. He arrived in Sioux City on August 9, 1954, three weeks before Jimmy Bremmers went missing.

When Triplett first approached Raymond Flood, owner of the Flood Music Company, about a job, Flood turned him down. But Triplett was persistent. He'd hang around the store all day, and Flood soon realized he really did have some knowledge of the music business. When Triplett proposed going door to door to sell music lessons on commission, Flood finally acquiesced. What did he have to lose? For the first week or so, Triplett would travel by bus to various neighborhoods. Then, Flood bought him a '41 Plymouth, green in color but with the paint so faded and deteriorated that the gray primer was visible. Flood also helped Triplett get a driver's license. Flood and his wife, Mary, thought he was a hard worker; their only complaint was that they wished he dressed a little better—those wash pants he insisted on wearing to the store were just not the image the Flood Music Company wanted to project. Eventually Mr. Flood bought him a suit and gave him nine of his old white shirts.

The job was perfectly suited for Triplett. His time was his own and he had a car. He didn't have to pay for gas—a local service station owner owed Mr. Flood money for a guitar that he paid off in part by filling up Triplett's tank. Triplett could stop for coffee and a roll whenever he wanted. If he got drunk on the job, no one really had to know; one afternoon, in Homer, Nebraska, a prairie town across the Missouri, he drank a bottle of wine and slept it off in the car. Children and teenagers were in and out of his car all the time as Triplett demonstrated the guitar and tried to cajole them into taking lessons.

On the morning of the day Jimmy Bremmers disappeared, Flood gave Triplett a dollar for lunch, and the salesman drove off in the Plymouth in the direction of Riverside, a neighborhood of modest bungalows west and north of downtown with the Big Sioux River behind it. He called on a Mrs. Carter, who had expressed an interest in an electric guitar but wasn't home. Then he proceeded to North Riverside, stopping at every house where there were bicycles or other indications of children in the household whom he might prevail on to take music lessons. Again he met with no success. He stopped for a beer and then headed to Jefferson, South Dakota, about eight miles away, but had no luck there either. He returned to Sioux City, made some more house calls, mostly in the Military Road area, and returned to the music store around 5 P.M., just as it was closing for dinner break. He told Mr. Flood that someone who lived up on Military Road was interested in an accordion. Mr. Flood gave him one, and he put it in the backseat of his car, alongside the accordion he regularly took on his rounds.

Shortly afterward, he went back to his hotel for about an

hour, read the newspaper, and apparently smoked part or all of a marijuana cigarette. He returned to the Military Road area to call on Mrs. Deloris Osborn, in the hope of talking her into accordion lessons for her son David. But he drove past the Osborn residence by mistake, continuing on to the house of another potential customer, Mr. and Mrs. Arthur Meisch. The Meisches lived on the corner of Casselman and West 22nd, just a few blocks from the Bremmerses. There was something about the salesman that particularly disturbed Mr. Meisch and led him, the following day, to call the police. Triplett "was sitting in my front room, just as I am sitting here, with his legs crossed," he said. "He didn't have any socks on.... He wore wash pants and a summer wash shirt, but I thought it odd he didn't have any socks on."

Then Triplett drove back to the Osborns'. There, he stood on the front porch talking to 8-year-old David while the boy's mother was in the garden. David later said that Triplett grabbed him by the wrist. A moment later, Mrs. Osborn appeared, carrying a basket of tomatoes. She gave one to Triplett. Inside the house, Mrs. Osborn noticed that the salesman seemed nervous and wouldn't look at her in the face. Triplett left the house at 7:55. Mrs. Osborn was sure of the time because it was just before the commercial preceding *Robert Montgomery Presents*, which began at 8 P.M. *Robert Montgomery Presents* was an hour-long dramatic series, and Mrs. Osborn watched it without fail.

After talking with Mrs. Osborn, Triplett seems to have had some kind of encounter with Jimmy Bremmers, an encounter that he was to characterize in various and often contradictory ways over the next few weeks and months.

Later, Triplett returned to the Bus Hotel and took his accordion up to his room. Then he headed downstairs to the lobby to watch TV. According to one of Triplett's accounts, he caught the end of *Robert Montgomery Presents* and settled back to watch the *Liberace Show*, which began at 9 P.M. In another account, he switched channels between *Liberace* and a program about "a ventriloquist and some counterfeit money." The second story would have placed him at the hotel a bit later. In any event, once Liberace had played his last arpeggio, Triplett went outside, moved his car, and unloaded the second accordion. Then he went to bed.

Shortly after that, at 11:26 P.M., the Sioux City police received a telephone call from Joseph Bremmers. He and his wife had been searching for their son Jimmy for almost three hours, he told the police, and Jimmy still had not come home.

On Wednesday, September 2, the morning after Jimmy Bremmers disappeared, Ernest Triplett went to work as usual at the Flood Music Company. He was still wearing the same clothes he had had on the day before, a fact that annoyed Mr. Flood. Triplett went out on his rounds but by noon he returned to the store. He told the Floods that someone in the neighborhood had informed him that a small boy was missing so it wasn't a good time to be going door to door. Mr. Flood suggested that he spend the rest of the day at the store.

At 7:30 the next morning, Russell White Sr., the assistant chief of police, telephoned the Floods at home. White told Mr. Flood that someone had tipped off the police that Triplett had been in the area where Jimmy Bremmers had disappeared; the police wanted to talk to him. He asked Flood to keep Triplett at the store until the police arrived. Mr. Flood promised to do so. When Flood told Triplett that the police wanted to interrogate him, Triplett appeared unconcerned. Only the Floods were anxious; a police investigation of their door-to-door salesman could hardly have a positive effect on a business that depended upon the confidence of parents. Mr. Flood insisted that Triplett accompany him to a nearby store, where he bought him a new pair of slacks and a shirt. It wasn't until about 1:30 that afternoon Lieutenant William Dennison and Sergeant Tony Bucchino showed up and took Triplett to the police station for questioning.

Triplett remained in police custody for the next two weeks, telling a series of confusing and contradictory stories about his movements on the night that Jimmy disappeared. He had no legal counsel, and no lawyer was ever present at any of his interrogations. At first he told police he had run into Jimmy Bremmers, talked to him about music lessons, and then returned immediately to his hotel. Then he changed his story. In the revised account he claimed he had seen Jimmy walking in a ditch alongside the road and that the boy had told him he was running away from home. Triplett tried to discourage him and gave him a ride home on his front left fender. The boy went inside the house, put on a plaid shirt, returned to talk to Triplett, and then disappeared around the back, and Triplett never saw him after that. In yet another conversation, Triplett embellished this account to say that after the boy disappeared behind the house, Triplett drove toward the Riverside area, and when he approached the first hill before Riverside, he saw Jimmy Bremmers alongside the road hitchhiking. But when Lieutenant Dennison informed him that this would have been a mile from the Bremmers household, Triplett changed his story again, saying it was perhaps not the same boy after all.

"I am very interested in clearing up this murder and cooperating in every way to have it cleared up," he told the police. However, no body had yet been discovered, and so far, there had been no indication that Jimmy was the victim of foul play.

Throughout two weeks of questioning and two lie detector tests, Triplett insisted that he was innocent of any crime.

All this was extremely frustrating to the police officers who interrogated him. Russell White, the assistant chief, said that if Triplett told one account and was proven wrong, he would immediately change his story. White found him "as hard a person to interrogate as I have ever encountered.... I don't think anybody during my time of being with him and listening to him was ever ahead of Ernest Triplett on interrogation." What Triplett was trying to do is unclear. Certainly, he had the police going around in circles. And that made them all the more suspicious that Triplett was responsible for Jimmy Bremmers's disappearance.

The Sioux City police were not a group to be toyed with. In that sense, they reflected the city in which they worked. Despite its outward aspect of church and family, Sioux City, like many river towns, was a rough, wide-open place. The sobriquet "Little Chicago" had come to mean not just stockyards but also gangsters and shoot-'em-ups. Back in the 1930s, an exposé of Sioux City corruption had won the editor of the *Cedar Rapids Gazette* a Pulitzer Prize. Al Capone had supposedly hid out in Sioux City on various occasions. The sale of liquor by the drink was against the law in Iowa, yet it was legal just across the river from Sioux City in Nebraska and South Dakota. Although nominally a dry town in a dry state, Sioux City was full of bars, largely concentrated at the "sharp end" of Lower Fourth Street. Prostitution was available in that part of town as well, at three or four hotels located on the second floor above the bars. Across the Missouri in North Sioux City, South Dakota, were the racetracks—the pari-mutuel track and Sodrac Park, where visitors bet on the greyhounds; downtown hotels advertised taxi services to both. All these things gave Sioux City the flavor of the Roaring Twenties well into the 1950s. Corruption and payoffs remained widespread; a lawyer who first began practicing in Sioux City at that time described the place as "inherently dishonest."

In an era when police work was far more physical than it is today, officers were hired primarily for their size and strength. Assistant Chief White, Lieutenant Bill Dennison, and Sergeant Tony Bucchino were "tough as junkyard dogs," in the estimation of a police officer of a later vintage who was acquainted with all three. Chief of Detectives Harry Gibbons had formerly been a boxer.

Gibbons was not known for his intelligence or investigative genius; someone who knew him suggested that he "probably failed to duck one punch he should have." But Gibbons's uncle happened to be the commissioner of public safety. He made sure that his nephew and Russell White received what amounted to lifetime tenure. They were the two most powerful men in the Sioux City police department, and they had virtual free rein with anyone who wound up in their custody.

White drove around in a Cadillac convertible that was brand new every year. R.H., as he was called, was a well-known "ladies' man" and a natty dresser who rated an honorable mention on *The Sioux City Journal*'s list of "best dressed men" for the 1954 fall season. It was said that you could wake him up at midnight and he would look as if he had just shaved and oiled his hair. "He had the air of a handsome, dashing bootlegger," says one old-time Sioux Cityan. He also tended to be a bit of a "showboat," frequently arriving at the scene of a crime at about the same time the photographers did. White was apparently unconcerned if his lax hours, flamboyant style, and interest in female companionship raised eyebrows; he had lifetime tenure, after all. But

21

despite his reputation for style and suavity, when it came to Ernest Triplett, White was totally stumped.

A week and a half after Triplett's arrest, on September 12, frustrated police officers asked Joseph Matousek to "take a crack" at Triplett. Matousek was a private detective whose brother-in-law was a Sioux City police officer and who had helped the police on a number of cases. He spent two hours with Triplett on a Sunday afternoon, finding him "cooperative to the point of exasperation." In the course of conversation, Matousek suggested to Triplett that if he admitted his guilt in the boy's disappearance, probably the worst that would happen would be that he would be committed to the state mental hospital at Cherokee for three or four years. For his part, Triplett told Matousek that he wanted to be helpful to the police. If Matousek would just explain to him how the boy was killed, he would sign a statement to that effect, he said. Matousek replied that it would be necessary for Triplett to tell him how the crime was committed; if Triplett committed the crime, he should know how he did it. Triplett then replied, "I have no idea how the crime was committed."

Matousek left the interrogation as baffled as anyone else as to how to deal with him. But he also left the interrogation pretty sure that Triplett didn't know anything about what had happened to Jimmy Bremmers.

If the police could not get Triplett to confess, they were eager to prove a pattern of "immoral sex practices" on Triplett's part that might indicate at least a motive for Jimmy's disappearance. This supposition had already found its way into *The Sioux City Journal*, which published it in its September 11 edition under the headline "[Police] Link Man Held in Hunt for Boy to Sex Cases." The article quoted Chief of Detectives Gibbons to the effect that the suspect had been involved in "sex deviations" and had admitted to having been arrested at various times in connection with sex offenses. But it was not until a September 15 interrogation of Triplett by three detectives that the police really made headway. In that interrogation the questions the police asked had little to do with the disappearance of Jimmy Bremmers and everything to do with Triplett's sexual proclivities and practices.

Did Triplett commit an "act of perversion" with a man named Buster DuBois back in Missouri Valley, Iowa, when Triplett was 15? The police wanted to know.

Yes, he had.

Did he "go down on him?" the police asked, using that exact phrase.

Triplett said he had.

How many times?

Three or four, he said.

Did he do this with anyone else?

There was also a painter in town. Triplett admitted he "went down on him" three times.

Then there was his sister-in-law. When Triplett was 16 or 17, he had discovered the woman lying naked on a bed in his mother's house. They had indulged in oral sex. When his mother found out, she kicked her out of the house.

And, finally, there was Doris Spencer, the prostitute who was Triplett's wife for six years.

Did he "go down" on her during the course of their marriage? He admitted he had done so.

Did she "go down" on him?

Yes, she did.

The police officers couldn't get enough of this. They seemed to believe that all sexual acts other than those performed in the missionary position were equally perverted, with each kind of perverted act leading inexorably to the next, as marijuana smoking was assumed to lead to heroin use. The 1950s were a period in which there was an increased awareness of sexual variation; Alfred Kinsey's *Sexual Behavior in the Human Male* had been first published six years before and was an instant bestseller. In the most extensive survey of American sexual habits ever undertaken, Kinsey found that 72% of heterosexual men had experimented with oral sex with wives, girlfriends, or prostitutes at some point in their lives. He also found that 37% of the male population had had at least some overt homosexual experience after the onset of adolescence. But if the Sioux City police officers were even vaguely familiar with Kinsey's findings, they didn't show it.

The cops asked Triplett about "immoral acts" in more recent years, when he was "on the bum." There was one, Triplett admitted. In New York State a couple of years before, he had met a man while hitchhiking. The man took him to his "little home in the country" to perform a sexual act. But Triplett had his "premium." He insisted on $5, which the man paid. Yes, Triplett had gone down on him. The whole incident, he insisted, had lasted only about 10 minutes.

Under further questioning, Triplett admitted that while in Sioux City, he had invited a number of boys into his car as he made his rounds. But he insisted that he had done so only to sell them music lessons or to demonstrate his guitar playing. Nothing untoward had occurred, he said.

The police pressed him for more descriptions of immoral acts and Triplett obligingly described how, at the age of 9, he had been sodomized by an older boy on a farm outside of his hometown of Woodbine. What the officers saw in Ernest Triplett was a lifelong pattern of immoral sex practices—from sodomy to "going down" on his sister-in-law and his wife to (perhaps) the molestation and murder of Jimmy Bremmers.

Eventually in that interview, the police officers did get around to asking Triplett about the missing boy. He had seen a boy on the side of the road on Casselman Street the night that Jimmy disappeared, he conceded. The boy was shirtless and appeared to be 10 or 12 years old. It was dark and he was able to see him with his headlights. Triplett asked the boy if he wanted to take music lessons, and he said no. Then, Triplett said, he drove off.

He wouldn't admit to a role in Jimmy's disappearance— yet—but the cops were convinced that he had a motive.

The Sioux City police had found their "sex fiend." But what to do with him? They couldn't keep him in jail indefinitely based on admissions of consensual acts of sodomy and oral sex that, while illegal, mostly took place 30 years before. They lacked sufficient evidence to charge him with any crime; in fact, the body of Jimmy Bremmers had not been found. At this point, Triplett made things easier for everyone. On September 16, he voluntarily committed himself to the state mental hospital at Cherokee. He made this decision without the benefit of any legal counsel. In the view of law enforcement officials, Cherokee was a convenient place to keep him, at least temporarily. In Triplett's view, it was more comfortable than the city jail, and a place where he could avoid relentless questioning. But what he didn't realize was that he had fallen into a trap.

CHAPTER 3

Truth Serum

The Mental Health Institute at Cherokee was the largest—and considered the best—of the four state mental hospitals in Iowa. A massive brick-and-stone structure that resembled a cross between a Bavarian castle and a Victorian workhouse, it loomed over the residential districts of Cherokee (population 16,000), an hour's drive northeast of Sioux City. The hospital was founded in 1894 and served 31 Iowa counties; at its high point it housed 1,720 patients. In the 1950s most stays at Cherokee were long-term: Tranquilizers and antipsychotic drugs had not yet come into widespread use. Almost the entire medical staff was composed of foreign-born doctors unable to obtain a license in the United States. "We paid quite low salaries and had to take what we could get," admitted Dr. Willard Brinegar, superintendent of Cherokee at the time. Nonetheless, Brinegar liked to boast about the exotic, if not aristocratic, connections of some of his staff: One psychiatrist, a highly regarded Russian-Jewish refugee named Flora Ginzberg, supposedly had been married to a member of the Russian royal family who had been executed by the Bolsheviks, and she herself had narrowly escaped the Nazis; another, an Iranian neurosurgeon, Azizollih (Asa) Azordegan, was a first cousin to the Shah and 114th in line for the Peacock throne, at least according to Brinegar's calculation.

Dr. Brinegar, who became superintendent of Cherokee in 1948, was himself a somewhat dubious figure. A nurse at the hospital claimed that by the time he departed Cherokee some years later, he was addicted to Demerol and morphine. "He left in a straightjacket," she claimed.

An even more questionable character than Brinegar was the hospital's assistant superintendent and clinical director, Dr. Anthony Sainz. According to people who worked at Cherokee at the time, the Cuban-born Sainz was an egomaniacal and unreliable figure who created a sense of mystery about himself, ingratiated himself with Dr. Brinegar, and functioned as his "court jester." Sainz was infatuated with anything new and trendy. His car was always the fastest, his research always the most cutting-edge. When nuclear medicine came into vogue, Sainz put a sign on his desk warning DANGER: RADIATION. One doctor who worked at Cherokee at the time claimed that Sainz had stolen his residency certificate and affixed his name to it. (The doctor needed a copy of the certificate, and in those days, before the widespread use of copying machines, Sainz offered to take a picture of the certificate and then never returned it.) The certificate stated that the doctor had performed his residency at St. Vincent's Hospital in New York City. Later the Iowa state medical board became suspicious of the fact that two doctors at Cherokee were listed as having completed their residency at St. Vincent's, and Sainz was found out. According to Dr. Brinegar, even after Sainz had left Iowa, the chairman of the Board of Registration of Medicine kept asking him, "Where is Sainz?" and "Do you suppose we can get him in some way?"

Dr. Sainz was extremely interested in experimental drugs. He wrote papers on the subject, gave talks at medical meetings, and possessed a special license to use all manner of "investigative" drugs. A new drug, Thorazine, particularly interested him and would soon revolutionize the treatment of schizophrenia. He was also intrigued by a hallucinogen known as lysergic acid diethylamide: LSD. At the time LSD was new and not well known. It had been discovered in 1943 by a researcher for the Sandoz drug company in Switzerland and was introduced for the first time in the United States in 1949 at the Boston Psychopathic Hospital. In the 1950s, long before LSD became the symbol of the drug culture of the Vietnam era, the drug was used experimentally by various medical researchers and investigators who suspected it might be useful as a therapeutic agent in areas including alcoholism, obsessional neurosis, and the rehabilitation of criminals. (Drug companies were happy to provide free supplies to physicians like Sainz who possessed the special license.) In fact, between 1950 and the mid 1960s, more than a thousand clinical papers were published on the therapeutic use of psychedelic drugs, discussing 40,000 patients.

Dr. Sainz was extremely secretive about his drug experiments; few at the hospital, including Brinegar, knew exactly what he was doing. One patient who was a subject of Dr. Sainz's experiments was Ernest Triplett. On September 24, after being at Cherokee for a little more than a week, Triplett was given a 40-milligram dose of a powerful amphetamine called Desoxyn, injected for immediate effect. The following day Triplett received his first ampoule of LSD. Then, on September 27, he received a combination of LSD—this time via injection—and sodium amytol, a drug considered to be a truth serum. These drugs were not given for therapeutic purposes but in an effort to get Triplett to confess to a role in the disappearance of Jimmy Bremmers. (Such combinations of drugs were tested in the 1950s by U.S. investigative agencies, notably the Central Intelligence Agency, as part of efforts to develop "miracle" truth drugs; in fact, LSD's earliest experimental use by the CIA was as a potential weapon in breaking down enemy agents during interrogation.)

But Triplett didn't confess. Instead he offered the doctors

disconnected fragments that were obviously hallucinations—images of Jimmy Bremmers running down a ravine at the back of his house to find a friend behind a coal chute, for example. Triplett had no idea what he was being given; later on he commented that he had "got on quite a few drunks over there" at Cherokee and had seen "fabulous pictures."

As doctors at Cherokee were using experimental truth drugs to get Triplett to admit his guilt, Sioux City authorities mounted their final all-out search for Jimmy Bremmers. On September 28, the day after Triplett had received his second dose of LSD, authorities mobilized some 200,000 people in four Iowa, Nebraska, and South Dakota counties. During the course of the day, all businesses, industrial firms, and residential and apartment dwellers were asked to search their immediate premises and areas nearby. As this was happening, the National Guard activated three telephones to receive calls for any clues in locating Jimmy. That same afternoon, 60 Boy Scouts from South Sioux City and Homer, Nebraska, began a search on the Nebraska side of the Missouri; police officers checked the Missouri and Big Sioux rivers. Even a fortune-teller was consulted. The police told *The Sioux City Journal* that if this final attempt failed, the case would be written off as "the most perfect crime in the annals of the police department."

And then, at about 11 o'clock the following morning, quite unexpectedly and unconnected with the search, a crew building a snow fence came upon the remains of Jimmy Bremmers in a rolling pasture north of Sioux City. The body was discovered four miles from the Bremmers's home, just beyond the city limits, in neighboring Plymouth County. The upper part of Jimmy's body had completely decomposed. The boy's crushed skull lay several feet away, apparently smashed by a blunt object. His bones had been scattered about, probably by birds and wild animals. His hands were missing.

Within hours of the discovery of the body, three Sioux City police officers arrived at Cherokee and took custody of Ernest Triplett. He was brought by squad car to the Sioux City police station and then to the place where Jimmy Bremmers's remains had been found. Sioux City Assistant Police Chief Russell White drove. Lieutenant Bill Dennison sat next to him in the front seat; Triplett sat in the back, sandwiched between Chief of Detectives Harry Gibbons and Dr. Sainz, who had come along to offer a scientific appraisal of Triplett's reactions. No one had told Triplett that the boy's body had been discovered or where they were going. In fact, Russell White was the only person in the car who knew they were headed to the site where the body had been found; White hadn't even informed Harry Gibbons of their destination.

Just over the Sioux City line, they turned off the Broken Kettle Highway onto a graveled stretch called Ridge Road and drove through rolling fields and pastures. The day Jimmy had vanished had been mild, the air fresh and lovely, and everything was a glorious green—the height of summer in northwest Iowa; by the day the body was found, the weather had turned cool, the cornfields had been plowed under, and the hills were covered in the autumnal yellows of goldenrod and the reds of sumac. Ridge Road was a relatively uninhabited area with hardly a farmhouse to be seen; it was known for being a lover's lane. Because of the hilly landscape and the expansive views, couples could park and have plenty of advance warning if a car approached in any direction.

After about half a mile, the police car pulled off to the right side and parked next to a five-foot ditch. On the other side of the ditch stood a high embankment. Beyond the embankment was a barbed-wire fence bordering a field where, 20 feet farther on, Jimmy's remains had been found. Since the field sloped away from the embankment, the site where the body had been found could not be seen from the road.

Police officers White and Dennison and Dr. Sainz got out of the car and stood in front. Triplett and Gibbons walked to the bottom of the ditch. The two stood there for a minute or two without saying a word. Suddenly, Triplett bounded up the bank, and Gibbons followed him. When Triplett got to the top, he grasped the barbed wire and looked out into the field in the direction of the covered spot where Jimmy Bremmers's body had been found.

"What's that?" Triplett asked Gibbons.

"Don't you know, Ernie?" Gibbons replied.

Triplett didn't respond. He removed his hands from the barbed wire, took a step half way down the bank, and stood there and looked at Gibbons again.

"That's Jimmy," Gibbons said.

Triplett dropped his head and grew very pale.

"Well, I don't know anything about that," he said.

Triplett then walked back down into the ditch. At that point Russell White, Bill Dennison, and Dr. Sainz went up the bank to examine the area where the body had been found. White stayed at the fence and continued to watch Triplett. He noted that it was four minutes by his watch before the color returned to Triplett's face; when it did, two red spots were suddenly visible, one on each cheek.

The police had been observing Triplett closely throughout this entire process, and his sudden pallor—and the emergence of the red spots on his cheeks—made a big impression on them. They were also struck by the fact that Triplett had immediately headed for the only spot from which the body could be viewed—all of which confirmed their suspicions that he was guilty.

For his part, Triplett would insist that he had been distracted by some people taking pictures of the site from the other side. "Anyway, the doctor gave me a shot of medicine before we left the hospital," he would say later. "I couldn't talk to Gibbons. I couldn't talk to nobody. He'd ask me a question, and I'd get about two words out of my mouth, then I'd forget it all of a sudden."

In fact, before leaving Cherokee that morning, Dr. Sainz had given Triplett a powerful combination of uppers and downers: 40 milligrams of Desoxyn (speed) and 10 milligrams of hyoscine (a barbiturate). He also had injected Triplett with 500 milligrams of LSD. None of that was known, however, until many years later.

Mr. and Mrs. Bremmers went out to Ridge Road shortly after Jimmy's remains were found. They were not permitted to see the body—it was so mutilated and decomposed by that point—but Mrs. Bremmers identified the clothing found with the body as belonging to her son. Sightseers flocked to the site, causing traffic jams; the police pleaded with people to stay away out of fear they might trample the ground and destroy possible clues. Meanwhile, friends, neighbors, and relatives crowded the living room of the Bremmers's Cottage Avenue home to try to comfort them in their grief. *The Sioux City Journal* published a front-page photograph of Jimmy Bremmers's forlorn black and white dog, Specks, sitting on a hassock. The caption read, "Just Waiting."

With all the notoriety surrounding the family, Mrs. Bremmers was particularly concerned about her two daughters,

Karen and Patty. "We are worried about the girls," she said. "They both are afraid now to step outside the door." Karen, the older of the girls and the one who had been in charge of Jimmy the night he had disappeared, took the discovery of the body particularly hard. When she was told her brother's body had been found, she was watching the World Series on TV in the school auditorium. She screamed and passed out.

Meanwhile, Ernest Triplett's seemingly revealing behavior at the scene of the crime, in addition to his varying accounts about his supposed encounter with Jimmy Bremmers, made the police even more certain they had "the right man." Chief of Detectives Gibbons used that very phrase to the newspaper the following day. Triplett is "a very, very odd person," Gibbons said. "I think he knows more about the case than he has admitted."

Instead of being returned to Cherokee, the suspect remained in police custody in Sioux City, subjected to round-the-clock grilling. In comments to the press, the police described Triplett as seemingly "unconcerned about the whole thing." Police Chief James O'Keefe told the *Journal* flatly that Triplett was "a psychotic and a homosexual." By now there was little doubt in the minds of the police that they were dealing not just with a vicious murder but also with a sex crime.

An attempt was also made to link Triplett to similar cases around the country. In Auburn, Maine, 12-year-old Daniel K. Wood had disappeared on July 22, after telephoning home that he was heading for nearby Lewiston in the company of a traveling salesman. His naked body was found in the Little Androscoggin River 12 days later; he had been struck several times in the head and had been sexually molested. With much fanfare, two officials from Maine flew to Sioux City to interview Triplett. But they returned home empty-handed, convinced that Triplett had a solid alibi: He had been working as a dishwasher in Newport, Rhode Island, and then had hitch-hiked to St. Joseph, Missouri, where he arrived the day after Wood had disappeared. For its part, the FBI was checking out the possibility that Triplett might have been involved in the unsolved kidnapping and murder of 10-year-old Charles Mattson of Tacoma, Washington, years before in 1936. But nothing came of that either.

Meanwhile, the Sioux City police department announced that during the month of September the department's youth bureau had received reports of 46 missing children. Except for Jimmy Bremmers, each child was found and returned home. The town was becoming increasingly agitated. One Sioux City boy who was nine at the time—and afraid he would be the next victim—expressed the general mood of the townspeople. After Jimmy vanished, he said, "Whenever I had to go any-where, I would always run. I was a good runner too." He grew up to be a police officer.

It had now been more than a month since Ernest Triplett had first been detained as a suspect in the disappearance of Jimmy Bremmers. Triplett still had not been charged with a crime and had never seen a lawyer. At Toller's, the restaurant on Pierce and Sixth that was a lunchtime hangout for Sioux City lawyers, some of the younger attorneys could be heard grumbling that Triplett's rights were being violated. Stanley Corbett, the president of the Sioux City Bar Association, took it upon himself to investigate, paying two visits to Triplett in the office of Chief of Detectives Gibbons on October 1 and 4. There he found Triplett holding court next to a coffee urn and a bunch of sweet rolls. Corbett explained to Triplett that if he wanted to secure a writ of habeas corpus to get out of jail, the bar association would furnish him with an attorney. But

Triplett appeared uninterested. "If I decide I want to go, I'll call your company," Triplett told Corbett. When a somewhat mystified Corbett repeated the offer, Triplett replied that he had no place to go if he were released. "I imagine my position [at the Flood Music Company] has been terminated," he noted. Corbett concluded that Triplett was not being held against his will and that his rights were not being violated.

But Triplett later offered a different interpretation. By rejecting the offer of legal assistance, he claimed, "Right then and there I was trying to prove to the detective force that I wasn't guilty, and I figured they would turn me loose; but they made a steady customer out of me, a steady customer, head-quarters man."

In some ways Triplett actually seemed to enjoy himself. He had a roof over his head—even if he had slept on steel mesh at first, until Gibbons gave him a mattress. He got three square meals a day and all the cigarettes he wanted, just as in "Hoover's time" when he and Doris had hitchhiked across Nebraska, perfecting the art of "eating off the sheriff." At the end of each day Triplett would give his dirty clothes to Gibbons, who took them home for his wife to launder. "I sat about 10 days in Gibbons's office up there helping him drink coffee and eat rolls, and I was in there continually with him, day in and day out," Triplett said later, as if the main reason he was in custody was to keep the chief of detectives enter-tained. He told Corbett that when the Bremmers case was cleared up, he wanted to come back and work for Gibbons because Gibbons treated him so well. Then he returned to spinning his web of tantalizing tales to Gibbons and the other interrogators.

Whatever his motives, Ernest Triplett was in way over his head. On October 5 he was ordered to appear before the

Woodbury County Insanity Commission. Again he had no legal representation. He was committed—this time involuntarily—to the state mental health facility at Cherokee.

The following morning, October 6, at Cherokee, doctors injected Triplett with 80 milligrams of the amphetamine Desoxyn and three grains of the barbiturate Seconal. (He was not given LSD this time.) He had not eaten since the previous day. He was then interrogated three times by Dr. Asa Azordegan—putatively 114th in line to the Iranian throne—and by Sioux City police officers Gibbons and Dennison, who had driven out to Cherokee that morning. In the first interview, at about 10:30 A.M., Triplett repeated the story he had told the police previously about how he had given Jimmy a lift home on the night of the murder and then how Jimmy had disappeared around the back of the house.

The second interview took place at about 1 in the afternoon in a small cubicle with two single beds. Triplett sat on the edge of one bed. Dennison, Gibbons, and Dr. Azordegan sat on the other. Bill Sangwin, a hospital attendant, was also present. Azordegen told Triplett, "I want to talk to you, and I want you to know that nobody is harassing you or pushing you. Do you know that?" Triplett replied in the affirmative. And in that interview, Ernest Triplett admitted that he had taken Jimmy Bremmers in his car to the field just off Ridge Road and that he had started to unzip Jimmy's pants. He said Jimmy had tried to run away and then he killed him.

The participants took a short break and met again for a third time in another room. This time, attendant Sangwin placed a tape recorder on the floor under a desk and a microphone upon the desk itself. He turned on the recorder, apparently without Triplett's knowledge. There, under prompting from the persuasive Azordegan, Triplett repeated his confession.

Ernest Triplett remained at Cherokee for the next five months. It was not until March 3, 1955, that he was formally charged with the murder of Jimmy Bremmers.

CHAPTER 4

"A Lover of Liberace" on Trial

On October 7, 1954, the day after his confession, Ernest Triplett received another megadose of amphetamines, barbiturates, and truth serum (sodium amytol) and was interrogated for an hour. But this was the last time. Sioux City police were confident they had all they needed to put Triplett behind bars, and anyway, soon after, Dr. Sainz left Cherokee to take a job as senior staff physician at the Veterans Hospital in Iowa City. For the rest of his stay at Cherokee, the only medication Triplett received was penicillin.

Three weeks after his confession, Triplett was transferred out of the mental hospital's maximum security ward. Doctors determined that he wasn't psychotic, after all; the paranoid ideas he'd displayed when he first came to Cherokee (perhaps with a little help from Dr. Sainz's drugs) had vanished, so he would now be treated like any ordinary mental patient. At Thanksgiving, Triplett was allowed to leave Cherokee for three days to visit his family near Missouri Valley. This was rather astonishing, given that he had been committed to the hospital involuntarily and had confessed his guilt in the most highly publicized murder case northwest Iowa had seen in years. He returned on time of his own volition.

Throughout this period, Triplett grew increasingly hopeful that he might be released, and he went back to denying that he had ever killed Jimmy Bremmers. He had still not been charged with the murder, and the Sioux City police were continuing their investigation. What appeared to be a promising development came in early November when Lyle Walter Palmer, a 36-year-old former resident of Sioux City, confessed to police in Portland, Oregon, that he had killed Jimmy. Palmer had been a patient at Cherokee for 12 years—he had been committed in 1942—until he had escaped the previous summer. Sioux City Police Chief James O'Keefe immediately flew to Portland and interrogated the suspect for almost three hours. Palmer told him he had brought Jimmy Bremmers to an old streetcar barn on West Third Street in Sioux City, where he took him into a dark corner, sodomized him, and choked him to death. The problem with his story was that the streetcar barn in question had been demolished 25 years before. Palmer also claimed to have murdered a woman on the fourth floor of the Oxford Hotel on Lower Fourth Street in Sioux City after engaging in sex with her. The hotel had only two floors, however, and there was no unsolved murder of that description on the books in Sioux City. Finally, an exasperated O'Keefe asked Palmer, "Why are you telling me this story?" And the former mental patient conceded that his main desire was to get sent back to Cherokee so he could be with his friends. No charges were filed against Palmer, and no other suspects emerged.

As time went on, Triplett appeared to be adjusting to life at Cherokee. "Patient quiet and cooperative," stated a ward note dated January 1, 1955. "Eats and sleeps well, helps with ward work. Attends entertainments. Enjoys playing cards. Neat and tidy in personal appearance."

On January 28, 1955, Cherokee doctors recommended that Triplett be discharged and prepared to notify the authorities to that effect.

But if the medical staff at Cherokee was prepared to let Triplett go, the authorities in Sioux City were not so inclined. On January 28, the same day that the doctors recommended Triplett's discharge, Don O'Brien, the county attorney in Sioux

City, wrote to Dr. Willard Brinegar, the superintendent at Cherokee, asking him what, if anything, he had found of "the record of the confession of Ernest Triplett."

O'Brien, 31 years old, had taken office only a few weeks before. He had been elected county attorney—the equivalent of district attorney—in an upset victory. During the election campaign, in the aftermath of Jimmy Bremmers's murder, when *The Sioux City Journal* surveyed various candidates as to their aims if elected, O'Brien replied, "I would use every legal means at my command to protect young people." This may have been code for cracking down on homosexuals and sexual deviates in general—or simply a political platitude. In any event, the politically ambitious county attorney wasn't about to allow the confessed murderer of Jimmy Bremmers to walk away scot-free.

Dr. Brinegar replied swiftly to O'Brien's request for the record of the confession. A tape recording did exist, he wrote O'Brien, and he would give it to him, but only on the condition that O'Brien obtain a court order. In his letter, Brinegar questioned whether Triplett's rights had been violated; he also mentioned drugs. Eight days later O'Brien got the necessary court order—and the tape.

Still, preparations were going forward at Cherokee for Triplett's release. On February 14, Dr. Brinegar wrote the clerk of the Woodbury County Insanity Commission that the staff at Cherokee had determined that Triplett was "not psychotic and, therefore, not committable.... We must, therefore, in accordance with the law, ask you to come and remove this patient at your earliest convenience." A copy of the letter was forwarded to O'Brien. O'Brien immediately requested that Triplett be kept at Cherokee for another two or three days.

Two or three days stretched into two and a half weeks. Finally, on March 3, law enforcement officials filed charges accusing Ernest Triplett of the murder of Jimmy Bremmers. But to the surprise of almost everyone, the charges were not filed in Sioux City. Since Jimmy's remains had been found just over the county line in Plymouth County, charges were filed there in the county seat of Le Mars. The trial would take place in Le Mars, and Woodbury County attorney Don O'Brien would not be the prosecutor; the case was now outside of his jurisdiction.

All of this was somewhat mysterious. Why was Triplett being tried outside Woodbury County, where the crime had likely been committed? Was the fact that the body was found just over the county line really the reason for the switch? Or did the Woodbury county prosecutor know something—that the confession had been drug-induced, for example—that made him not want to prosecute? In any event, O'Brien transferred all his information on Triplett, including the tape, to Bill Sturges, the Plymouth County attorney.

The day the charges were filed, the Plymouth county sheriff arrived at Cherokee to take Triplett into custody. Triplett was brought to Le Mars to appear before the justice of the peace and removed to the Plymouth County jail.

On April 12, after hearing the testimony of 25 witnesses, the Plymouth County grand jury indicted Triplett for murder. The indictment did not specify any specific degree of murder, giving the prosecution leeway to attempt to prove the defendant guilty of murder in the first degree. In Iowa, at the time, first degree murder was punishable by hanging. Although Triplett did not appear before the grand jury in person, the officers who saw him in jail described him as "pale, wan, weak, and thin." At his arraignment six days later, Triplett pleaded not guilty.

The trial of Ernest Triplett was the most sensational event to take place in the town of Le Mars since the Farmer's

Holiday movement of the Great Depression. Back then, on April 27, 1933, a mob of 300 to 400 farmers, enraged at foreclosures of farms by banks and insurance companies, dragged district judge C.C. Bradley from his Le Mars courtroom and took him to a crossroads a mile and a half southeast of town. There, they demanded that Bradley promise not to sign any more mortgage foreclosures. When he refused he was blindfolded and covered with grease and dirt, and a half-inch rope was placed tightly around his neck. The crowd eventually scattered, and the son of a local clergyman drove him back to his office. The following day the governor declared martial law in Plymouth County and sent in National Guard troops.

The origins of Le Mars itself were more genteel. A pleasant and prosperous town of some 8,000 people about a half hour's journey by car from Sioux City, it was originally settled in the 1880s by a London-based land company that recruited the second sons of well-to-do English families to farm in the surrounding area. By 1891, at the height of the boom years in northwest Iowa, Le Mars was the third largest city in the state, boasting an opera house and a polo team. The British aristocrats preferred horse racing and pubs to farming, however, and soon departed. But they did leave one important legacy: Le Mars increasingly gained a reputation as the seat of the "wettest" county in Iowa. In 1955 Le Mars was the scene of continuing strife between the young and newly elected Iowa attorney general, Dayton Countryman, and the young and newly elected Plymouth County attorney, Bill Sturges, over raids by state troopers on Plymouth County pubs. Countryman was determined to make Iowa "cracker dry," as the expression went, and Sturges was equally determined to uphold the county's proud "wet" traditions.

The decision to try the Triplett case in Plymouth County meant that the prosecution fell to the 27-year-old Sturges. Until that point, Sturges had had no contact with the case. More importantly, he had never before prosecuted a criminal case. A native of Le Mars, where his father had been county attorney during the time of the Farmer's Holiday, Sturges had graduated from law school only the previous June. For Sturges, the winter of 1955 was eventful: He took office on January 3, got married on February 3, and on March 3 charged Ernest Triplett with murder. As county attorney, he was earning $1,500 a month and had no assistants or paralegals. "The Triplett case was dumped in my lap," Sturges said years later. "I came to it late. I didn't get a lot of help from the Sioux City police. Every police officer wanted to be a hero. They were jealous of the others. They wouldn't tell the others the evidence they had."

Sturges was aware of the difficulties with the prosecution's case—one of which was the long period Triplett had spent in police custody without a lawyer or being charged. That might not be enough to get the case thrown out, but it certainly didn't look good. In addition, the evidence against Triplett, if not exactly weak, was problematic. There was the tape-recorded confession, of course, as well as Triplett's odd behavior at the site where Jimmy Bremmers's body had been found. There were the contradictory stories the defendant had told the police. But that was essentially it. There was no physical evidence—no fingerprints or blood stains in Triplett's car, no blood stains on his clothing, no murder weapon, no proof that Triplett had even been on Ridge Road the night of August 31. If the confession could be tarnished in any way, the prosecution's case could collapse. And Sturges was unaware of how tarnished the confession really was; no one had bothered to tell him that Triplett had been given mind-altering drugs at Cherokee.

Aware of his own lack of trial experience, Sturges asked his nemesis, Attorney General Countryman, to appoint a special prosecutor to assist him. But the attorney general's office informed him that it had already used up its appropriations for such purposes. So Sturges prevailed upon a Sioux City attorney, Robert Beebe, to help prosecute the case, and the Plymouth County board of supervisors named Beebe a special assistant county attorney. The 41-year-old Beebe had been practicing law in Sioux City since 1940 and had been an FBI agent as well as an assistant county attorney. He had a good deal of experience as a prosecutor as well as a reputation for being professional and thorough. When Sturges first approached him, Beebe reacted cautiously. "That guy was kept in jail too long!" he said. But he soon relented.

Then there was the question of who would defend Ernest Triplett. Public defenders didn't exist in Iowa in those days, and the itinerant music salesman who had been arrested with less than a dollar in his pocket and all his worldly goods in a paper bag couldn't afford a lawyer on his own. Finally, Thomas O. Tacy, a 68-year-old attorney from Council Bluffs, not far from where Triplett's family lived, stepped forward. As a court-appointed lawyer, he would receive $20 a day. Tacy had a reputation for courtroom oratorical "stem-winders"; *The Le Mars Globe-Post* constantly referred to him as "the Clarence Darrow of the Midwest." (That label made little sense since Darrow, the most famous defense attorney of his time, was born in Ohio and had practiced law in Chicago.) A former schoolteacher, Tacy had never attended law school. He had studied for the bar in a Council Bluffs law office, which was permitted under Iowa law in those days. In 1951, however, Tacy lost his license to practice. In four different cases, he had taken fees from clients but had failed to perform legal services in return. Although he regained his license two years later, his reputation had suffered greatly. Sturges suspected that Tacy had taken on the Triplett case in an effort to reestablish his career. Rumors also circulated that he drank.

Jury selection began on Monday, June 6, 1955, in the same courtroom in Le Mars from which the rebellious farmers had removed Judge Bradley 22 years before. The Plymouth County courthouse, which sits in the middle of a residential neighborhood of frame houses and wide lawns, is an impressive building, like many small-town Iowa courthouses. Built in 1901, it is constructed of red sandstone in a beaux arts style, with Corinthian columns and a grand stairway that leads to the main entrance.

Inside the second-floor courtroom, with its high ceilings, elaborate moldings, and floor-to-ceiling windows, the prosecution and defense presented a study in contrasts. Prosecutors Beebe and Sturges both sported crew cuts, presenting an impression of youth and energy and a "straight-arrow" approach to the law and public morals. Defense attorney Tacy, who could have been Sturges's grandfather, cut an old-fashioned courthouse figure with his bow ties and white hair. Still, there was a shabbiness about him. His suits didn't fit, and one local wag thought he looked as if he had a notary seal in one jacket pocket and his lunch in the other. As for Triplett, he made his best effort to appear respectable. He dressed in a suit and tie and, even while slumped in his chair—his usual pose—he appeared more robust than when he had been indicted two months before. If Sturges and Beebe looked straight out of a promotional ad for the Boy Scouts and Tacy out of a production of *Inherit the Wind* (the Clarence Darrow connection), Triplett gave the impression of a character from one of William Burroughs's novels. In fact, Burroughs probably would have been drawn to Triplett—the marijuana smoking, the transgressive sex, the vagabond lifestyle.

District Judge R.G. Rodman Jr. presided over the case. In his late 50s, the balding, freckle-headed Rodman was a colorful figure with a reputation for plain speaking. He had just one leg, which he never let inhibit him in any way. Sturges recalled going to Rodman's house one day on a legal matter to find the judge up on the roof doing some shingling. He swung his leg around and practically bounded down the ladder. Rodman had been the county attorney in nearby Cherokee County during the period of the Farmer's Holiday movement. When the angry mob of farmers went looking for Judge Bradley, they stopped at the courthouse in the town of Cherokee first, thinking he might be there. Frustrated at their inability to find the judge, they pushed their way into Rodman's office. Rodman, so the story goes, removed two six-shooters from his desk drawer, pointed them in the direction of the mob, and announced, "You'll probably get me, but I'll get 12 of you first!" The farmers made a speedy exit and headed for Le Mars, where they found Judge Bradley and put the noose around his neck.

Rodman took a stern approach to the Triplett trial. At the beginning of the proceedings, he announced that children under 18 would be barred from the courtroom since the testimony might be too explicit. He did urge parents of young children to come and view the trial, however. No matter who killed Jimmy Bremmers, he said, the case offered an important lesson for parents to make sure their children stayed away from strangers.

The jury pool was quickly whittled down. When the panel of seven men and seven women (including alternates) was finally chosen, it included an Iowa Public Service lineman, a resort operator, a livestock feeder, a poultry raiser, and four farm wives. Most of the farmers in the original jury pool were dismissed—they had more important things to do. All but one of the jurors was married, with children or grandchildren.

The trial opened on Wednesday, June 8. The weather was comfortable, with the temperature in the 60s. On that first day, the courtroom was not particularly crowded, though the crowds eventually swelled during the course of the trial. Some of the parents whom Judge Rodman had urged to attend were present, however, as well as a cameraman from a Sioux City television station; the trial marked the first time that TV cameras were permitted in an Iowa courtroom.

In his opening argument Bob Beebe laid out the prosecution's case. The prosecutors would prove the scenario set forth in Triplett's tape-recorded confession: that the defendant had made sexual advances toward Jimmy Bremmers, that the boy had tried to run away, and that Triplett had killed him. And Beebe offered a tantalizing preview of what the jury would hear when the tape was played: how Triplett had "loved up" Jimmy and tried to unzip his trousers. Clearly, Triplett's sexual predilections would play a major role in the prosecution's case. They expected this to play well in a small town where the jurors were all good, church-going people.

In his remarks, Tacy framed the defense arguments in loftier and less emotional terms, emphasizing that Triplett's rights had been violated during his long stay in police custody and that his confession was of questionable validity.

A parade of witnesses took the stand for the prosecution. Woodbury County Coroner Thomas Coriden told the jury that a blow from a hard object was most likely responsible for Jimmy's death. He also revealed that when the boy's body was found, his trousers were unzipped an inch from the top. Arthur Meisch described how, on the night of the murder, Triplett had come to his house to sell him music lessons for his son and raised Meisch's suspicions by not wearing socks. Thirteen-year-old Steve Counterman related in tender terms his last glimpse of Jimmy. Mr. and Mrs. Bremmers recalled their last evening with their son.

In his cross-examination, Tacy was particularly harsh on Mr. Bremmers, asking him point blank if he had killed Jimmy. Trying to portray Mr. Bremmers as a greedy man who had perhaps killed his son for money, he questioned him about the insurance policies he had taken out on his children. He also alluded to the fact that Mr. Bremmers had sued *The Sioux City Journal* after the newspaper had published a gruesome picture of Jimmy's body. But Tacy made little headway with this approach, beyond generating increased sympathy for the grieving parents. And if there was a truly dramatic moment that first day of the trial, it came during the testimony of Plymouth County Coroner S.H. Luken. When Luken stated that all parts of Jimmy's mutilated body had been found except for the hands, the entire courtroom could see Triplett flush a deep red.

Over the next few days, a number of Sioux City police officers testified for the prosecution, charting the twists and turns of Triplett's stories during his days in police custody. Assistant Police Chief Russell White detailed the defendant's reactions at the site where Jimmy Bremmers's body had been found—his paleness and the two red spots that appeared on his cheeks. "I don't believe the reactions of an innocent party would be the same as Ernest Triplett's out at the scene," he said.

The officer who spent the most time on the stand was Lieutenant William A. Dennison. Tall and heavyset with thinning hair, Dennison had been on the police force for 20 years.

Like his colleague Russell White, he had made honorable mention on *The Sioux City Journal*'s list of "best dressed men." One Lower Fourth Street bar owner of the period recalled that Dennison telephoned him regularly to ask him to pick up his shirts at the dry cleaners across the street. The bar owner obliged, but Dennison never offered to reimburse him; footing the dry cleaning bill for a well-dressed cop was part of the price of running a tavern in Sioux City. In the courtroom, Dennison was calm and deliberate in his manner and continually paused to consider every question defense attorney Tacy put to him. This drove Tacy to distraction.

In one of the trial's lighter moments, Tacy questioned the police lieutenant about an interest his wife had in a Sioux City establishment, Ye Old Tavern. "Does your wife have a license to sell beer?" Tacy demanded.

"We sell root beer," said Dennison.

"But it is called a tavern, isn't it?" Tacy persisted.

"That's because we sell tavern sandwiches," replied the policeman. (A "tavern sandwich" is Iowa lingo for a loose-meat sandwich, a sloppy joe.)

Dennison then went on to explain that they hadn't had a beer license for four years. Convinced that, despite its name, Ye Old Tavern was "cracker dry," Tacy moved on to weightier matters.

Dennison's most important role at the trial was to link the defendant to both marijuana use and to "unnatural sexual practices." So Dennison told the court that, in their conversations, Triplett had admitted to smoking marijuana regularly. According to what Triplett had told Dennison, marijuana wasn't hard to find—the plants "grew along the highways and railroad tracks, and you could pluck off the leaves and put them in your hat band and in two or three days' time that they were dried out enough to smoke." (Iowa marijuana,

49

known as "ditch weed," had been planted by farmers during World War II as a source for rope, out of fear that foreign hemp sources might be cut off by the Japanese.) Dennison testified that Triplett had admitted to probably smoking a marijuana cigarette or a part of one on the evening that Jimmy had disappeared. Over heated defense objections, Beebe pressed him on the subject:

Beebe: Mr. Dennison, did you have any further conversations with Mr. Triplett concerning his use of marijuana?

Dennison: Yes, I did.

Beebe: What did you ask him?

Dennison: I asked him what effect the smoking of marijuana had on his physical condition.

Beebe: What was his answer?

Dennison: He said it stimulated him sexually.

Beebe: Did you have any further discussion?

Dennison: I did.

Beebe: What was that?

Dennison: About whether his sexual desires pertained to men or women.

Beebe: What was his answer?

Dennison: He said that he had committed acts of perversion with both sexes.

Dennison's testimony enabled the prosecution to bring out a motive for the slaying: a "reefer madness" that had inflamed Triplett's libido and perverted sexual desires and led him to attempt to seduce Jimmy Bremmers; when Jimmy resisted, Triplett killed him. Moreover, both Dennison and Harry Gibbons testified that in interviews on the day of his confession,

Triplett had told them he had intended to commit an act of sodomy on Jimmy the evening he killed him.

Other testimony appeared to confirm Triplett's sexual interest in young children. Eight-year-old David Osborn told the court that Triplett had put his hand on his wrist when he had come to his house to sell music lessons. The implication was that Triplett had tried to abduct him but failed when David's mother suddenly appeared; unsuccessful in that attempt, Triplett moved on to Jimmy Bremmers. And late in the trial came the testimony of Mrs. Luella Edwards, who stated she had complained to Mr. Flood, Triplett's boss, that Triplett had attempted to persuade children to get into the car with him, "and he would play his music and say, 'Oh, come get on my knee,' and so forth."

The prosecution didn't have much trouble proving that Triplett was immoral. But harder evidence was needed, and the prosecution provided this with the intensely awaited tape recording of Triplett's confession. After much sparring over its admissibility, on the sixth day of the trial, Monday, June 13, the recording was finally played. This was the first time a tape had been played as evidence in an Iowa courtroom. As a piece of legal theater, however, it was far from a success. For one thing, the tape was extremely difficult to understand. There was a great deal of background noise, apparently the result of previous recordings that had not been completely erased. The recording was overmodulated, and Triplett's slurred speech made his answers difficult to make out.

In the courtroom, Sturges asked repeatedly for parts of the tape to be replayed so the court reporter could take down every word and identify who was speaking. *The Le Mars Globe-Post* noted that "Every time the tape was run backward for such reruns, it sounded like a Donald Duck recording."

Eventually, the recording was successfully transcribed, and

51

Judge Rodman asked that the transcript of the confession be read to the jury. In the recording, Dr. Asa Azordegan led Triplett through the events after Triplett brought Jimmy in his car to Ridge Road:

Azordegan: As soon as you stop the car, now tell me everything you told me before. (Pause.) You stop the car... What happened?...

Triplett: Well, I go around the car to where he is...and...we stand there talking at the edge of the car.

Azordegan: Good. Are you playing with the boy?

Triplett: Well...yes.

Azordegan: What kind of play was it? (Slight pause.) Kiss him. Did you play with his hair?

Triplett: I kissed him and loved him up, and he didn't seem to mind so much.

Azordegan: I don't get it. What happened?

Triplett: He didn't seem to mind so much.

Azordegan: And what happened later?

Triplett: It seems to me I can't exactly tell you what happened. The picture...'cause my mind is not clear on it.

Azordegan: But you do remember you started to open his pants?

Triplett: Yes.

Azordegan: For what intention did you open his pants?

Triplett: Whether I thought he was girl or a boy I didn't know.

Under Azordegan's prodding, Triplett related how Jimmy began to run away toward the fence, how Triplett ran after him and grabbed him and hit him with his hand, and the boy fell on a stone. Although Azordegan tried to encourage Triplett to state that he hit him with something other than his hand, Triplett was not forthcoming on this point. The tape continued:

Azordegan: Can you tell us, after he fell down, you found him dead?
Triplett: No, I didn't know he was dead.
Azordegan: How did you find him?
Triplett: Lying on his face.
Azordegan: Uh-uh. Crying? Make noise?
Triplett: No.
Azordegan: Without any noise?
Triplett: Yes.
Azordegan: How did you find he was dead?
Triplett: Well, I didn't. I just took him, put him through the fence and over there and let him lay.
Azordegan: Let him lay?
Triplett: Yes.

It was devastating stuff, and the best that Tacy could do was to try to cast doubt on Triplett's state of mind when the tape was recorded. In his cross-examination of Dennison, Tacy pressed him on this point: Could Dr. Azordegan have given Triplett sedation or drugs or "a sort of brainwashing"? The police lieutenant was adamant. He knew nothing about any drugs and wouldn't even admit that Triplett sounded any differently on the tape than he did in his normal manner of speaking.

Later in the trial, when Triplett took the stand in his own defense, Tacy brought up the subject again, asking why his voice on the tape sounded different than in the courtroom. Triplett conceded that on the tape he spoke in a "deeper, sleepy voice, and I did notice there was something wrong there in particular with that."

Tacy asked whether he had felt sleepy at the time.

"Well, I didn't feel natural, that I'll grant you," the defendant replied.

Despite this line of questioning, Tacy never presented any direct evidence that Triplett was under the influence of drugs when he confessed or when he was taken to the site of Jimmy Bremmers's body. Even though he had a waiver from Triplett to do so, Tacy never went to Cherokee to examine the records of Triplett's treatment. Dr. Azordegan never appeared as a witness—he was out of the country at the time of the trial—and Dr. Sainz never testified either.

When Triplett finally took the stand, he repudiated the taped confession and the many stories he had related under police interrogation. "I'm denying everything I told the police," Triplett said, adding, "I'm sworn in here. You ain't going to get me for perjury." In this new version of events, he had never seen or met Jimmy Bremmers. "I never killed the kid," he insisted. On the night of the murder he said he had visited the Meisches and the Osborns, gone back to his hotel, and "played a little bit on the guitar before I heard this piano player coming on" TV. (The piano player was Liberace.) He insisted that in his many interviews with the police, he had agreed with or confirmed certain things simply to be helpful or to get them off his back. When Sturges asked him on cross-examination whether he ever told officers Bucchino and Davidchik that he had talked to Jimmy Bremmers, their exchange went as follows:

Triplett: I think there might have been something said about that because, after all, you can only stand so much.

Sturges: Didn't you tell the officers, on this same day, Jimmy Bremmers talked to you about running away?

Triplett: I finally let them go ahead and let them go ahead, when they commenced—

Sturges: Didn't you tell the officers—

Tacy (intervening): Just a moment. Let him finish his answer.

Triplett: I just quit denying everything and let them go ahead and build it up to suit themselves, because if they can convict an innocent man that's better than I could do, or would want to do.

At certain points Triplett's testimony actually undermined the defense case. When Tacy tried to get him to agree that the police interrogations had exhausted him so completely that he'd say just about anything, Triplett responded, "Well, I wouldn't say I wore out too easily. I know I put a few of them big boys to sleep down there on the desk, all exhausted, and I was still sitting there smoking a cigarette and wondering why they was going to sleep on me."

Triplett's veracity came into question on a number of smaller matters as well. On cross-examination, Sturges asked him if he had ever been acquainted with Doris Spencer, the prostitute who had been his wife during "Hoover's Time." A clearly agitated Triplett denied he had any idea who Doris Spencer was. Finally, he admitted knowing her. He justified his memory lapse, however, saying, "When I get rid of somebody, I forget about 'em." It was an unfortunate phrase.

Other moments of his testimony were vintage Triplett. He showed his feisty side, informing Sturges in response to one question, "I think you've got your wires crossed on that." He referred to the ward attendants at Cherokee as the "tenants," to the mystification of the prosecution, and noted that the other patients were so "out" that "you couldn't even get a good card game started." When Sturges asked how many times he had gone to Cherokee, Triplett replied, "I believe it was two. They tried to get rid of me in the first place. He [Chief of Detectives Gibbons] threw me over there for insanity and rigged it in the paper. He said, 'That's all I want to do with Triplett. You better keep him there. No court for him.' That's Gibbons, quote. Here we are in court; now we can fight it out."

At one point Sturges was asking Triplett a series of written questions, and Triplett became increasingly testy. Co-prosecutor Beebe called Sturges to the side. "Put your notes down," he whispered. "You've got him going!"

Outside the courtroom, the twice-weekly *Le Mars Globe-Post*, which boasted a hard-boiled style and a bent for sensationalism the equal to that of any big-city tabloid, was having a field day with Triplett's testimony. "Triplett Clowns—But the Jury Doesn't Join in Any Laughter" read one *Globe-Post* headline. The subhead went: "Implication: Admirer of Liberace Wouldn't Miss TV Program Just to Commit a Foul Sex Murder!" The newspaper had particular fun with the Liberace connection, with hints that Triplett and the flamboyant pianist might share a special bond. (The public mania for Liberace, who extolled the virtues of his mother and offered a sanitized approach to the classics that infuriated music critics, was beginning to give way to backlash and to insinuations about his sexuality.) The *Globe-Post* article began:

> For a time today, it seemed to some of the spectators at the Triplett murder trial that Triplett, through his shrewd and learned counsel, Robert O. Tacy, of Council Bluffs, was trying to put over the idea that as a lover of Liberace, the pianist who uses candelabra

instead of electric lights for illumination, it was temperamentally impossible for him to stay away from Liberace's TV program at the very time Jimmy Bremmer[s] was murdered.

That wasn't really the point, of course. The point was that if Triplett actually watched the TV show, it's an alibi. The state, however, figures that as a lover of Liberace, Triplett would know all about the Liberace program even if he was out murdering Jimmy Bremmer[s] at the time and would naturally offer it as a false alibi.

The paper couldn't resist mining this vein a bit more:

This is part of the crosscurrent of opinion among the spectators, some of whom openly said that Triplett could not be guilty if he loves Liberace. But other spectators expressed the opinion that as a lover of Liberace, Triplett deserves hanging.

The Liberace connection resurfaced after the verdict when the *Globe-Post* quoted one juror as saying, "They had a very weak case against Triplett, but he admitted in open court that he listened to Liberace on the radio, and a man who does that is liable to do anything."

Through all this, the prosecution was well aware that it had no physical evidence linking Ernest Triplett to the crime or the crime scene. The testimony of police officer Louis Peterson was offered to counteract this. Peterson told the court he had observed numerous striations on the cowl on the driver's side of Ernest Triplett's Plymouth. These striations weren't exactly a "proof print"—they were too smeared for that—but they showed "indications of small fingers." On the outside of the car, protruding from the handle of the left front door, were more striations both of small fingers and what appeared to be longer fingers. The striations that came down from the door handle were "a little outstanding," Peterson told the court, "as if there had been a struggle and someone was reaching for the door handle to grab it." But there was no proof that the striations of "small fingers," if they existed at all, were those of Jimmy Bremmers, and the notion of some sort of struggle was very much Peterson's interpretation. Still, the testimony achieved what it was supposed to—to give the illusion of physical evidence where none existed.

There were other witnesses as well. Triplett's employers, Raymond and Mary Flood, tried to back up Triplett, denying they had received complaints about his behavior on the job. Willard Brinegar, the superintendent of Cherokee, took the stand but was never asked whether Triplett was given drugs at the hospital, nor did he offer the information. Tacy queried the testifying police officers about other suspects besides Triplett, including a neighbor of the Bremmerses who at one point claimed he had kept Jimmy tied up in the cellar. (The police concluded that the man was guilty only of "idle talk"; previously, he had also been a patient at Cherokee.) There was an attempt by the prosecution to prove that a guitar steel the size of a 12-gauge shotgun shell missing from the Flood Music Company might have been the murder weapon. None of this changed the course of the trial very much, though, and by this point the verdict seemed a foregone conclusion.

In his final summation, prosecutor Sturges called for the death penalty. He quoted Genesis 9:6: "Whoso sheddeth man's blood, by man shall his blood be shed." Life had taken a strange turn for the young county attorney; while in law school, he had written a paper opposing capital punishment. Now he was advocating death for Triplett and was absolutely convinced it was the right course. Triplett, it seemed, was that evil.

Co-prosecutor Beebe, appearing to barely contain his anger, denounced Triplett as "a homosexual pervert inflamed by marijuana." Dramatically pointing at the defendant, he asked the jury to keep "men like that" away from "my child, your children, and your grandchildren."

In his remarks, Tacy quoted the Bible back at Sturges and tried to rebut Beebe by telling jurors they needed more than a dislike of the defendant's "bad habits" to find him guilty of murder. He blasted the state's case, noting that no evidence placed Triplett at the scene of the crime; that no weapon was ever found; that there was no evidence that the murder even took place in Plymouth County; and that Triplett was drugged and pressured in order to obtain a rehearsed confession. Nonetheless, his summation was something less than the Second Coming of Clarence Darrow.

The jury deliberated for four hours and 15 minutes. By the end of the first half hour, the jurors all agreed that Ernest Triplett had murdered Jimmy Bremmers. For the rest of the time they debated whether the crime was premeditated (first degree murder, punishable by death) or whether, in the words of the *Globe-Post*, Triplett had killed the boy "in the excitement and frustration of an unsuccessful homosexual attack" (second degree murder, punishable by life in prison).

At 10:35 P.M. on Friday, June 17—the 10th day of the trial—the jury informed Judge Rodman that it had reached its verdict: Triplett was found guilty of murder in the second degree. He had been spared hanging. Judge Rodman thanked the jurors, saying, "This case should cause all decent persons—

not only parents—to take warning. They should shudder at the very thought that other brutal, bestial slayers with the same inclinations may still be at large."

As the verdict was read, Triplett sat with a frown on his face, but Tacy appeared relieved. He turned to Triplett and said, "That's not so bad."

Triplett was unimpressed. "It ain't so good either," he replied.

Yet Triplett seemed not to realize the full measure of what was happening. As he left the courtroom he was overheard saying, "Does that mean I have to stay here all summer, Tacy?"

The *Globe-Post* headline in its Monday edition was "Prisoner Not Grateful for Having Neck Saved."

Triplett remained in the Plymouth County jail for three more weeks until his sentencing. His mood was surprisingly cheerful. Tacy intended to appeal the verdict; perhaps this gave him heart. Sheriff Frank Scholer told the *Globe-Post* that the prisoner was spending most of his time singing to himself. "Nothing seems to bother him," the sheriff said. "He's too cool to let anything bother him." When the *Globe-Post* reporter asked what kinds of songs Triplett was singing (perhaps religious hymns? he wondered), the sheriff replied, "I didn't pay close attention. Sometimes he just sings good and loud. At others he just hums."

At 10 A.M. on Thursday, July 7, 1955, Judge Rodman sentenced Triplett to life imprisonment at the state penitentiary at Fort Madison. He pledged his "vigorous opposition" to any efforts to parole the prisoner or to commute his sentence. In pronouncing sentence, the judge could not resist one last salvo in Triplett's direction. Judge Rodman stated, "He has led a lecherous life of sexual debauchery and, in my opinion, is a perverted, depraved, and sadistic murderer, utterly devoid of the slightest conception of moral obligations under the laws of either God or men."

A few hours after his sentencing, at about 2 in the afternoon, Ernest Triplett was driven to Fort Madison in Sheriff Scholer's Nash car. Bill Sturges sat in the front seat next to the sheriff, while the bailiff, Greg Featherstone, and Triplett sat in the back. Triplett had a chain around his midsection to which his arms were handcuffed; his legs were also chained. Fort Madison was at the other end of the state, a journey of nearly 12 hours. Despite the nature of his destination, Triplett was his usual talkative self, discoursing on the trial, the weather, and a dozen other topics. Midway, everyone stopped for a bite to eat. Sitting in a restaurant booth shackled to the sheriff, Triplett engaged Sturges in conversation across the table. "Looks to me that you did a better job than my lawyer," Triplett said to his prosecutor. "Would you represent me on my appeal?"

It was almost midnight when the Nash pulled up in front of Fort Madison. The massive door clanged shut, and Bill Sturges thought that was finally the end of the case—and of Ernest Triplett.

Yet something nagged at Sturges, even as he savored his first courtroom triumph, even as he received the compliments of the strange man he had helped send to prison. He had never talked to any of the jurors after the trial, but he couldn't help wonder whether they had convicted Triplett because they believed he murdered Jimmy Bremmers or because he was a sex pervert. "You always wonder what they were thinking," he said years later. "You see, that was the attitude at the time. Sex perverts and murderers—they put them both in the same category."

CHAPTER 5

The Body in the Cornfield

Ernest Triplett awoke the following morning, Friday, July 8, 1955, at the state penitentiary at Fort Madison, the impregnable, medieval-looking fortress on the banks of the Mississippi River that houses Iowa's most violent criminals. Triplett still clung to the hope that his lawyer would successfully appeal his case, but the prospects were dim. Judge Rodman's words at Triplett's sentencing—that he was "utterly devoid of the slightest concept of moral obligations under the laws of either God or men"—hung over the case and over Triplett. But for Triplett there was a more immediate and ominous question: Could a convicted child murderer survive at Fort Madison? In any event, Sioux City could finally rest calmly—the man convicted in the death of Jimmy Bremmers was more than 350 miles away and under lock and key, presumably forever.

But all would not remain calm. The very next night, Saturday, at midnight, Sioux City's flood sirens began to wail, awakening the entire town. It had begun to rain a few hours before, and by now the rain was falling in torrents. Low-lying sections of the east and west sides were already underwater. Police patrolled the streets in boats to evacuate stranded residents. At the drive-in theater just outside of town, couples broke off their embraces, abandoned their cars, and waded through high water to take shelter at a nearby furniture store. Fallen limbs and downed power lines made streets impassable. A fire broke out at a lumber company plant, and fire trucks were unable to make their way through the clogged streets to extinguish the blaze. Iowa Public Service Company employees worked throughout the night to restore electricity. Sioux City was no stranger to storms and floods and extremes of weather of all sorts, but this one was so unexpected, so intense, that it took everyone by surprise, conjuring up memories of the terrible flood two years before.

By early Sunday, July 10, it was all over: The rains had stopped and the waters were receding. As the cleanup continued, life in Sioux City began to return to normal. The stock car races went on as scheduled at Riverview Stadium; Les Elgart and his orchestra appeared onstage at the Shore Acres ballroom. Movie theaters reopened. At the Uptown, there was a double-feature starring Jane Russell; in one of the movies, appropriately titled *Underwater*, the voluptuous actress played a skin diver.

That evening, Mrs. James Davis tucked her 22-month-old daughter, Donna Sue, into her crib in the first-floor bedroom of their modest two-story frame house on Isabella Street, on Sioux City's west side. "Three to get ready. And four to go—to bed," she told her daughter as she kissed her good night. It was late, past 9 P.M., and Donna Sue was in her pink pajamas. She had bright blue eyes and a mass of curly blond hair; neighbors described her as the "darling of the neighborhood." It was an uncomfortably hot night—with the temperature still in the 80s when Donna Sue went to bed—so her bedroom window was wide open. A massive 100-year-old maple tree loomed over the side of the house where Donna Sue's bedroom was located, keeping it cool by day and in deep shadow at night. Isabella was a quiet side street. The Davises' block ran between well-traveled Villa Avenue and the more obscure West 14th Street. It was about 12 blocks from the neighborhood where Jimmy Bremmers had been abducted slightly less than a year before.

Mrs. Davis went to sit in the kitchen, where she caught up on the Sunday newspaper. That day's *Sioux City Journal* featured a pictorial spread of the annual comedy golf event at the Morningside Country Club. In one photo, golfers attempted to hit lemons instead of golf balls as they approached the green on the fifth hole; in another, one golfer tried to drive the ball blindfolded, while a second attempted his shot from a bedspring. The newspaper ran a feature on walking shorts for men, which had recently come into fashion and were still quite controversial. "No matter how one feels on the subject," the article began, "the harbinger [of summer] is the sudden, shocking glimpse of bare male knees, on the golf course, the backyard, and—steady there, fellows—on Fifth Avenue."

Mr. Davis, a clerk for the Chicago and Northwestern Railway, was watching TV in the living room. The couple's other two children, Mary Claire, 11, and Tim, 7, were asleep in the next room. It was a peaceful midsummer evening after the wild rain and unsettling alarms of the night before.

About a half hour later, when Mr. Davis got up to go to bed, he looked in on Donna Sue. Her room appeared just as it always was: her crib against the outer wall; a cedar chest just off to the left under the open window; a child's telephone and a book featuring the cowboy stars of the day, Roy Rogers and Dale Evans, on a night table. But in the dark room, the one thing Mr. Davis couldn't see was his infant daughter. She must be hiding under the bedcovers, he thought. "Where's Donna?" he called out to his wife. Then he noticed that the window screen had been removed. Donna Sue was gone.

Mr. Davis jumped into his car and began a frantic search of every nearby street, alley, and back lot. When he couldn't find his daughter, he became so distraught that he drove his car into a ditch; friends had to pull him out. The police arrived to take over the investigation. This was a more populated and urbanized part of town than where Jimmy Bremmers had vanished the summer before; that made the search easier and more difficult at the same time.

A little earlier that evening, Mr. and Mrs. Laif Fjeldos, who lived on West 14th Street, heard their dog Rex barking at the back door. The Fjeldoses lived around the corner from the Davises', just two houses away; their back lots bordered each other, separated by mulberry and hackberry trees. Rex was a hero in the Fjeldos household. Just two weeks before, someone had been vandalizing the family car; Rex sounded the alarm, and a young man was apprehended. Tonight when Mrs. Fjeldos got up to let Rex in, she saw a man skulking along the alley that extended along the other side of their house from the Davises'. The stranger appeared to be carrying a bundle. She immediately called her husband, who grabbed a flashlight and shone it in the direction of the man, who was hiding behind a bush. Mr. Fjeldos's first thought was that the stranger might be carrying meat to poison the neighborhood dogs. He handed the flashlight to his wife and told her to keep the light on the man while he called the police. By the time he got off the phone, the man had fled. It was just after 9:37 P.M. A few minutes later, as Mr. Fjeldos was telling two neighbors what he had seen, they heard the screams of a woman: "My baby is gone!" And then the same voice, softer now and more plaintive: "Help, help, help."

Shortly afterward, Sid Goldberg, a Sioux City resident, was driving through the nearby town of Elk Point, South Dakota. Just outside a motel, Mr. Goldberg had seen a man in a white T-shirt and khaki trousers standing on the road beside a black Chevrolet sedan. The man was holding a baby in his arms. After he heard a report of the missing child on the radio, Mr. Goldberg immediately telephoned the police. But by the time the Elk Point police arrived at the motel, the sedan was gone.

The following afternoon, Monday, a local farmer, Ernest Oehlerking, was driving his tractor into town from his hog farm on the outskirts of South Sioux City, Nebraska, just across the Missouri River, to buy oats. His nephew and two teenage boys, who were helping him tear down a corncrib on the farm, followed in a wagon. About 100 feet from the farmhouse, Mr. Oehlerking noticed something strange in a ditch alongside the road: the lower part of a baby's pajamas and a rubber diaper. He returned home and called the police. He also told his wife, who went to pick up their six daughters at Girl Scout camp. On her way back, she stopped at the home of her sister-in-law, Mrs. William Oehlerking. On a hunch that the newspapers later attributed to "women's intuition," the women set out in two cars to search for Donna Sue. Mrs. Ernest Oehlerking's six children were with her in her car, along with her 13-year-old niece; her sister-in-law drove alone. They passed the Oehlerking farm and continued for about half a mile down the back road leading from South Sioux City toward Dakota City. Suddenly and in unison, the children let out a scream: In the first row of a cornfield, just a few feet from the road, lay the body of a little girl. It was Donna Sue. Her pink pajama top was wound around her neck.

Mrs. Ernest Oehlerking went home to call the police. It was about 4:15 P.M. Her sister-in-law remained with the lifeless body of Donna Sue. It was a blisteringly hot afternoon—96 degrees—and there was little shade in the open field. The child appeared almost as if she were asleep; her arms were resting about her head. Mrs. Oehlerking found an old paper sack and covered the body.

Identification was made by the brother and sister of Donna Sue's mother. The sister, Mrs. J.R. Stokes, broke the news to Mr. and Mrs. Davis. Neither parent came to view the body. "They had already seen the clothes, and I believe they were prepared for the worst," said Mrs. Stokes. "When I told them that the child was dead, they did not cry but just sat and stared."

An autopsy was performed later that day at a Sioux City funeral home. The coroner concluded that by the time the body was found, Donna Sue had been dead for 10 to 12 hours. He attributed her death to a massive brain hemorrhage resulting from a severe blow to the head. Donna Sue's lower left jaw was broken, and there were severe bruises on other parts of the body. Her buttocks were covered with burns from a cigarette or cigarette lighter. She had been raped and sodomized.

Sioux City was in an uproar over Donna Sue's death. The police department was inundated with phone calls. *Sioux City Journal* reporter Bob Gunsolley was covering a city council meeting when the news arrived that the body had been discovered. At the meeting, the mayor, George Young, practically went berserk when he heard the report and started cursing. Emotions were running high—much higher, Gunsolley thought, than when Jimmy Bremmers had disappeared. "Sadistic Rapist Kills Child; Body Found Near South Sioux," read the banner headline in the *Journal* the next morning. In South Sioux City, the weekly *Dakota County Star* quoted one housewife as saying, "He just has to be caught; he has to die for it." The *Star* noted that some people believed that if a suspect had been apprehended on Monday evening or Tuesday "when the public was at a fever pitch," angry crowds might have resorted to violence.

The fact that a two-year-old girl was snatched out of her crib on a midsummer night and brutally raped and murdered—in addition to the previous summer's murder of Jimmy Bremmers—shocked and terrified the citizenry. Years later, Sioux Cityans could tell you exactly where they were when they heard the news of Donna Sue's death. Hardware stores reported a run on locks and screen latches. Lights burned through the night in frightened homes across the city. When county attorney Don O'Brien saw the little girl's body, he was horrified. "When people ask me today whether I'm for the death penalty, I say I'm not sure," he said years later. "But I sure was for it the day I saw Donna Sue Davis."

Donna Sue's funeral took place that Wednesday at the St. Boniface Catholic Church in Sioux City. It was as much a canonization as a funeral. The crowd of 350 people stood silently as the small, white, flower-crested casket was wheeled down the aisle; Mr. and Mrs. Davis and their two remaining children followed. In the eulogy, the priest said the little girl had died in defense of purity and compared her killing to those of small Jewish boys in biblical times. She was now "to many hearts St. Donna," he went on, and the mourners "might well pray to her rather than for her in order they might all be childlike." After the funeral 40 cars accompanied the little girl's body to Calvary cemetery, where four young boys carried the casket to its resting place on a green hilltop.

The same day at his press conference in Des Moines, Gov. Leo A. Hoegh suggested that the killer of Donna Sue "must have been insane." The whole matter was "a serious situation that should be given the attention of state officials," said the governor. He added that perhaps "more should be done in the field of preventing mental disease."

The Sioux City Journal offered a reward of $1,000 for information leading to the murderer's arrest and conviction and promised to increase that amount as contributions came in. The *Journal* was still smarting from the bad publicity it had received the previous year when it published a gruesome photo of Jimmy Bremmers's body and was sued by the boy's parents. In a front page "Open Letter to the Man Who Murdered Donna Sue Davis," the newspaper editorialized:

> You cannot undo the terrible wrong you have done. That has been chalked up against you, and you must pay the consequences. But you can demonstrate whether you have any remaining spark of decency, whether there is enough good left in you to want to protect other innocent children from a person like yourself. This you can do by giving yourself up to the FBI or any local police officer wherever you may be. It is up to you.

In Washington, D.C., when FBI Director J. Edgar Hoover was informed of the sadistic nature of the murder of Donna Sue Davis, he was said to have responded simply, "Get him!"

And "get him" was what the police and the FBI were determined to do. The FBI regional office in Omaha joined the Sioux City police in directing the investigation, practically taking over a floor of the federal building downtown. Some 20 to 30 FBI officers came into town; agents were paired up with Sioux City police officers. (The FBI became involved because the body had been found across the state line in Nebraska.) "I never saw better police work than in the Donna Sue Davis case, not even the Lindbergh kidnapping," one Sioux City lawyer close to the case would say later. "Chief Gibbons had a number of big spiral notebooks. They were all cross-indexed. Each tip, each report would go into the central system. If a name popped up twice, they'd go after it. It was a like a computer. Everything was checked out. Someone would call and say, 'I was walking my granddaughter and a guy smiled at her.' That would be checked out. They rounded up anyone they could think of. And whenever they'd pick up anybody, they'd forget about rights."

Woodbury County attorney Don O'Brien had never seen the FBI more involved than in the Davis case. "They were constantly bringing people in," he said. "Richard Tedrow was the court reporter, and the FBI had him taking statements. They took statements from half the people in town." Suspects who didn't have a reasonable alibi were sent to Des Moines, the state capital, for lie detector tests; later a polygraph was set up in the federal building in Sioux City. Don Doyle, a state legislator from Sioux City at the time, noted that the police and the FBI "questioned every neighbor, anyone ever arrested for anything." Two years after the Davis murder, Doyle received a phone call from a constituent who told him that his son had been turned down for admission to Officer Candidates School because he had been questioned in the Davis case. There had been no evidence against the young man, and the police had only interrogated him on one occasion; it was just that practically everyone was questioned.

On Wednesday, the same day as Donna Sue's funeral, the first promising development in the investigation emerged when a farmhand named Otto E. Wennekamp was apprehended near South Sioux City. Wennekamp had bought a used car, trading in his old one as part of the deal; he had gone off in the newly purchased car supposedly to get the money for payment but had never returned. In his absence, the seller noted a number of cigarette burns on the dashboard of the man's old car. Donna Sue's body had been covered with cigarette burns, and the similarity led the South Sioux sheriff to believe that Wennekamp might be the killer. But after intense questioning by the FBI and Sioux City police detectives at the city council chambers in South Sioux City, Wennekamp was cleared. "His alibi checks," the police officers announced. He was held only for auto theft.

Then, that same day, a 42-year-old drifter named Audrey Brandt told the police in Joplin, Missouri, that he had killed Donna Sue. Brandt's confession, produced after nine hours of interrogation, made banner headlines in the Sioux City and Des Moines newspapers. Then four hours after he signed a written confession, Brandt admitted to the authorities it had all been a hoax. He had lied, he said, because he had gotten "all riled up." Relatives and friends told the police that at the age of 16, Brandt had still been in the first grade. "He has the mentality of a child of 2," said a Joplin police detective. "If we had asked him if he had been in the Brinks robbery he might have said 'yes.'" After it was determined that he had been traveling with a carnival in Missouri on the night Donna Sue was abducted, he was eliminated as a suspect.

As the week dragged on, despite the zeal of the FBI and the Sioux City police and despite the large number of people brought in for questioning, the case was going nowhere. An Indiana man wanted on a parole violation was held for four days in Dubuque and then let go when it was confirmed that he hadn't even been in Sioux City on the weekend of the kidnapping. Two other men who had been held in other cities were dismissed as suspects as well. In Sioux City, the police arrested a 19-year-old Kansas man and charged him with lascivious acts with a child. But since nothing was found to link him with Donna Sue's murder, he was released on bond.

With the murderer still at large, the citizens of Sioux City and neighboring towns remained extremely tense. Parents refused to let their children out of sight. Numerous people called the police to report neighborhood prowlers. When officers arrived to investigate, they were met by irate citizens carrying loaded shotguns and other firearms with safety catches off. There were several cases of Sioux Cityans firing guns into the air to scare off possible marauders. When a South Sioux City man returned home from a meeting that had kept him out until 11 P.M., he found his wife sitting anxiously in the living room, a rifle at her side.

The police began to worry that the situation might get out of hand. Sioux City Police Captain John A. Rispalje stated that while he understood the depth of popular feeling and "while everyone has a right to defend his own property, I would like to ask that people use a little caution in exercising that right. We don't want to have a police officer or another citizen injured or killed." Rispalje urged that anyone concerned about prowlers turn on all the available lights in the vicinity instead of getting "careless with a gun." And he implored anyone firing a gun into the air to ward off a prowler to report their firing to the police in order to avoid "unnecessary duplication in investigating gunfire."

The anxiety extended to Des Moines, 200 miles away. Two days after the murder, Captain R.E. (Mickey) O'Brien, chief of the Des Moines police department detective bureau, urged citizens to notify the police immediately if they saw a prowler. "A lot of people don't like to because they think it might be an innocent party," he said. "In such a case, we wouldn't embarrass anyone. We'd rather have 20 misses than to let one prowler get away."

In Sunday sermons, some Sioux City ministers used the murder of Donna Sue as a lesson in the evils of improper attire. One pastor asked women to avoid appearing on the streets in scanty dress that was appropriate "possibly only on the beach." Another urged parents to see that their children were properly dressed; certain types of attire created by "pagan designers" might arouse the passions and baser instincts of "sex maniacs." Whether the minister believed that Donna Sue Davis's pink pajamas fit that category was unclear.

The failure of law enforcement officials to find the killer also provided fodder for gossip and rumor. "There are enough rumors going around about the recent sex killings in Sioux City to keep tongues wagging for some time," wrote the young editor, Henry Trysla, in his column in *The Dakota County Star*. A lot of "nice people" were being asked "routine questions," he noted. That was the FBI's job, after all. But Trysla was concerned that innocent people might be harmed because of some folks' "irresponsible chattering." Just let the town gossip get hold of "something like that," he wrote, and "before you know it, they'll have a man persecuted."

That was exactly what was happening. The wildest and ugliest rumor of all was beginning to float around Sioux City—that the father of Jimmy Bremmers had killed both his son and Donna Sue Davis. The report first surfaced in *The Le Mars Globe-Post*, notorious for publishing unfounded rumors and then assuring the public there was no truth to them. Mr. Bremmers's automobile had been damaged in a car crash and had been taken to a local body shop for repair, the paper said. A mechanic noticed some stains on the car's interior and immediately suspected they were blood stains. Sioux City police analyzed them and concluded that the stains were the result of leaking rainwater.

Mr. Bremmers appeared at the police station apparently to ask the police what could be done to stop the rumors, but this only further inflamed the situation. Chief of Detectives Harry Gibbons told the *Globe-Post* that he was "more than ever convinced" that the jury in the Triplett case "did the only thing that sane people could, confronted by the evidence. Triplett is the most vicious sex pervert in the experience of the Sioux City police department." Robert Beebe, co-prosecutor in the Triplett case, wrote a letter to *The Sioux City Journal* assailing the dissemination of "vicious, unsubstantiated, and untrue rumors" concerning the Bremmers family.

For his part, Bill Sturges, the Plymouth County attorney, told the *Globe-Post* that he had recently gone to the Sioux City Police Department's detective bureau to examine the files in the Davis case. He concluded that the evidence in the Jimmy Bremmers and the Donna Sue Davis murders was completely dissimilar; the same person would not have committed both crimes. Triplett had killed Jimmy Bremmers in a "frustrated rage" after his attempt to commit a sex act was rebuffed, said Sturges. The rape and murder of Donna Sue, on the other hand, was "the deliberate act of a sadist" who had "tortured her to death for the sheer joy of it." While both murders involved "sex perversion so vicious they defy the imagination of normal people and almost benumb the mind," according to Sturges, the motivations of the two were plainly different. For this reason, Triplett would hardly be suspected of the Davis murder even if he had been free to commit it. "The murderer of the Davis baby deliberately abducted a helpless baby—not a boy of Jimmy Bremmers's size," Sturges told the newspaper. "Triplett and the Davis baby's murderers are both as vicious as ever found, but their diseased minds are basically different."

On July 22, eleven days after the murder, the Davis family broke its silence to thank the public for its support. The family had received some 500 cards and letters from all over the world, expressing prayers and sympathy. "So many persons did so many things for us that we are not able to remember all the kindnesses," said Mrs. Davis.

On that same day, *The Sioux City Journal* reported that its reward fund for information leading to Donna Sue's killer had reached $1,344. A week later, the amount had grown to $2,387. One Sioux City television station promised $500, and Governor Hoegh offered $500 on behalf of the state of Iowa. It was the first time the state had ever offered a reward in a criminal case.

Needed: 25 Sexual Psychopaths

It wasn't enough merely to find the killer of Donna Sue Davis. What was needed was a means of stopping such men before they murdered and raped and sodomized. And suddenly, talk of Iowa's sexual psychopath law—a law few people had paid any attention to when the governor had signed it a few months before—was on everyone's lips.

On January 31, 1955, five months to the day after the abduction of Jimmy Bremmers and five months before the murder of Donna Sue Davis, a group of legislators introduced a bill in the Iowa House of Representatives whose purpose was "to provide for the confinement of persons who are dangerous criminal sexual psychopaths." Two of the four sponsors—representatives Jacob Van Zwol and Wendell Pendleton—represented counties near Sioux City and were obviously aware of the public outrage over the young boy's death. Under the legislation, anyone charged with a public offense and who possessed "criminal propensities toward the commission of sex offenses" could be declared by the local county attorney to be a criminal sexual psychopath. The county attorney would submit a petition to that effect, a hearing would take place, and a judge could then commit the accused person to a state mental hospital. There, the person would be detained and treated indefinitely or until he was certified as "cured." The bill essentially amounted to preventive detention.

In introducing such a bill, the legislators proposed that Iowa join 25 other states and the District of Columbia, which had all enacted such legislation, usually in the aftermath of vicious sex crimes.

The term *sexual psychopath* was invented in the 1930s, according to Estelle B. Freedman, a historian who has studied and written on the subject. During this period, American criminologists became interested in the link between sexual abnormality and sex crimes. Increasingly, the male sexual deviant was a subject of social concern, particularly as a threat to children. It was the Great Depression, and jobless men roamed the countryside, hopping freights and wandering into unfamiliar towns in search of work or a free meal. The traditional social structures that had kept such men in check were crumbling. Enter the notion of the sexual psychopath. "From the origin of the concept, the psychopath had been perceived as a drifter, an unemployed man who lived beyond the boundaries of familial and social controls," Freedman wrote in her essay " 'Uncontrolled Desires': The Response to the Sexual Psychopath, 1920-1960." "Unemployed men and vagabonds populated the depression-era landscape, signaling actual family dissolution and symbolizing potential social and political disruption." The drifter had acquired a sexual dimension, and a new and sinister category of criminal was born. Ernest Triplett was the perfect prototype of this new category.

The first period of major sex-crime panics (also called moral panics) occurred between 1937 and 1940, Freedman writes. In August 1937, following two child murders, residents of Queens in New York City demanded that the police be given greater power "to take suspicious characters in hand before they commit the crimes," according to a *New York Times* report cited by Freedman. That same year, in Chicago, the rape and murder of two nurses led to the formation of a police squad to "round up attackers," according to the *Times*. In Inglewood, California, a mob threatened to lynch the suspected murderers of three local girls. Meanwhile, in a 1937

New York Herald Tribune article, FBI Director J. Edgar Hoover was quoted as calling for a "war on the sex criminal," whom he characterized as "the most loathsome of all the vast army of crime." In this charged atmosphere, five states—Michigan, Illinois, Minnesota, Ohio, and California—enacted sexual psychopath laws.

The second period, between 1949 and 1955, followed a similar pattern. In November 1949, a six-year-old Los Angeles girl was brutally murdered by a retired baker already charged in a sexual molestation case. A week later a thousand people attended a mass meeting and drew up a petition proposing that anyone convicted of a sex crime involving children be jailed for life. The magazine published by the American Legion called for life sentences without parole for sex offenders. J. Edgar Hoover warned that crime by "degenerate sex offenders" represented the most rapidly increasing type of criminal activity, "taking its toll at the rate of a criminal assault every 43 minutes, day and night, in the United States." Writing in *The Saturday Evening Post*, David G. Wittels asserted that most sex killers were psychopathic personalities and estimated "at least tens of thousands of them are loose in the country today."

The atmosphere of fear and paranoia that characterized America in 1950s gave the sex-crime panics of that decade a particular flavor and intensity. The Cold War was at its height, Sen. Joseph McCarthy was engaged in his campaign against domestic subversion, and national attention was focused on the "enemy within." At the same time, much of the anxiety of the period centered around the most vulnerable of souls—children. The polio epidemic was a major source of concern for parents, and the most commonplace locales—public swimming pools, for instance—took on a menacing quality. The 953 cases in Woodbury County (Sioux City) in 1952—out of 60,000 in the entire nation that year—underscored how widespread the epidemic was, particularly in the Midwest.

At the same time, to even the most casual reader of *The Sioux City Journal*, America was a country characterized by almost daily incidents of missing children, child kidnappings, and child murders. During the period of the deaths of Jimmy Bremmers and Donna Sue Davis, the otherwise staid *Journal* offered a drumbeat of headlines that played upon these fears:

WHOLE TOWN HUNTS BOY, 4: CHILD MISSING IN COLD OF NORTH DAKOTA SINCE SUNDAY
(October 19, 1954; Powers Lake, N.D.)

GIRL MURDERED BY SEX MANIAC
(November 6, 1954; Norwood, Mass.)

FIND MISSING GIRL'S BLOUSE: AUNT IDENTIFIES STAINED GARMENT; UNCLE MUM
(November 21, 1954; Lebanon, Mo.)

NAB SUSPECT IN KIDNAPPING OF YOUTH; VICTIM ESCAPES; $100,000 RANSOM UNPAID. JOBLESS MAN ADMITS CRIME; BOY HELD IN CELLAR
(January 10, 1955; Freehold, N.J.)

RAPES AND KILLS BROTHER'S WIFE AND BABY: 25-YEAR-OLD MAN ADMITS SHOCKING CRIME TO OFFICERS: SAYS HE WOULD BE CHRISTIAN, BUT ACTS LIKE A MANIAC
(July 13, 1955; Jamestown, N.Y.)

From 1947 to 1955—roughly corresponding to what Freedman describes as the second period of sex-crime panics—an additional 21 states and the District of Columbia enacted sex psychopath laws. There were sensible reasons for such legislation—at least at first glance. Prosecuting sex criminals was often difficult, and when they were prosecuted, they were often locked up only for short periods. Psychiatric treatment was rare. For those reasons, Plymouth County attorney and Triplett prosecutor Bill Sturges lobbied for the passage of Iowa's sexual psychopath law. "Sex crimes usually don't happen on a street corner," Sturges would say later. "There is seldom proof of the crime. It is difficult to get convictions. So if you couldn't convict, at least under a sex psychopath law, you could get them treated." Sexual psychopath laws gave prosecutors a new weapon for dealing with sex crimes. When the evidence in a particular case was weak, instead of going to trial and risking losing the case, the prosecutor could now merely file a petition that the defendant was a sexual psychopath and have him put away indefinitely.

There were other arguments in favor of sexual psychopath laws as well. The record of rehabilitation of such offenders was poor; when they were released from prison, they often committed the same crime again. Clearly, a new solution was needed, and increasingly, the mental hospital was viewed as the solution—and an enlightened one at that. Proponents of this approach ranged from Max Lerner, the highly respected columnist for the liberal *New York Post,* to the hard-line J. Edgar Hoover. "Sex criminals must be studied and treated by psychiatrists, not cooped up in Sing Sing," wrote Lerner. "And they ought to be treated in mental hospitals, not prisons." For his part, Hoover criticized the existing practice of treating sex offenders like any other criminals rather than giving them a psychiatric examination or medical attention. "Nothing could be less realistic," he stated.

In the case of Iowa, Hoover's comments were perfectly timed: They were reported in *The Des Moines Register* on February 24, 1955, the day after the sexual psychopath bill passed the Iowa House of Representatives and was sent on to the Senate for approval.

Across the country, there was an alarming vagueness in legal definitions as to who might be classified as a sexual psychopath. State laws defined a sexual psychopath as someone who had "propensity" to commit sex offenses (Michigan and Missouri) or who "lacked the power to control his sexual impulses" (Massachusetts and Nebraska). In most states, however, authorities couldn't just pluck such a person off the street and label him a sexual psychopath. In Alabama, for instance, the suspect had to be convicted of a sex crime first. Under the proposed Iowa legislation, such a person had to be charged with—but not necessarily convicted of—a "public offense." In Nebraska, on the other hand, a suspect didn't have to be charged; all that was needed were certain facts showing "good cause" and the process of classification as a sexual psychopath could begin. And in Minnesota, the only requirements were a petition by a county attorney and an examination by "two duly licensed doctors of medicine."

Whatever their individual wordings, such laws were intended to bring about indefinite detention of dangerous or socially undesirable people. In all these states, a sexual psychopath could not be released from detention until psychiatrists ruled that he was "cured" or at the very least no longer posed a threat to society.

Despite their good intentions, sexual psychopath laws invariably took a catch-all approach to sexual offenses. The intended targets may have been rapists and murderers, but in almost every state with a sexual psychopath law, little or no distinction

81

was made between nonviolent and violent offenses, between consensual and nonconsensual behavior, or between harmless "sexual deviates" and dangerous sex criminals. An adult homosexual man who had sex with his lover in the privacy of his bedroom was as deviant as a child murderer. A person who had a pornographic book or photograph hidden in a night table faced the same punishment as a rapist. All these people were lumped in one category—that of the sexual psychopath—and could be incarcerated in a state hospital indefinitely.

New York lawyer and judge Morris Ploscowe, one of the most prominent critics of sexual psychopath laws at the time, found that these were most often used to punish and isolate minor offenders rather than dangerous predators. In Minnesota, which enacted its sexual psychopath law in the '30s, some 200 people were committed to state hospitals in the first 10 years of the law's existence, according to Ploscowe. Most were detained for homosexual activity, not for being hard-core sex criminals.

Ploscowe also disputed assertions that such laws encouraged the psychiatric treatment of sex offenders. In reality, he said, the treatment for sexual psychopaths usually involved little more than warehousing them, whether in a state mental hospital or a penitentiary. State hospital administrators were unhappy about taking on sexual psychopaths as patients, he noted; they often didn't have adequate facilities to deal with the patients they already had. And Ploscowe further argued that individuals committed under the sexual psychopath laws were frequently discharged based on the needs of the institutions rather than those of the patient.

Such critiques made little impression on Iowa legislators as they considered sexual psychopath legislation. In fact, some of Ploscowe's criticisms—that such laws were used primarily to punish minor sexual offenders, for instance—were seen as reasons for passage. To Rep. Wendell Pendleton, one of the cosponsors of the Iowa bill, the entire point of the legislation was to screen minor offenders so they wouldn't go on to become major ones. A sexually oriented minor crime, such as exhibitionism or "window peeping," could be a tip-off that the perpetrator "wasn't thinking straight" and should be "screened," he said many years later. "The idea we had at the time," he continued, "was that possibly by screening them, we might be able to define those who might pose a threat to society, who might commit violent acts. We thought maybe we could head off something."

When it was introduced in the 1955 legislative session, the Iowa sexual psychopath bill was "amazingly noncontroversial," recalled former state representative Jack Milroy, another of the bill's co-sponsors. Milroy, a first term legislator from Vinton, near Cedar Rapids, apparently stumbled into sponsoring the bill without knowing much about it. According to his account, he was talked into it by Rep. Jacob Van Zwol, a legislator from Paullina, in O'Brien County, north of Sioux City. Van Zwol told him that it was simply a bill that called for the treatment of some people who had "problems" as mentally ill, not as criminals. At that point, Van Zwol didn't use the term "sexual psychopath."

"It's a good bill," Van Zwol added, noting that Wendell Pendleton, the legislator from Storm Lake, near Cherokee, was cosponsoring it. "Penny," as he was known, was a well-respected, three-term legislator, the speaker pro tempore of the House and chairman of the Rules Committee.

"Would you like to go in on it too?" Van Zwol asked.

"Sure," said Milroy.

Milroy said later he didn't bother to read the bill; he just took Van Zwol's word for it. Then one Friday night, the legislator got home and settled back with the *Cedar Rapids Gazette*, only to see his picture and that of his colleague, Rep. Bob Carson, as co-sponsors of the sexual psychopath bill. "I didn't know anything about it," Milroy insisted years later. "That is how it happened."

During the period of its consideration by the Iowa legislature, the sexual psychopath bill received scant attention. *The Des Moines Register*, the state's most influential newspaper, completely ignored it both in its news and editorial pages until the following summer, and by then it was already law. Opposition did come from the Board of Control, the state agency that governed Iowa's four state mental hospitals. To many, however, the Board of Control's position appeared self-serving: State mental hospitals just didn't want to cope with a new and potentially dangerous patient population or take responsibility for certifying sexual psychopaths as "cured."

In any event, with the death of Jimmy Bremmers fresh in the public mind, the bill sailed through the Iowa legislature. On February 23, 1955, it passed the House by a 100-0 vote; Senate approval, 49-0, came on March 28. Gov. Leo Hoegh signed the bill three days later, and on April 14, 1955, it became law.

The Iowa sexual psychopath law was never applied in the case of Ernest Triplett, however, since he was indicted two days before the new law went into effect. And the legislation, after all, was intended primarily as a preventive measure. Nonetheless, in the days immediately following the murder of Donna Sue Davis, the three-month-old law began to be viewed as a panacea for the sex crimes that were bringing Sioux City—and, increasingly, the rest of Iowa—to near mayhem. It was quickly becoming a matter of "lock 'em up" and ask questions later. And what more humane and politically appealing way to lock up potential child killers and child molesters than under the guise of treatment?

Newspaper editorialists were the first to raise their voices. The day after Donna Sue's body was found, *The Sioux City Journal* demanded that Sioux City be made "the most feared town in America for the sex deviate. That's the job as quickly as the murder of Donna Sue Davis is solved." In the following day's issue, the *Journal* published an editorial cartoon featuring a little boy and girl walking through a jungle labeled "Our Cities." Blocking their path was a menacing panther, labeled "Human Depravity" and a giant snake, coiled and ready to strike, labeled "Sex Perverts." The caption of the cartoon was "Civilized Jungle."

Urgent calls for action filled the Letters to the Editor section of the *Journal*: "Urges Commitment of Every Sex Offender"; "Stern Punishment for Sex Offenders Urged"; "Law in Sex Cases Termed Inadequate."

Meanwhile, on the day after Donna Sue's funeral, *The Des Moines Register* reported that the Des Moines police department was taking the first steps to certify a pedophile as a sexual psychopath. Under the headline "Sex Offender Law Is Unused," the newspaper quoted the Board of Control as saying that until now, no criminal sexual psychopaths had been committed to a state hospital under the new law. The implication of the article was that it was about time they should be. Perhaps seeking maximum impact, the *Register*'s editors placed the article on page 3, next to a picture of Mr. and Mrs. Davis and their children grieving in front of Donna Sue's casket.

Taking their lead from the *Register*, newspapers around the state urged that the sexual psychopath law be used as the legal basis for a roundup. In Council Bluffs, the daily *Non-Pareil* demanded that anyone who showed "an inclination to molest children and commit offenses which indicate perversion should be committed to an institution for observation and treatment.... If something isn't done, and done quickly, no child will be safe, and there will be frequent repetitions of the horrible tragedy in Sioux City."

The Storm Lake Register, the newspaper in Rep. Pendleton's district, concurred. Why, the newspaper asked, had Ernest Triplett, "a known screwball," been "running loose" at the time of Jimmy Bremmers's murder? Why, it demanded, had Audrey Brandt, the farmhand who had confessed to the murder of Donna Sue Davis and then recanted, been wandering the streets to begin with? In enacting the sexual psychopath law, the paper wrote:

> Our Iowa legislature last winter took notice of the dangers that arise from permitting sex-deviates, homo-sexuals and the entire disgusting ilk to run at large.... Certainly, permitting such scum as Triplett and Brandt to roam at large is a reflection upon the intelligence with which we of this modern age are supposed to be endowed!

Although its news article had sparked the campaign to put the sexual psychopath law into practice, the editorial page of *The Des Moines Register* was the only place where reservations were expressed. In a July 15 editorial, the newspaper noted that sexual psychopaths remained "among the most puzzling and difficult cases." In view of a nationwide shortage of psychiatrists, a shortage that was particularly acute in Iowa's state mental hospitals, "no magic cures can be expected and grave administrative problems can arise in trying to care for such people in crowded institutions."

The *Register*'s words of caution, however, proved to be too little, too late. On the day the editorial was published, Leo Tapscott, the county attorney in Des Moines, filed a court petition asking that a Des Moines man named Richard Jennings, aged 23, be declared a criminal sexual psychopath and sent to a mental hospital. Jennings had been arrested earlier that week, charged with molesting a 7-year-old girl. (It was his case that was referred to in the initial *Register* article.) Jennings was said to possess "strong pedophiliac tendencies" and "a peeping mania."

A week later Tapscott filed a second petition asking that Floyd Kamerick, a 29-year-old Des Moines musician and music instructor, also be judged as a sexual psychopath. Kamerick had been arrested on two morals charges involving 10- and 12-year-old boys.

Not to be upstaged, Gov. Leo Hoegh moved quickly to respond to the public clamor. Hoegh was a first-term Republican and decorated World War II lieutenant colonel, known primarily for his crew haircut, charming wife, and strong opposition to the sale of liquor by the drink. (The recipe for a cool—and non alcoholic—"Hoegh Cocktail," served when committees met in the governor's office, was said to be: "Fill tall glasses with ice; add tea, with sugar or lemon, if desired.") On July 15, the same day that the county attorney filed his first petition, the governor announced that he was calling a special meeting of the Board of Control and the superintendents of the state's four mental hospitals. The meeting was set for Friday of the following week. In the meantime, he asked the Board to come up with a plan for incarcerating sexual deviates. "We're trying to work out some plan whereby we can take care of people processed under the new law," said the governor at a press conference. "We're concerned about the facilities and also the technicians, but I believe we can get the technicians."

At the July 23 meeting, the governor announced that the state was establishing a special ward for criminal sexual psychopaths. The ward would be set up at the state mental hospital at Mount Pleasant, in the southeast corner of the state. Mount Pleasant was selected because of its proximity to the University of Iowa hospitals in Iowa City, where psychiatrists were available. Dr. Charles C. Graves, director of mental health services for the Board of Control, suggested the ward could also be used for a "personality research" project, in cooperation with state colleges.

Some at the meeting expressed skepticism, which wasn't entirely surprising because the Board of Control had originally opposed the sexual psychopath bill at the time it was introduced. When the board's chairman asked how many people he and his colleagues should prepare for in the new ward, Hoegh randomly picked the number 25. "When we get 15, we'll start thinking of the next 25," the governor said.

Dr. W.B. Brown, the superintendent of Mount Pleasant, appeared less than enthusiastic at the prospect of an influx of sexual psychopaths to his institution. He had attended a national meeting of psychiatrists that April in Atlantic City, where speakers had argued that there was yet "no specific and adequate treatment after which it can be said that a deviate has been cured."

Governor Hoegh, however, was determined to act. "The guy I want to treat," he said, is the sex deviate "who is now roaming the street but never committed a crime." This statement would have enormous consequences.

A week after the meeting, the Board of Control informed the governor that a special ward to house 25 sexual psychopaths had been established at Mount Pleasant. The ward had already found its technicians—two young psychologists just out of graduate school who had been summer interns at the mental hospital and agreed to stay on for the year to treat the inmates of the new ward. Everything was ready at Mount Pleasant. All that was required now was some sexual psychopaths to fill the ward to give the impression that the state of Iowa was doing something about the problem. But where to find them?

PART 2: THE ROUNDUP

<u>SIOUX CITY, IOWA, SEPTEMBER 1955</u>

"[A]s 'birds of a feather flock together,' deviates tend to do the same, and as soon as one or two are discovered, the rest are soon known to the authorities, though they may never be picked up for any actual crime. The fact is that sex deviates often lead normal, respectable lives, with the exception of...one peculiarity, and this has led to their being overlooked in the past, except when one 'goes off the deep end,' resulting in some shocking crime, such as the Jimmy Bremmer[s] murder or the murder of Donna Sue Davis."

—*The Le Mars Globe-Post,* September 8, 1955

Pinched

Things had gotten rocky between Doug Thorson and Duane Wheeler, so Doug had gone off by himself to the *Holiday on Ice* show at the Sioux City Auditorium. Doug wanted the freedom to go out with other men; Duane was the marrying kind. The two were on the verge of a breakup.

Doug and Duane had been seeing a lot of each other since Doug had gotten out of the Air Force six months before in February 1955. Doug, 23, had grown up on a mink farm on the outskirts of a small town near Fort Dodge, about two hours east of Sioux City. In high school he directed the band, drove a school bus, and helped lead the basketball team to the state finals three years in a row. Eager to see the wide world, he joined the service right after graduation. He had a top security clearance, and his job was cryptography—coding and decoding messages. In the Marshall Islands in the Pacific Ocean, he witnessed the first hydrogen bomb tests. Later he was stationed at Andrews Air Force base in Maryland. His parents had divorced, and while Doug was in the Air Force, his mother remarried. Her new husband was a custodian at Morningside College, the liberal arts school in Sioux City, so the family moved there. Two of Doug's three brothers enrolled at Morningside, where they played on the varsity football team.

In Sioux City on leave, Doug met Duane at a skinny-dipping party at the gravel pits over in Plymouth County. When Doug got out of the service he moved to Sioux City, where he got his job as a management trainee at Kresge's. Kresge's was known for its popular lunch counter and for a white-haired woman who sat just inside the entrance and played tunes like "Over the Rainbow" and "My Funny Valentine" on the piano all day long. He also got his own apartment—a hole-in-the-wall up the hill off Nebraska Street, a few blocks from Kresge's. He could walk to work and was just far enough from his mother and brothers over in Morningside, across the viaduct, to feel that he was on his own.

Outside of his family, Doug knew few people in Sioux City, so one of the first things he did when he got back to town was to look up Duane Wheeler. Doug had a basketball player's physique—tall and lean—with dirty blond hair, and was rather wild. He could be rough and prickly and fly off the handle, and when he drank too much, he made passes at people. There was the time he bit Billy Ivers on the back of the neck at a drive-in restaurant over in Riverside; Billy, who was only 18 at the time, never forgot it, though Doug later insisted that Billy had made the whole thing up. Doug possessed a fiercely independent streak that probably came from his learning to fend for himself early on. When he was 12 years old, he spent the summer busing tables at a hotel in Fort Dodge and living at the YMCA. In his high school years, he worked three nights a week waiting tables at a roadhouse owned by a Chicago gangster. The gangster's bodyguard took a fancy to him, buying him clothes and even a broken-down car. He was the first man with whom Doug had ever had sex.

If Doug was a little rough for some people, everybody was crazy about Duane Wheeler. A Korean War vet who was four years older than Doug, good-looking and witty and with a lot of friends, he had polish. In some ways he was Doug's opposite—a devout Catholic, for one thing. "I'd go to a bar, and Duane would go to Mass," Doug liked to say. Marie Ellis's School of Cosmetology, where Duane was a student, was just down the block from Kresge's, above Niesner's dime store. Cosmetology school is where Duane dyed his hair blond. He had grown up in Sioux City, where his father was a railroad engineer, and served in the Navy for four years after he had finished at Central High. Duane was on the campy side, "a real lady," as one of his friends put it. (That wasn't the way Doug Thorson saw it: He insisted that "You'd never know that Duane was gay.") He had wanted to go into the Marines like his older brother Bob, but Bob discouraged him. "You'll get clean sheets in the Navy," he told him. Bob knew Duane wasn't cut out for the Marines. In the Central High School yearbook, his classmates wrote about Duane, "It's the quiet kind that is dangerous."

The Friday evening of Labor Day weekend, 1955—a month and a half after the murder of Donna Sue Davis—seemed to be as fine a moment as any for Doug to begin to assert his independence. All seemed right with the world. The hottest August in Sioux City in 87 years was finally over. Sioux City can be intensely hot in summer: The scorching Plains winds make you feel as if you are in the middle of a giant baking oven. But today had been a glorious day—not a cloud in the sky and the temperature in the high 70s. At the movies, *Love Is a Many-Splendored Thing* with William Holden and Jennifer Jones was playing at the "scientifically cool" Capitol. *The McConnell Story*, starring Alan Ladd as a heroic Korean War flying ace and June Allyson as his devoted wife, Butch, was showing at the Orpheum. ("Go ahead, tiger—you own the sky!" was the film's most famous line.) Doug couldn't wait to see both films. He loved the movies; when things were good between them, he and Duane would go all the time.

After he finished work, Doug headed over to the Martin Hotel, a few doors from Kresge's, for dinner. There he struck up a conversation with an out-of-towner in Sioux City for a convention. Sioux City was a big convention town in those days. Kiwanians and dentists and teachers were constantly booked into the Martin or the Warrior, drawn in part by the city's shiny new art deco auditorium and plethora of hotel facilities but also by the bars and prostitutes on Lower Fourth Street. There was always somebody new in town. For gay men, that was a particular boon. After all, Sioux City was a town of only 80,000 people where there weren't too many options for homosexual sex or romance, and where most gay men were coupled off or married to women or so deeply closeted that the only social appearances they made were in the bathroom of the Warrior Hotel for a clandestine encounter. Thus, out-of-towners were highly desirable commodities. The two men went back to Doug's apartment and had sex.

Doug was pleased with his good fortune. He certainly had shown up Duane Wheeler. But Doug wasn't going to let the satisfactions of an early evening encounter with a visitor from out of town keep him from attending the *Holiday on Ice* show. He had been planning on it for too long. By the time he got to the auditorium, the place was already packed. The two dozen female skaters, known as the Glamour Icers, and their male escorts, the Ice Squires, had already taken their places. There were eight production numbers, but the highlight was clearly Ravel's "Bolero." That number featured drumbeats, skaters tapping their sticks on the ice to the music, and one performer who dazzled the audience as an Aztec statue covered in gold paint. In the background, a volcano smoldered. When Doug was a kid they would flood a field on his grandfather's mink farm for ice skating in the winter. But ice on Labor Day weekend—and drumbeats too! There was something thrilling about that.

On his way home after the show, Doug stopped for a drink at the Warrior Hotel. The hotel bar, located on the ground floor and called the Tom Tom Room, had been steadily losing popularity since the end of World War II when it used to be filled with GIs from the large Army air base outside of town. (It was then known as the Bomber Room.) On weeknights, if there wasn't a convention in town, it was virtually empty. That was when it started to attract a gay clientele, although it was not strictly a gay bar by any means; Sioux City didn't have such a thing and wouldn't until the New Black Coach opened in the 1970s. The Tom Tom Room was dimly lit and woody in the manner of hotel bars—classy, Doug always thought—with booths off to one side.

When the Warrior Hotel first opened downtown in 1930, at the cost of a million and a half dollars, it was the toast of Sioux City—ten stories on Sixth and Nebraska, brick and terra cotta on the outside, in the art deco style. Inside there were 250 rooms and 30 deluxe apartments, as well as an "ultra modernistic grill" that touted itself as the "most ornate coffee shop in the Middle West." By the 1950s, the Warrior was still a pretty posh place: A grand staircase led to the second-floor lobby, which featured marble columns, overstuffed chairs, and crystal chandeliers. Almost every aspect of the hotel had an Indian motif: There were oil paintings of Indian scenes in the lobby, murals of Indians in full regalia on the walls of the coffee shop, and even the dinner plates featured Indian heads surrounded by gold leaf. At the winter quarters of the Sioux City Country Club, located at the hotel, the city's top business executives played poker—and sometimes, slot machines—long past midnight. Political figures and celebrities also stayed at the Warrior: Adlai Stevenson, Sonja Henie, and Liberace. When Elvis stayed there, young women tried to sneak up the back stairway into his room.

Doug was wearing a suit and tie, his *Holiday on Ice* program tucked conspicuously under his arm; it was his badge of freedom, after all. He noticed that the usual barmaid who was friendly with the gay clientele was nowhere to be found. Someone new was behind the bar asking the regulars their names and where they lived. "I've got to get your name and addresses, so I know who you guys are," he remembered her telling him. Doug gave the woman his name, without paying much attention. He was still basking in the glow of the performance: the guardsmen in their military costumes doing their precision marches across the ice as if it were half-time at a football game, the acrobatic skating, the jugglers, the clowns. He was recounting all this with great enthusiasm to Floyd Edwards, a window dresser at a downtown department store, who plopped himself down next to him at the bar. As usual, Floyd was trying to pick Doug up, but he always tried to pick up everybody, so Doug didn't pay him much attention. Doug was hopeful some of the male skaters from *Holiday on Ice* might show up. When the ice show came to town, new faces usually showed up at the Warrior. Even back then, male skaters had a certain reputation.

There was a new face at the bar that night, but Doug didn't remember him from *Holiday on Ice*. He was tall, well built, with dark hair; "a good looking son of a bitch," Doug thought. The new face came in with another man and sat on a barstool next to Doug. Noticing Doug's *Holiday on Ice* program, he struck up a conversation about the performance. After a while, the man turned back to his friend. Floyd, who was still sitting on the other side, revived a noisy attempt to persuade Doug to go home with him. Floyd was beginning to get on Doug's nerves, so Doug decided it was time to go. When he left the bar, he noticed that the newcomer had left too—alone.

Doug walked up Nebraska Street and turned in at another bar he knew. The man followed behind him. Once inside, the man approached Doug, and they talked some more. "Where can we go for a drink?" the man asked. The guy was handsome, no doubt about it, even if he lacked Duane Wheeler's easy charm. But Doug had already made his point once that night; he really didn't need to tumble into bed with another stranger. He hesitated, but only briefly. "I've got some booze at home," he said.

Back at Doug's apartment the two drank a little of Doug's prize scotch. It was getting late so Doug offered to let the man sleep on the couch. The visitor lay down on Doug's bed instead. Doug lay beside him and dozed off. In Doug's version of the story, he was soon awakened by his bedmate, who had begun to fondle him, and one thing led to another. After they had finished, Doug stepped into the kitchen for a cigarette. When he returned, his visitor was standing with a gun in his hand. "You're pinched," he announced, flashing his badge. "Get dressed."

The man handcuffed Doug and telephoned his partner, who showed up a few minutes later in a squad car. Doug recognized the second policeman as the other newcomer who had been at the Warrior earlier that evening. He was another "good-looking SOB" with reddish-blond hair; actually better looking than his partner, Doug thought. But this was not the moment for that kind of observation. It was now 1:30 A.M., and it was clear that Doug would not be sleeping in his own bed that night.

When he was booked at the police station, the cops asked him, "Are you queer?"

Doug replied fiercely: "Do you want to pump my stomach and find out?"

Police patrolman Dick Burke loved sting operations. He relished the challenge, the chance to outwit an opponent, to show who was in charge. Probably the only activity he enjoyed more than doing these things was bragging about them. For example, there was the case of the fellow who kept robbing the collection box at a Catholic church downtown; Burke rigged up an alarm, which he hid in the collection box. He got his man. Then there was the matter of the editor of the *Press-Dispatch*, a Sioux City weekly, who was extorting money from tavern owners in the days when liquor by the drink was still illegal in Iowa. Burke persuaded the owner of one bar to hide a tape recorder under a newspaper the next time the editor came by to shake her down. The ploy worked. Later, the editor—by then the ex-editor—wrote Burke letters from prison. Burke's wife would tell him admiringly, "You get people sent up for 10 years or 15 years, and they shake hands with you and thank you." He kept a scrapbook full of newspaper clippings about his exploits.

By the summer of 1955, Burke had been on the police force for six years; before that, he had spent three years as a private detective. He hadn't really wanted to become a cop. He liked being a private dick, being his own boss, but a friend talked him into it. When he first went to work as a police officer, he was making just $190 a month. A patrolman just starting out had to buy his own uniform and gun, and Burke took out a $500 loan to cover these expenses. He was married and there were kids coming along, so in order to make some extra cash, he worked as an off-duty cop at a bar that catered to packinghouse workers on Lower Fourth Street, where fights broke out constantly. "It was like Madison Square Garden down there on Lower Fourth," he would say. But he was in good shape in those days and managed pretty well. Burke soon found a more lucrative way of earning money as the "champion of Fourth Street in bumper pool." He would make $35 or $40 a night playing pool, on top of the $8 he made doing details.

Burke was 30 at the time, tall, his dark hair parted on the side; he was also rather vain. Years later, in his old age, hunched over with back problems, he was still handsome, with blue eyes, silver hair, his forearms still strong, and an aggressive, if not intimidating, presence. And his vanity was intact. He described a recent function where, as he was arriving, the bartender called in his direction, "There goes Jimmy Stewart!" Burke just waved. At the end of the evening, as he was leaving, the bartender called out, "Bye, Jimmy." Burke was convinced the guy thought he really was Jimmy Stewart. In his younger days, it was probably more a dark-haired Gary Cooper that he resembled.

One sting operation at which Burke excelled was rounding up homosexuals. Although the Sioux City police didn't have a special squad for that purpose, as did some larger cities like Washington, D.C., the chief knew who to turn to when it was useful to arrest some "deviates." In Sioux City, they called it "fruit picking." The long Labor Day weekend was a good time to do it. "That way we didn't have to file charges for three days," said Burke. "It wouldn't get out in the paper, so people wouldn't find out what we were doing and lie low. That gave us three days to clean house."

Even after he had quit the police force and went into the polygraph business, Burke was still proud of what he had learned on the homosexual beat. At a convention of the

American Polygraph Association, he attended a seminar at which the subject of sexual deviates as potential security risks came up. Burke explained to investigators from the Secret Service and the Naval Intelligence Service how to catch a homosexual. He described how he and his partner, Ed Verbeski, spent three days hiding out in a cleaning closet just above the men's room at the Warrior Hotel looking through a ceiling grate to see what was going on. (After a while, Burke insisted upon a mattress.) Although a number of men wandered in and out of the men's room, the two officers couldn't catch anyone in the act or figure out what was going on. Burke was mystified. There was a partition between each bathroom stall with an opening at the bottom. And Burke's eyes soon focused on that open space between the stalls. He began to watch the men's feet. It was then that he stumbled upon what he called the "international code" of homosexuality. A guy in one stall would raise the sole of his foot and move it to the right or left; the guy in the next stall would do the same, move his foot in the direction of the guy in the first stall. That was the signal, the international code, known apparently from Sioux City to Singapore. Soon enough, Burke tried it out for himself. He'd sit in a stall at the Warrior, moving his feet like a practiced dancer, passing written notes to his neighbors—all to entrap Sioux City homosexuals. He'd always wear shiny shoes; in the world of bathroom sex, shiny shoes had cachet, like a crisp fedora or a new suit.

When you rounded up homosexuals, he explained, the key was to find some ingenious way of trapping the first one. Once you did, you'd persuade him to give you a name, and then you'd bring in the person he named and get the second person to give you another name, and you were off and running. "If one admitted against another that he had been with him, that was enough," he said. "They were considered co-conspirators." Burke kept a card file on homosexuals. After he'd talked to one and gotten the name of someone that person had had sex with, he'd put it on a 3-by-5 card. Maybe he wouldn't arrest the second person right away, but he'd have the name if he ever needed it. He had a file in his locker filled with these 3-by-5 cards with names of men from three states. Cops from as far away as Omaha would come to Sioux City to consult with Burke and his index cards.

But how to find that first homosexual? It was tricky. Years later, Burke volunteered an example of how he operated. It was Labor Day weekend, 1955. He went up to the Warrior Hotel bar, which he knew to be a homosexual hangout. There were seven or eight men there. They all had butch-style haircuts and looked like they were "part of a baseball team—they looked like all-American guys." The way Burke told it, when he left the Warrior, one of the guys followed him down Nebraska Street. Burke turned into another bar he knew, where he told the bartender, "Don't mention anything about the police department." The guy who had been following him came in and sat down, and the two of them talked for a while. Burke pretended he had too much to drink. "You shouldn't drive," the guy told him. "I've got an apartment nearby." Burke agreed to go with him. The apartment was a short walk up Nebraska Street.

When they got to the apartment, Burke said he had to go to the bathroom. He noticed a white cabinet next to the sink and carefully stashed his badge and holster behind it. When he returned to the living room, the two men had a drink and talked for a while longer. "You shouldn't be driving," his host repeated. Burke conceded the point and stripped down to his T-shirt and shorts and lay down. After a minute or two he felt a hand on his leg. "Wait a minute," Burke said. "I have to go to the bathroom." A minute later he emerged, still in his T-shirt and shorts, but this time with his badge and shoulder holster. "You're pinched," he told the man. He called his partner, Ed Verbeski, and a squad car arrived and took them to the police station.

Dick Burke proudly recorded it all in his scrapbook.

CHAPTER 8

Enemies Within

It wasn't easy being a homosexual in the 1950s, especially in a town like Sioux City. In the postwar rush to normalization and in the tense political atmosphere of the early days of the Cold War, the fear of the other became a major component of American life. Those who didn't fit the mold—from bachelors to beatniks to teenage rebels without a cause—were viewed with grave suspicion. The two worst things you could be in the 1950s were a Communist or a homosexual; they were the invisible, undetectable "enemies within," the great skeletons in the closet of the books and plays of the period.

In February 1950, three weeks after Wisconsin senator Joe McCarthy made his famous speech in Wheeling, West Virginia, alleging that Communists had infiltrated the U.S. State Department, Undersecretary of State John Peurifoy was testifying before a Senate committee. In the course of his testimony, he was asked how many State Department employees had resigned during the previous three years while under investigation as potential security risks. "Ninety-one persons in the shady category," replied the undersecretary. "Most of these were homosexuals."

Seemingly out of nowhere, another domestic enemy had emerged—homosexuals, also known as "perverts" or "deviates" in the language of the time. (The word *gay* hadn't come into widespread use; even *The New York Times* used the word *perverts* in its headlines.) The Red Scare quickly merged with the Lavender Scare. The chairman of the Republican National Committee, Guy George Gabrielson, warned in a letter to the party faithful that "perhaps as dangerous as the actual

Communists are the sexual perverts who have infiltrated our Government in recent years.... It is the talk of Washington." A Washington, D.C., vice squad officer told the Senate that there were 5,000 "perverts" in the nation's capital, the vast majority employed by government agencies. A Senate subcommittee immediately launched an investigation. Meanwhile, Nebraska senator Kenneth Wherry, the Republican floor leader, was telling *New York Post* columnist Max Lerner, "You can hardly separate homosexuals from subversives. Mind you, I don't say every homosexual is a subversive, and I don't say every subversive is a homosexual. But a man of low morality is a menace in the government, wherever he is, and they are all tied together."

Once the outcry about homosexuals in high places began in the winter and spring of 1950, large numbers of gays and lesbians were dismissed from civilian governmental posts—an average of 60 a month over the next year and a half. Under the federal government's loyalty-security program, amended in 1953, "sexual perversion" was sufficient and necessary grounds for the termination of a federal employee.

The FBI's job in all this was to supply the Civil Service Commission with background information on employees and applicants for employment. The bureau's regional offices compiled lists of homosexual bars and gathering places and kept in close contact with vice squad officers from various police departments who in turn supplied arrests records on morals charges. The fact that FBI Director Hoover had lived for many years with his second in command, Clyde Tolson, in what was, at the very least, an intimate friendship—and perhaps much more than that—may have made him even more zealous.

Senator McCarthy and his chief counsel, Roy Cohn—the leading anti-Communist crusaders of the period—had no compunction about using allegations of homosexuality to discredit their enemies. Cohn, a closeted homosexual, had his homosexuality thrown back at him by his opponents (most famously at the Army-McCarthy hearings when the word "fairy" was coyly bandied about by the Army's counsel and Cohn was asked whether he had a "special interest" in his friend G. David Schine, a McCarthy committee aide). At the same time rumors circulated that McCarthy himself might share Cohn's proclivities; the senator's marriage at age 45 to his secretary, Jean Kerr, in September 1953, was viewed in some quarters as an effort to counteract these rumors. In the polarized political climate of the 1950s, "queer baiting" became a weapon used by both McCarthyites and their enemies.

Ironically, the queer baiting of the period was only possible because the previously taboo subject was beginning to gain more attention. During World War II, for the first time, draft boards screened for homosexuality, asking young men "Do you like girls?" and homosexual GIs from around the country came into contact with each other in the mass mobilization of the war years. Historian John D'Emilio has characterized this period as "something of a national coming-out experience for gays and lesbians." After the war, gay and lesbian GIs who didn't want to return home—or who were reluctant to do so because they had received an "undesirable" discharge for homosexuality—swelled the population of cities such as New York, Chicago, and San Francisco. The findings of the Kinsey Reports, published in 1948 and 1953, indicating that 8% of American men were exclusively homosexual for at least three years during their adult lives (the percentages for women were lower) stunned the public, causing many to realize that same-sex relationships were more prevalent than many had imagined. The first U.S. gay organization, the Mattachine Society, and first lesbian organization, the Daughters of Bilitis, were founded in 1950 and 1955 respectively, in part as a response to the greater openness of the war years and in part as a reaction to the repression of the 1950s.

The search for "sexual perverts" in the 1950s went far beyond weeding out a few homosexuals in State Department posts. An atmosphere of purge and persecution was prevalent nationwide. Homosexual acts were against the law in every state in the union; in Iowa, for example, consensual sodomy was punishable by 10 years in prison, and conspiracy to commit a felony (sodomy) was punishable by three years. In Washington, D.C., arrests of gay men numbered 1,000 a year in the 1950s, with police entrapping men in parks and movie houses. Four detectives on that city's vice squad were exclusively involved in cracking down on homosexual men. Raids on gay bars were commonplace in many cities, and those arrested usually found their names and addresses published in the newspaper the next day. On a single night in Baltimore in October 1955, 162 men were arrested at a gay club. In gay bars, men would be dancing with men and women with women; a red light would flash on the dance floor, announcing a police raid, and the same-sex couples would quickly switch partners. Often, the police weren't fooled and arrested everyone anyway.

One of the most grievous instances of antigay persecution took place in Boise, Idaho, beginning in November 1955. The arrest of three men on charges of sexual activity with teenage boys precipitated a massive witch hunt. An investigator who had worked purging homosexuals in the State Department was called to Boise to clean up the city. (Under the headline "Crush the Monster," a November 3, 1955, *Idaho Daily Statesman* editorial called for "immediate and systematic cauterization" in the wake of the first arrests.) Over a 15-month period, some 1,472 men were brought in for questioning, 16 were charged—several were sentenced to long prison terms—and large numbers of gay men fled the Idaho capital. The widely accepted belief that gay men sought to recruit young men into homosexuality was behind this and other roundups of the period.

Given the forces arrayed against them, gays and lesbians could defend themselves in few ways. Even the American Civil Liberties Union refused to come to their assistance. The fledgling gay organizations—the Mattachine Society and the Daughters of Bilitis—were extremely weak and took a low profile, eschewing political activism and relying on heterosexual experts—sociologists, psychologists, and legal and medical figures—who could provide support for their cause. During this period, leaders of the Mattachine Society almost always used pseudonyms, with good reason. FBI and police informants regularly attended the organization's meetings, collected the names of those in attendance, and tape recorded the group's lectures.

In the 1950s, homosexuality was considered an illness. The belief that homosexuals could be changed into heterosexuals through psychoanalysis was a dogma that few questioned. That one could be a homosexual and still have a meaningful and satisfying life was assumed to be impossible. In 1952, when the American Psychiatric Association issued its first official catalog of mental disorders, homosexuality was listed prominently among the sociopathic personality disturbances. Psychiatric hospitals often treated gay men and women with shock treatments, lobotomies, and aversion therapies.

At this time, the terms *homosexual, pervert, sexual deviate, pedophile, sex criminal, sex offender*, and *sexual psychopath* often overlapped and were used interchangeably. This was more than just a matter of linguistic sloppiness: The use of such imprecise language played a role in forming and confirming public views about homosexuals. Historian Estelle Freedman raises the question of whether the term *psychopath* served as "part of a code for homosexual" at a time of heightened public consciousness about homosexuality. In his lurid but influential book, *The Sexual Criminal*, published in 1949, J. Paul de River, a criminal psychiatrist and founder of the Sex Offense Bureau of the city of Los Angeles, called the homosexual "a psychopath rather than a neurotic" and portrayed homosexuals as prone to violence. Medical history was "rich" with case reports of homosexual sadism and masochism, he wrote, and "it is not unusual to find sadistic homicide, particularly among the male homosexuals."

In the introduction to de River's book, Eugene D. Williams, former chief deputy district attorney of Los Angeles County, went even further. "The sex pervert, in his more innocuous form, is too frequently regarded as merely a 'queer' individual who never hurts anyone but himself," he wrote. "All too often we lose sight of the fact that the homosexual is an inveterate seducer of the young of both sexes and that he presents a social problem because he is not content with being degenerate himself; he must have degenerate companions, and is ever seeking for younger victims."

In this social climate, it was no wonder that a gay man or a lesbian in Sioux City and a thousand towns like it lived lives of fear and desperation. There was virtually no avenue for articulating the view that being homosexual was anything other than a mental illness or pathology. If you were a gay man in Sioux City, you married your high school sweetheart and tried to put any sexual desire for men out of your mind, or you never married and lived quietly with your mother, cultivating an interest in antiques or community theater, or you simply left town. Maybe, once in a while you stopped in for a quickie at the Warrior Hotel bathroom. If you were bold or lucky, perhaps you discovered some like-minded people and established your own private social world. If you were bolder or luckier still, you might have a lover, might even live with a lover, though that was extremely difficult in a town the size of Sioux City, where everyone knew everyone.

One thing was clear to all but a handful of gay men and lesbians: Homosexuality had to be hidden at all costs. In most cases, exposure meant the loss of livelihood, family, and social position, for homosexuals were as marginal a group as there was in Sioux City. Although the early publications of the Mattachine Society and the Daughters of Bilitis attempted to counteract the silence and condemnation surrounding the subject, their readership was tiny, and their membership was concentrated within a few large urban areas, mostly on the East and West coasts. Certainly, the news that homosexuality was anything other than sick or subversive had not yet reached Sioux City, Iowa.

CHAPTER 9

Naming Names

Doug Thorson was sharing a cell in the Sioux City jail with a man arrested for bigamy. They each slept on a steel frame with no mattress or blankets. The August heat spell was just a memory; as the calendar moved toward the middle of September, the nights grew increasingly chilly. The food was dreadful—mostly beans. Doug's cellmate had three wives. "What are you in here for?" the bigamist asked. "They say I'm queer," Doug said.

The bigamist just shrugged.

Jail brought out Doug's cantankerousness. "Who's on the other side? Who's over there?" he'd call in a loud voice each morning.

On Doug's second day in jail, Harold McBride shouted his name.

"Harold! Not you too!" Doug exclaimed.

Harold McBride owned a beauty shop in Kingsley, a lonesome, windswept town 45 minutes east of Sioux City dominated by a grain elevator. Doug had met him through Duane Wheeler. Harold, who was 35, was married and had three children—two boys and a girl—aged 11, 10, and 8. Hairdressing ran in Harold's family; his mother's two brothers cut hair for a living, and Harold was the 17th blood relative to become a hairdresser. Harold was serious and intelligent, with a self-deprecating humor and a tendency to worry. He grew up in Woodward, near Des Moines, and enrolled in a pre-med course at the University of Omaha. But his studies were interrupted by the war. He married in 1943 while he was a pharmacist mate second class in the Coast Guard in Southern

California. In the military he developed ear problems and received a medical discharge; doctors feared he might go insane if he got near an explosion. He needed to find work quickly, so he chose the family profession. "I became the first veteran in the state of California to study hairdressing under the GI bill," he would say later.

Harold came back to Iowa to raise his family and sell beauty products. In 1949 he opened a hair salon in Kingsley. He had researched the subject and found that Kingsley had the second biggest drawing area for potential clients in the state; after all, farmers' wives needed to get their hair done too. Harold was the first male hairdresser Kingsley had ever seen, and business at his House of Beauty was good. Plus, Harold had a gimmick. Any bride who had him do her hair before her wedding could bring her veil along to the salon, and Harold would snap her picture once he was finished. That day, in church, Harold would then put her veil on for her and make sure her hair was perfect. Pictures of young brides covered the walls of the House of Beauty.

Harold was also the president of the Sioux City Coiffure Guild, an affiliate of the state cosmetology association. One of his best friends, Eugene Bergstrom, headed up the affiliate in nearby Sioux Falls, South Dakota, where he also owned a beauty shop. (He was known professionally as "Mr. Eugene.") Gene had grown up in Le Mars, a town not far from Kingsley. Harold and Gene had something else in common: They both liked men, although Harold was married, and Gene, a large man who was very much the old-fashioned queen, would later marry, much to the bemusement of his friends. (Gene's wife, even larger than he was, would be known as "Mrs. Eugene.")

Harold had a male "friend" in Storm Lake, whom he would visit now and then. For several years he had also been involved with an English teacher in a nearby town; Harold had helped get him his first teaching job. Harold had never told his wife, Glenda, any of this. If she had any suspicions, she kept them to herself.

Still, they had a good life together. Harold and Glenda and another couple from Moville, a town between Kingsley and Sioux City, participated in community theater; in the summer, the two couples went on trips to the Colorado Rockies and the Black Hills of South Dakota.

On the late Saturday afternoon of Labor Day weekend, 1955, Harold drove to Moville in his new-model Pontiac to get a haircut. "Daddy, can I go with you?" his daughter pleaded. Harold said no. "I'll be right back," he promised. After the haircut, he decided to continue on to Sioux City and see his friend Marie Ellis, who ran the Sioux City School of Cosmetology, where Duane Wheeler was studying. Harold felt guilty not going right home as he had promised his daughter, so somewhere between Moville and Sioux City he pulled over to the side of the road, intending to turn back. But he kept on to Sioux City.

He parked his car in the lot behind the Warrior Hotel and met Marie at a nearby bar. They chatted for about an hour or so, and then Harold headed back to his car. As he walked along Sixth Street, he peered into the lighted window of the Tom Tom Room and spotted his friend Gene Bergstrom sitting with a group of men whom he didn't recognize. Harold didn't know too many of the men who frequented the Warrior. He never spent time at the bar or cruised the men's room there; the only time he had gone to the bars in Sioux City was with a group of other hairdressers. It was around 8:30—time to be getting home—but he decided to go inside to join them for a quick drink.

114

Gene was his hostly and gregarious self. Although he lived in Sioux Falls, he often spent weekends in Sioux City; for a gay man, it was easier to be more open in another town, and, anyway, Sioux City was a lot livelier than Sioux Falls in those days. "A born promoter," Harold would say of Gene. "He could sell ice to the Eskimos." Gene was glad to see Harold, as always. He was camping it up; that was Sioux City gay style and Gene's style in particular. Harold hadn't been there for more than 15 minutes when two men in business suits entered the bar from the hotel side. They identified themselves as police officers and asked everyone for IDs. "Come with us," they said. Harold McBride and Gene Bergstrom had been pinched.

At the police station, they were taken off separately for interrogation. Harold was terrified. The questions were coming at him fast and furious: When had he had his first "immoral sexual relations" with another man? Who was it with? What type of sexual relations had they had? Who else had he had sex with? Who was the "aggressor"? Did he realize these immoral sexual relations were violations of the laws of the state of Iowa? No lawyer was present, and Harold told them far more than he should have.

The police then called Harold's wife. A friend drove her into Sioux City so she could retrieve the Pontiac from the Warrior parking lot.

In the days that followed, the cells in the Sioux City jail were filling up with homosexual and bisexual men. Doug knew some of them, but others he had never seen before. Harold didn't know anyone except for Doug—and Gene, of course. The police brought in Floyd Edwards, the window dresser who had tried to pick up Doug at the Warrior bar the

115

night Doug had taken the cop back to his apartment. There was a hairdresser who had moved to Sioux City a few years before from a South Dakota town, and his lover, a mysterious fellow with a slight foreign accent who taught dancing at Arthur Murray. An older Jewish man who owned a shop on Fourth Street was brought in, as well as a salesman at Younker-Davidson's department store. There was a farmer from nearby Homer, Nebraska, and a clerk from Le Mars who worked at the state liquor store there. By the end of the week, the number of men arrested was close to 20—virtually anyone in Sioux City and the surrounding towns who had ever poked his head out of his closet door.

Eventually, Duane Wheeler was also brought in. Doug always said you'd never know that Duane was gay, but in the end that didn't save him. The police had called Duane on the phone. He met them on the street corner, where they then handcuffed him and took him to jail. Doug insisted that he never gave the police Duane's name.

Doug was convinced that the new barmaid at the Warrior took down the names and addresses of a number of the men and gave them to the police. Later he ran into the regular barmaid, who said she had taken a two-week vacation during the period the arrests occurred. "If I had known, I'd have warned all of you," she told him.

For his part, Harold McBride would recall a male, not a female bartender, although this discrepancy may have been due to the fact that he was arrested on a different night than Doug and generally didn't spend as much time at the Warrior anyway. "Eugene always felt that the bartender called the police," said Harold. "Maybe he was alerted to the fact that they were on a roundup. I remember Eugene saying 'That bartender, he's the one who turned us in!' "

116

Dick Burke also debunked the story that the police had planted a barmaid at the Warrior. "We didn't operate that way," he insisted. But perhaps he just wanted all the credit.

The following Thursday, September 8, 1955, *The Sioux City Journal* published an account of the arrests, under the headline "Several Face Morals Charge After Roundup." The newspaper reported that 19 men had been arrested, most of whom would be charged with offenses related to sexual deviation. The roundup, the newspaper wrote, had begun that weekend at a downtown tavern and "as more names were mentioned, the pickups continued." The *Journal* did not list the names of the arrested men until later.

On the same day, *The Le Mars Globe-Post*, always on the lookout for sensation and scandal, made its first reference to the arrests in a front-page story headlined "Crackdown On 'Queers' Has Begun." Three men from the Le Mars area had been brought in in the roundup, the newspaper reported, without revealing names. The *Globe-Post* also wrote that Plymouth County attorney Bill Sturges, fresh from his successful prosecution of Ernest Triplett, had compiled a "secret dossier" of Plymouth County residents suspected of homosexuality. (Sturges later vehemently denied this.) The purpose of the dossier was to give the police a definite "prospect list" to check when crimes were fresh, a tactic the newspaper asserted had been standard practice in European cities for the past 50 years.

In its September 19 article, the *Globe-Post* named Harold McBride and Eugene Bergstrom as two of the local men arrested in Sioux City. In the same article, the newspaper noted, "Quite a number of the men arrested are beauty shop operators." There were three, to be exact, plus two beauty school students.

Meanwhile, at the Sioux City jail, the police grilled the men, pressing them to name names of other men they'd slept with, assuring them it would make it easier for them if they did. Floyd Edwards, the window dresser, implicated Billy Ivers, who was studying hairdressing with Duane Wheeler—or so Billy was convinced. Billy was just a kid, a couple of years out of high school. (Floyd himself had been arrested after officers Burke and Verbeski had overheard him trying to pick up Doug Thorson that night at the Warrior bar; that was apparently enough to bring him in.) Frank Hildebrandt, the hairdresser, and his lover, Karl Schmidt, the dance instructor, implicated each other. Harold McBride admitted he'd had homosexual contacts while on the road but insisted he never told the police the names of his sexual partners, and, in fact, they were never brought in. The police tried to get Doug Thorson to go out "spotting" with them and identify other homosexuals. He refused, he said, but others agreed to do so. "The cops would promise you anything," Doug explained. "They behaved differently with each person. You just didn't know what to do."

In such circumstances, the men could do little but agree to whatever the police wanted. They couldn't get out on bail, and many had no legal representation to speak of. Doug's brother asked his lawyer to represent Doug, but the lawyer told him he'd heard it was a losing battle and wouldn't take the case. Years later neither Doug nor Harold remembered seeing a lawyer at all. Court records state that Doug was represented by M.E. Rawlings, a former county attorney known for his role in cleaning up corruption in Sioux City in the 1930s. More than likely, Rawlings merely signed the documents without doing any other legal work in the case.

During the interrogations, one topic that particularly interested the police was the murder of Donna Sue Davis, which had occurred less than two months before. "They questioned us all on that crime," Doug recalled. "They kept saying, 'You did it! You know you did it!' " Doug was able to tell the police exactly where he had been that Sunday night when Donna Sue was taken, however. The unexpected flooding had washed out the roads the night before, and he had stayed over at Duane's. Doug and Duane spent the entire next day together and went to the movies that night; the show was just ending around the time of Donna Sue's abduction. The flood made it easy for everybody in Sioux City to remember their whereabouts that July night.

Doug and Duane's names do not appear in the directory of suspects in Chief Gibbons's voluminous notebooks regarding the little girl's murder. Years later Harold McBride had no recollection of being questioned about the murder during his interrogation, and his name does not appear in the list of suspects either.

Staring at the bare walls in his Sioux City jail cell, Harold McBride surveyed the ruin of a once well-ordered life. Who would take care of his family? What would happen to his marriage? His business? He was overwhelmed with guilt; if he had only listened to his 8-year-old daughter and let her come with him to get a haircut that Saturday evening.... Why had he insisted on driving to Sioux City, when he obviously should have gone home to be with his family? Glenda, his wife, came to visit him in jail; she was standing by him. That was some comfort, but it also intensified his feelings of guilt at having betrayed those who most depended upon him. Two of Harold's Shriner brothers paid a visit too. Harold was a member of the Shriners (an auxiliary order of the Masons), and he asked his Shriner brothers to help him get out of jail. They refused. Later, he said, these same brothers helped get him expelled from the Masons.

Doug Thorson was just plain angry. On his third day in jail, he discovered that he had a nasty case of trench mouth. His family doctor arrived to treat him. "Maybe I got it from the cop I slept with," he told a guard, bitterly. "Yeah, right," said the guard, unimpressed. Then again, maybe it was that conventioneer from out of town.

Doug was angry at himself too. Before he started going out with Duane, he had dated a guy who, unbeknownst to Doug, had been previously arrested on a morals charge. The guy was on probation, and he insisted that he and Doug have sex only over in Plymouth County, where no one knew him. It wasn't until their third or fourth date that Doug's friend explained why they had to drive to the next county for their liaisons. Doug was furious and pulled the car over the side of the road and told the guy to get out. The entire experience should have taught him to be more careful. But it hadn't. He had always been reckless, and now he had gone and gotten himself in a real mess.

One day, Karl Schmidt, the Arthur Murray dance teacher in the cell next to Doug, passed him a note that said, "I Love You," with the words cut out of a magazine. But the dance teacher had never known Doug before they were put behind bars, and, even in jail, he had never seen him, just heard his voice. It was just weird, Doug recalled later, part of the weirdness of the whole experience. He didn't reply to the note.

Meanwhile, autumn was approaching. The temperatures were falling into the 30s at night, and the prisoners still weren't given blankets. Doug's brother brought him a sweater. His mother came too. She met with county attorney Don O'Brien, as did all of the families of the men.

"We can't let that type of people run loose in this town," she recalled the county attorney telling her. "They need to be locked up."

"What type of people do you mean?" she asked O'Brien.

That was how Doug Thorson's mother learned that her son was homosexual.

Less than two weeks after his arrest, Doug pleaded guilty to conspiracy to commit a felony (sodomy)—punishable by three years in jail. He was in a bind: He had to plead guilty to the conspiracy charge or face the harsher charge of sodomy, which carried a penalty of 10 years. Gene Bergstrom did the same. At first, Duane Wheeler refused to plead guilty to even the lesser charge, but the county attorney's office pressured him, charging him with sodomy and dangling in front of him the possibility of spending 10 years in prison. At that point, Duane changed his plea to guilty, and the sodomy charge was reduced to the lesser conspiracy charge. Harold McBride pleaded guilty to the charge of lascivious acts with a child— defined as someone under the age of 16—punishable by four years in prison. (The name of the "child" was never revealed, and, years later, Harold was unaware what the charge had been and was thoroughly puzzled by it.)

But instead of prison, the authorities had something else in mind for Harold McBride and Doug Thorson and Duane Wheeler and Gene Bergstrom and the other men they'd rounded up. County attorney Don O'Brien asked the court to declare them all "criminal sexual psychopaths" under the state law enacted several months before.

On September 8, George W. Prichard, judge of the Fourth Judicial District of Iowa, "ordered, adjudged, and decreed" that Harold McBride be declared a criminal sexual psychopath. The

121

judge committed him to the state hospital for the insane at Mount Pleasant. A week later, on September 15, another district court judge, L.B. Forsling, classified Doug Thorson as a criminal sexual psychopath and ordered him to Mount Pleasant as well. Eugene Bergstrom was committed on the 21st and Duane Wheeler on the 22nd. The other arrested men suffered the same fate. By the end of the month, some 20 men from Sioux City were officially declared to be sexual psychopaths and ordered to Mount Pleasant. All were judged to be suffering from a "mental disorder." Their sentences were indefinite; they would remain at the mental hospital until it was determined that they were "cured."

Governor Hoegh, with the assistance of the Woodbury County attorney Don O'Brien, had found the first 15 men and more that he had been looking for to pacify public opinion and fill up his special ward at Mount Pleasant. The governor had said that he wanted to treat the sex deviate "who is now roaming the street but never committed a crime." The state was doing something. It was far easier to find homosexual men to fill up that ward than to track down child molesters and child murderers. And as it was in Sioux City in those days, the general public believed that homosexuals were dangerous and prone to violence anyway. The way to prevent future Jimmy Bremmerses and Donna Sue Davises was to lock up any sexual deviate the police could get their hands on. As a Sioux City lawyer explained it, "People thought that anyone with any sexual aberration could do anything. If you loved boys, you could kill little girls."

After their sentencing, Doug Thorson and the other men were transferred from the city jail to the Woodbury County jail, where conditions were better. They had mattresses to sleep on, the food was tolerable, and there were even recent magazines to read. Doug heard people talking about Mount Pleasant, but he still wasn't sure what the place was exactly. Was it a state prison? Someone had said it was an insane asylum, but that didn't make sense. But Harold McBride knew exactly what Mount Pleasant was. Back in his hometown, before he went off to the service, he had worked as a ward supervisor at the Woodward State Hospital for Epileptics and the Feeble-minded. He had seen shock treatments and knew what such places were like. He knew that once you were committed to a state hospital, the authorities could do anything they wanted to you. Anything.

On September 26, Harold McBride was driven to Mount Pleasant Hospital. Doug Thorson and Duane Wheeler went three days later. On that trip, Doug and Duane were the only passengers. Two other men who had been transported to Mount Pleasant in the same car a few days earlier had been handcuffed in the backseat; the door handles and window handles had been removed so they couldn't escape. Doug and Duane weren't handcuffed, but the door handles were still missing. The two of them were together again, but not in a way they had ever imagined.

Meanwhile, in Sioux City, the killer of Donna Sue Davis remained at large.

CHAPTER 10

Morals Crusader

When Donald Eugene O'Brien was elected the Woodbury County attorney in November 1954, Sioux City's political and legal worlds were stunned. O'Brien was only 31, had never run for elective office, and was a Democrat in a traditionally Republican county. The county attorney whom he unseated, Wally Huff, was experienced and well-respected. But in trying to stamp out corruption in Sioux City municipal government, Huff had stepped on too many toes. He brought graft and bribery indictments against a number of influential city officials, including the public safety, parks, and finance commissioners; the city purchasing agent was forced to resign under pressure. As *The Sioux City Journal* (which supported Huff) noted, "This was perhaps the first time in Sioux City's history when a county attorney made such an action stick." Business, liquor, and gambling interests were determined to oust Huff from office: Sioux City had traditionally been a wide-open Little Chicago, after all, and an awful lot of people were determined to keep it that way.

So Huff's opponents backed O'Brien, a relatively unknown attorney in the city's legal department. His campaign ads revealed little about the candidate or what he stood for: "Don O'Brien: Who he is: married, 31 years old, veteran of World War II, seven years of active law practice, awarded Distinguished Flying Cross, five years city prosecutor of Sioux City." When *The Sioux City Journal* queried candidates about their aims if elected, O'Brien responded, "I believe that it is the duty of the county attorney to see that all laws are enforced." He did promise to place special emphasis on preventing juvenile delinquency and on "protecting young people." And while some might take this latter promise as a pledge to crack down on sex deviates in the wake of the Jimmy Bremmers case, this was as specific as he got. O'Brien's platform was deliberately bland, barely a platform at all. The main thing in his favor was that Don O'Brien wasn't Wally Huff.

And while Huff was overconfident, O'Brien campaigned hard, upsetting the incumbent 16,348 to 15,810—the only Democrat to win in an election year in which Republicans swept the other seven races for county-wide office. Still, the vote was so close that Huff demanded a recount, and it wasn't until mid December—just two and a half weeks before the new county attorney's term was set to begin—that he finally conceded defeat and invited O'Brien to his office for a courtesy briefing on the county's legal case load.

For O'Brien, the 1954 election marked the beginning of a distinguished political and legal career. He would eventually make some important political friends—John and Robert F. Kennedy, among them—and become a U.S. attorney and a federal judge known for his principled (and sometimes unpopular) stands on civil liberties, prisoners' rights, and Native American issues. He and his brother Jack would emerge as dominant figures in the local Democratic Party—with Jack in the role of political operative and Don as statesman. In later years, a representative of the next generation, Dave O'Brien, would run unsuccessfully for the U.S. House.

When Don O'Brien took office in January 1955, he was ambitious but inexperienced, and so was his staff. He appointed two other young Sioux City lawyers—Bill Forker and John F. Clemens—as his assistant county attorneys; both were just a few years out of law school and had no prosecutorial experience.

The grand jury was sitting for its winter term on the day after O'Brien took office. The first case before it was a murder involving the death of a woman during a botched backroom abortion. Neither O'Brien nor his deputies, however, had ever been inside a grand jury room, and O'Brien had never prosecuted a murder case. O'Brien eventually won a conviction, but it was a rocky beginning.

Another of the leftover matters facing the novice county attorney was the case of Ernest Triplett, still a patient at Cherokee and yet to be indicted. O'Brien maneuvered skillfully. By making sure the case would be prosecuted, O'Brien fulfilled his campaign promise: "to protect children." By making sure it was tried in neighboring Plymouth rather than Woodbury County, he spared himself the headache of prosecuting a case in which the only hard evidence was a confession obtained under the effect of mind-altering drugs, a fact that O'Brien may or may not have been aware of at the time. (He later would deny any knowledge of this.) In his handling of the Triplett case, he had dodged a bullet.

Then, six months after O'Brien took office, Donna Sue Davis was murdered. The inability of the Sioux City police to find the culprit amidst public outrage reflected poorly on both the department and the county attorney. Moreover, O'Brien had seen Donna Sue's body and had been horrified. The Iowa sexual psychopath law had recently been enacted, and local prosecutors received copies of the law and suggestions as to how to put it into effect. The governor was pressing for somebody to populate his newly established sexual psychopath ward at Mount Pleasant. The young county attorney saw an opportunity. The local police force rounded up as many sex deviates as Sioux City could furnish. There is no proof that O'Brien gave the initial order for the roundup; it is possible that the police acted first, and O'Brien saw his opportunity after that. On matters like this, however, the county attorney and the police tended to work hand in hand.

By the end of September 1955, two and a half months after Donna Sue's murder, a total of 22 men had been arrested for morals offenses, almost all from Sioux City and nearby towns. Seventeen pleaded guilty to "conspiracy to commit a felony," the lesser version of a sodomy charge. Another four pleaded guilty to "lascivious acts with a child." Still another pleaded guilty to possession of obscene books and pictures. And if there remains some question as to whether O'Brien authorized the roundup, one thing is clear: He did petition the court to certify the men as sexual psychopaths.

Within days of the arrests, Woodbury County district court judges George W. Prichard and L.B. Forsling acceded to the county attorney's request, sentencing the men to Mount Pleasant Hospital for an indefinite period. All but two eventually went to the mental hospital. By occupation and hometown, the men included:

3 window dressers (Sioux City)
a hairdressing student (Sioux City)
a hairdressing student (South Sioux City, Nebraska)
a hairdresser (Kingsley, Iowa)
a hairdresser (Sioux Falls, S.D.)
a hairdresser (Sioux City)
a dance teacher (Sioux City)
a department store trainee (Sioux City)
a cook (Sioux City)
a clothing-store clerk (Sioux City)
an unemployed man (Sioux City)

a towel-service employee (Sioux City)
a service station attendant (Sioux City)
a farmer (Homer, Nebraska)
a store clerk (Le Mars, Iowa)
a student (South Sioux City, Nebraska)
a hospital worker (Cherokee, Iowa)
an unemployed man (Dakota City, Nebraska)
a clothing designer (Chicago)
a man of unknown occupation (California)

The chance for quick action in these cases was enhanced by the presence of Judge George W. Prichard on the district court bench. Prichard had a reputation for brooking no delays in sentencing. Other judges tended to give attorneys a good deal of leeway, accepting requests for continuances and delays, often to the dismay of the county attorney's office. But not Prichard. When he took charge of the criminal docket, as he did every fall, justice was rapidly dispensed in cases that had been hanging around for months. So when O'Brien submitted his requests to have the men certified as sexual psychopaths, he knew the court would move swiftly.

To county attorney O'Brien, Sioux City was in a predicament that required immediate action. "You have to go by what had happened in this town at the time," he said many years later. "It was a fact that kids weren't safe. No one was letting their kids out of their sight. The Donna Sue case was going every day. The gays at the time probably thought we were overdoing it. It wasn't a universal thing. There were two gay doctors in town and they weren't picked up. I think those who know me over the years would not counsel you that I was somehow a gay basher. The point was the fear of losing kids and grandkids was very important in this town. The crime had to have been done by someone who had inappropriate tendencies. The FBI was looking into everybody who might have such tendencies."

He never personally tried to figure out the appropriate treatment or punishment. "Someone persuaded the legislature to pass the sexual psychopath law," he said. "Prosecutors got copies of the law. It wouldn't be surprising if prosecutors thought about using it. The only city with two bad incidents happened to be us."

The indictments against the 17 charged with conspiracy to commit a felony paired each defendant with a co-conspirator. Thus, Doug Thorson was accused of "conspiring, agreeing, and confederating together" to commit a felony with Duane Wheeler, on or about July 16, 1955, and "at divers times" after that date. In layman's language, it meant the two had had sex on July 16 and again later, presumably in the privacy of their bedroom. Frank Hildebrandt, the Sioux City hairdresser, was accused of a similar conspiracy with his lover, dance instructor Karl Schmidt. Eugene Harbeck, a South Sioux City student, was charged with conspiracy to commit a felony with his lover, Gregg Phillips, a Sioux City cook. And on and on.

As Officer Dick Burke would point out, all that was needed was for one person to name someone else and to admit he'd had homosexual relations with him; the other man could then be charged as a "co-conspirator." This was the 1950s: Whether the object was rooting out Communists or sexual deviates, naming names was acceptable, admirable, practically a patriotic duty. In some cases—like that of Duane Wheeler—the police called the men on the telephone and brought them to the station after someone had given their names. In at least one case—that of a 31-year-old cook named Wayne Reed—the "crime" had taken place long before. Reed was accused of conspiracy to commit a felony with Floyd Edwards. On Reed's court documents, the date of the offense was listed as June 1952, with Floyd listed as the "only witness for the state." The most likely explanation is that under police pressure, Floyd dredged up the name of someone with whom he'd had sex three years before. Both were sent to Mount Pleasant.

Court records in these cases show some glaring inaccuracies. In four cases, county attorney O'Brien's petitions to declare certain individuals as sexual psychopaths stated that they "contributed to the delinquency of a minor." This was apparently an effort to strengthen the county attorney's arguments. But in all four cases, the "minors" turn out unquestionably to have been adults. Doug Thorson, 23, was accused of contributing to the delinquency of "a minor," Duane Wheeler; records at the Woodbury County courthouse, however, confirm that Duane was 28. The petition to declare Frank Hildebrandt, the 29-year-old Sioux City hairdresser, as a sexual psychopath linked him with a so-called minor as well—the dance teacher Karl Schmidt; in fact, Schmidt was 28. Floyd Edwards, 29, was listed as being responsible for corrupting underage Le Mars store clerk Charles Schroeder; according to his own court record, Schroeder was 31. And the petition declaring Greg Phillips, a 23-year-old Sioux City cook, to be a sexual psychopath claimed that he had contributed to the delinquency of South Sioux City student, Eugene Harbeck. Harbeck, it turns out, was 32, nine years older than Phillips.

When Judge Donald O'Brien was shown copies of these petitions many years after the cases were prosecuted, he immediately recognized the incorrect characterizations of adults as minors. "This is bad news," he said, increasingly distressed as he leafed through the documents. "I can't explain these. George Prichard was a fair judge who didn't let us run over

130

anybody, although we didn't try. He wouldn't have permitted it. There must be some explanation." Judge O'Brien had reason to be distressed. His signature was on those petitions, and the information contained in at least four of them was false.

In 1995, when questioned about the cases, Judge O'Brien was eager to prove that he was not a "gay basher," in his words; the social climate had changed. But back in 1955, two and a half months after the roundup had begun, county attorney O'Brien certainly sounded like he was on a moral crusade. In an interview with *The Des Moines Register*, published on November 23, 1955, he proclaimed "The word is out they're not welcome in Sioux City anymore," referring to sexual deviates. A boy of 13 had been picked up as he walked along the street in Sioux City soliciting others, O'Brien told the newspaper. "You have to protect the young people from other things than murder," he said. "Sometimes things like this can be worse."

The boy in question was Gary Paul Marsh, and he was actually 15 and a half at the time, though he looked younger. He was arrested at the urinal in the bathroom of the Warrior Hotel, where he had made the mistake of trying to pick up a police officer.

Gary was about to enter his sophomore year at Central High School. He was the fifth child in a family of seven. His father, a linotypist at *The Sioux City Journal,* was an alcoholic; he'd receive his paycheck on Friday and vanish until Sunday night. Gary's mother worked cleaning houses and essentially supported the family. His parents divorced around this time, and his mother soon remarried. Gary was an average student, doing just what he needed to receive passing grades. He liked to watch sports and play canasta. Throughout most of his high school years, he dated a girl from Heelan, the local Catholic high school. As a result, he got to take advantage of "double everything": two proms, two sets of football games, etc.

But Gary was also a "horny little kid," as he would describe himself. On Saturday afternoons he would take the bus downtown and go to the movies. Afterward, he'd stand on the corner of Fourth and Pierce, trying to get picked up, watching the cars cruising the loop, up Nebraska Street past the high school to 21st and then down Pierce to Fourth and back again. (This was the cruising route for both heterosexuals and homosexuals in Sioux City.) By the time of his arrest, he had been spending his Saturdays like this for two years. Eventually, he discovered the active bathrooms of Sioux City—the Warrior Hotel, the Orpheum Theater, and the public library. He'd have sex with men there or go somewhere else with them. It was "Wham, bam, thank you, ma'am" sex, in Gary's words; oral sex only—no necking or foreplay and certainly no anal intercourse. Gary never exchanged names with the men he met and never had sex with the same man twice. (One of them, if court records are to be believed, was "Mr. Eugene," the Sioux Falls hairdresser.) Although Gary was attracted to other boys in high school, he'd never have sex with them, afraid of being discovered. It was safer with older men, he was convinced. That was a reasonable supposition, but it turned out to be false.

It was Labor Day weekend, 1955. School hadn't started yet. Gary stood at a urinal at the Warrior bathroom, as he had done many times. At the urinal next to him stood a man of 30 or so. The Warrior men's room was spacious and sheathed in gray marble: There were a couple of sinks, then the urinals, and four stalls. It was well situated for anonymous sex. You could enter the bathroom down a corridor from the Nebraska Street entrance of the Warrior without going through the hotel lobby; no one could see you go in. That evening, Gary and the man at the next urinal were the only people present. The two stood there eyeing each other. Gary had an erection, and the other man kept looking in his direction. Gary extended his hand toward his neighbor's private parts—or was it the other way around? Gary can't remember. The man showed him his badge. Gary Paul Marsh was pinched.

The cop took him to the police station, and the officers called Gary's mother. He was sent to a juvenile detention center where he was kept for two weeks. Nothing really happened; he just stayed there. One day his mother came and picked him up and took him to the family doctor. The doctor said there was nothing wrong with him "except for one hell of a case of the crabs." Later his mother drove him to Iowa City for a few days of psychological testing and a talk with a psychologist. But further psychological help for Gary was not suggested. Everyone seemed convinced that he was going through a phase, that he had been the victim of everyone's lusts but his own, that he had been seduced by a series of older men.

When Gary was first brought to the police station, the cops asked him "Do you know what the word homosexual means?" He said, "No," and it was the truth. If they had asked him what a blow job was, he wouldn't have known either, he says. He was that naive. But he knew what he liked. Over the next few weeks the police would pick him up at the youth center and bring him to view a lineup. Four or five men would stand in a row, and Gary would pick out someone with whom he'd had one of those "Wham, bam, thank you, ma'am" encounters. He was scared—scared to death—and he would say or do anything the police wanted.

By the end of the month he was back in school. It was as if nothing out of the ordinary had happened. He told teachers and classmates he had been home sick. Since he rarely had

133

friends over to his house, no one questioned this or suspected anything. Unlike the adults involved in these cases, his name never appeared in the newspaper; he was a juvenile, to be protected. He went back to being a typical teenager. In his later recollections, he said he thought that the police had come and taken him out of school to view some lineups. Then again, maybe they didn't. Gary's memory of this entire period is hazy; he made a concerted effort to erase it from his mind, and he mostly succeeded.

For Gary, it was a narrow escape. Although the whole thing frightened him for a while and he stayed away from the Warrior, it wasn't long before he went back to having anonymous sex with men. After all, he was still the same "horny kid" as before. He worked as an usher at the Orpheum Theater after school and on weekends and frequently had sex in the men's room there. One time, after the movie was over, he went with a man in the man's car to a deserted road several miles out of town. It was 1 A.M. Suddenly, from nowhere, a police car appeared behind them. The driver headed over the next rise, and Gary pushed the door open and fled into the darkness. He walked all the way home, arriving just before dawn, exhausted and covered with mud. His mother, who had never lectured or criticized him during the period of his arrest, gave him a dressing down this time.

According to court records, at least five men were classified as sexual psychopaths as a result of Gary's identifications. But Gary himself never knew what happened to the men he picked out of those lineups. He wasn't aware that anyone was sent to Mount Pleasant; 40 years later, he had never heard of the place. "It was such a short period, just three weeks out of my life," he said. "I never went to a shrink or anything. I don't even know if my father knew about this. I never went to court.

I never read the newspaper at the time. I never really thought about it much afterwards."

While at the juvenile detention center, Gary Paul Marsh remembers being brought to a nearby hospital to identify a man named Ralph Eckert. Ralph was 22 at the time, a well-liked man who in later years would run a design studio in South Sioux City and live relatively openly with his male lover. But that day he was gray, ashen, the only one of the men Gary identified who stuck in his mind. As a result of that identification, Ralph Eckert was charged with conspiracy to commit a felony (with Gary as co-conspirator) and committed to Mount Pleasant Hospital as a sexual psychopath. But unlike the other men, Ralph never went. Instead, his lawyer convinced Judge Prichard that he was suffering from "active cancer of the blood." His commitment order was withheld to permit him to be sent to the Veterans Administration Hospital in Sioux Falls as a regular patient.

Ralph's health may have been a factor in his special treatment. But there was perhaps another reason. Unlike most of the other arrested men, he came from a relatively well-off family. His father owned a service station in Sioux City, where Ralph was employed at the time. One man who knew the family quite well believes Ralph's father paid off the police over the years to get his son out of trouble; the cops would bring in Ralph periodically on some morals charge or other in order to "shake down" the father. On this particular occasion, the police convinced the judge that the whole thing was "killing Ralph," according to the family friend. "He had a weak heart," he said. "They all had weak hearts in that family."

A good lawyer and a well-to-do family also saved Maynard Post from Mount Pleasant. Known for his sharp tongue and biting, often unkind wit, Maynard was an odd man out in Sioux City: "brilliant, mysterious, more of a New York, East Coast type of person," as a friend of the time described him. Maynard and Duane Wheeler had been high school classmates, and Duane's campy style reflected Maynard's influence. The friend tells of one occasion when Maynard, Duane, and a couple of other men were cruising the loop from 21st Street down Pierce to Fourth Street and back. Duane drove, and Maynard navigated from the backseat, his eyes glued to a pair of binoculars for a close look at whoever might be wandering down Pierce Street. "Hurry!" Maynard would shout. "There's a trick standing on the next corner!" Doug Thorson, who knew him through Duane, found Maynard embarrassingly flamboyant. Doug would never go to a restaurant with him; in fact, he didn't like to be seen with him at all. In the 1947 Central High School yearbook, one of Maynard's fellow students wrote of him, "His cracks make the class roar." Maynard was also very talented, creating a 13-piece costume that won first prize at the beaux arts ball in Omaha. (He later had a successful career in the fashion industry, designing, among other things, stewardess uniforms for various airlines.)

In September 1955, Maynard was living in Chicago. He was apparently boarding a train at the Sioux City station to return there when the police arrested him. He was declared a sexual psychopath and ordered committed to Mount Pleasant. *The Sioux City Journal* reported his conviction and commitment to the mental hospital in its September 30 edition. But he never went. His father owned two drug stores in Sioux City, and his lawyer arranged for Maynard to take private psychiatric treatment instead. In Maynard's court records, still on file at the Woodbury County courthouse, the judgment and decree are crossed out with a large "X." Another document, stamped by the sheriff, states, "Not served. Defendant not delivered to Mount Pleasant."

(Doug Thorson told the story another way. He said that Maynard was still living in Sioux City prior to his arrest, but that his father received a telephone call telling him to get his son out of town. At this point, Maynard fled to Chicago. He was arrested on his return to Sioux City a few weeks later, apparently believing that the heat was off. Maynard was one of the last people arrested in the roundup, lending credence to Doug's version.)

The fact that Maynard was already living (or taking refuge) in Chicago probably helped him; if the idea was to get sexual deviates of Sioux City out of town for a while, Maynard was already gone. As for Ralph Eckert, his fragile health offered a convenient excuse to spare him. Don O'Brien was right when he said, "It wasn't a universal thing. You can't prove the premise that if you were gay you went to Mount Pleasant." Apparently, if your family was rich or influential enough, you could avoid being sent there.

It was evident that in cracking down on the sex deviates of Sioux City and petitioning the court to sentence them to a state mental hospital, O'Brien had found a popular issue. At the very least, he was able to deflect attention from the failure to find Donna Sue Davis's killer. No doubt, O'Brien wasn't completely motivated by political expediency: He probably believed he was contributing to public morals and public safety. And there were plenty of others in town who would say, "What a great thing they are doing in the courthouse with those funny people!" During this period, a Sioux City lawyer who had doubts about the whole business was having a conversation with a judge who had a reputation for being a womanizer.

"Judge, how long would you have to spend at Mount Pleasant to change so you wouldn't like women?" the lawyer asked. "Don't be ridiculous!" the judge replied. "That's how God made me."

In those days, the lawyer liked to say, judges in Iowa were still wearing high-button shoes.

During the 1956 election campaign, a year after the men were first sent to Mount Pleasant, *The Sioux City Journal* once again surveyed the various candidates as to what they wished to accomplish in office. County attorney O'Brien replied, "If reelected, I would continue to operate the office in the same manner as I have for the last 33 months, placing special stress in the enforcement against sex offenders, particularly those involving minors." In that election, O'Brien was easily reelected over his Republican opponent by 24,811 to 18,654. He ran slightly behind Herschel C. Loveless, Democratic candidate for governor, but well ahead of Adlai Stevenson. Don O'Brien was a known quantity now, and the voters liked what they saw.

PART 3:
THE SEXUAL PSYCHOPATH WARD

"At about 20 he noticed some homosexual inclinations. At 21½ first homosexual connection with some salesman in form of fellatio. After that he had numerous sexual relations with different men.... At same time patient was engaged to a girl with whom he was also having normal heterosexual relations. That girl knows about his deviation and still wants to marry him and to straighten him out."

—J. Klodnycky, MD,
parole consideration note on Doug Thorson, January 25, 1956

CHAPTER 11

The Arrival

Doug Thorson and Duane Wheeler were roommates in the sexual psychopath ward. It was odd, a stroke of luck really. It was also a stroke of luck when they were driven to Mount Pleasant together, with no one else in the car except for the old man and the old woman who took turns at the wheel.

The four of them chatted cordially during the 10-hour trip. The old couple—hired by the Woodbury County sheriff's department—told Doug and Duane they couldn't understand why they were being sent to the hospital, but perhaps they were just being polite. Doug and Duane hadn't been able to have a private conversation since their arrests. But on that drive, a kind of understanding emerged between the two men, one that didn't need words. They were dependent on each other now. In the future there would be no more experiments in independence, no running off with out-of-towners or "good-looking SOBs" met at the Warrior bar. But what would happen to them at Mount Pleasant? And would there ever be a future to share? The anxiety increased as they passed through Des Moines and along the blacktopped Highway 6 to Iowa City and continued south—almost Missouri now, with rolling hills, not like the flat country of north central Iowa where Doug had grown up.

And then the nightmare really began: The ominous-looking building, the doctor with the strange accent asking them questions like "Do you know what your name is?" as if they truly were insane, the change of clothes into the same blue work shirts and blue jeans that the mental patients wore, the attendant with the jangling keys. Worst of all, the march through the "untidy ward" with the ghastly smell of human waste that Doug and Duane would never forget, that years later would resurface seemingly out of nowhere to haunt them and bring them back to that first day at Mount Pleasant. And then finally Ward 15 East, the sexual psychopath ward.

Fifteen East was much like other wards in the hospital. A 10-foot-wide corridor with an oak floor ran the length of the ward. As you entered from the "untidy ward" through the heavy, locked wooden door, you came upon the attendant's office and the bathroom (with one bathtub for what would soon number 35 patients). On the other side of the corridor was a dormitory room, with six to 10 single beds. Next came a series of double rooms, cubicles really. At the end of the corridor was a seclusion room and a large day room with chairs and a card table. Finally, there was another locked door that led to the next ward, the "violent" ward.

Doug and Duane were assigned to the same tiny room—bare, except for two cots which barely fit end to end. Doug couldn't get over their being put together; after all, the purpose of incarcerating them at Mount Pleasant was to cure them of their homosexuality, wasn't it? The hospital had received Doug and Duane's police interrogation reports and court documents in which it was stated that Doug Thorson had "conspired" and "confederated" with Duane Wheeler to commit a felony on "divers occasions." Perhaps whoever had assigned rooms hadn't been paying attention. Or could someone actually be trying to help them out, make their time there more bearable?

In the room just across from them were Harold McBride and Frank Hildebrandt. Just down the hall was Karl Schmidt, who had passed Doug the "I Love You" note in the Sioux City jail. Gene Bergstrom ("Mr. Eugene"), Harold's friend, was a couple of doors away.

142

It was all very cozy, except that they were in a locked ward in a state mental hospital, surrounded on one side by a ward of men who spent their days smearing feces on the wall and on the other side by inmates so violent that they weren't allowed to take their meals with the other patients.

Not surprisingly, the day after their arrival, Doug made an effort to convince Dr. Klodnycky, the physician in charge of 15 East, that he really wasn't homosexual. He had previously been engaged to a young woman, he told the doctor, and they'd had sexual relations regularly. "He says that the girl knows all about him and she still wants to marry him and straighten him out," Dr. Klodnycky wrote in his notes on the session. Such a girl had once indeed existed—sort of—but that was long before Duane had come along. If Doug thought stories like this were going to get him out of Mount Pleasant any time soon, he was mistaken.

Roy and Jackie Yamahiro were intrigued by the arrival of the men everyone at the hospital would soon refer to as the "sexual psychopaths." The couple had originally come to Mount Pleasant in June for Roy's three-month summer internship. Roy, 26, had just completed his master's degree in psychology at Drake University in Des Moines and was starting work on his Ph.D. in the fall. Roy and Jackie had met in an undergraduate psychology class at the University of Wisconsin. Jackie, 23, had received her bachelor's in psychology and had studied a year toward an advanced degree in childhood education.

Another young psychologist was also interning at Mount Pleasant for the summer—Dick Gundersen, 25, who had just finished his master's degree the month before at the University of Northern Colorado in Greeley.

143

When they first arrived, the young interns were eager and idealistic. But their enthusiasm was quickly tempered by the realities of Mount Pleasant. What they found was an enclosed world, one that was set in its ways; an institution where treatment options were few, where the doctors knew next to nothing about mental illness, and the attendants were primarily interested in keeping patients under control. In many respects, it was nothing but a human warehouse. Shortly before they arrived, the chief psychologist had left, and the position hadn't been filled yet. For the moment, the two interns, fresh out of grad school, constituted the entire psychology department for a hospital with a population of close to 1,500 patients.

In the 1950s, the Mental Health Institute for the Insane and Inebriates at Mount Pleasant—its official name—was still in its glory days. It had opened in 1865, the second state facility of its kind west of the Mississippi. Like the other state mental hospitals in Iowa, Mount Pleasant was almost entirely self-sufficient. It had its own dairy farm, vegetable garden, slaughterhouse, hog farm, cannery, bakery, orchard, timber pasture, electric power system, even its own fire department. The only essentials the kitchen needed to purchase were flour, sugar, coffee, grapefruits, oranges, and spices. Everything else was produced right on Mount Pleasant's 1,410 acres. It had an acre of rhubarb and a vineyard, and from the greenhouse came lilies at Easter and poinsettias at Christmas. At its high point, the hospital's cannery produced 50,000 cans of food a year; it even canned its own popcorn. Patients did almost all the work, although a group of prisoners from nearby Fort Madison worked in the dairy barns and were responsible for the planting and the harvesting; those activities were too vital to the running of the hospital be left to the mental patients. The hospital also had its own barbershop, beauty salon, and dentist's office. There were a couple of facilities unrelated to the mental hospital as well: a tuberculosis sanatorium and a "farmer's lodge"—an old-age home with nearly 100 residents.

Almost all the employees, including doctors and nurses, lived on the grounds. By and large, the townspeople of Mount Pleasant—a town that thought quite highly of itself—were loath to work at a mental hospital. So most of the employees were brought in from the economically depressed farm towns of southern Illinois. Wages at Mount Pleasant ran higher than in southern Illinois, and the word spread quickly. Some of the employees were "old bughousers," mental hospital slang for the now vanished species of itinerant ward attendants who migrated from one state hospital to another, by mood or by season, working up north in the summer and heading south in the winter.

That first summer, Jackie Yamahiro was working at the reception desk at the entrance to the main building. Behind her desk along a wide corridor were the visitors' lounge and doctors' offices. After about 50 feet, another corridor intersected, leading to more offices and eventually to the wards. The spot where the two corridors intersected was the crossroads of the hospital: Mount Pleasant's version of Grand Central Station. Roy and Jackie would meet there to go to lunch; employees and staff ran into one another and exchanged gossip; doctors and patients crossed paths.

To Jackie, the hospital was like a small town where the staff lived at close quarters and everybody knew everybody else's business. "You worked on the first floor, ate on the second floor, and slept on the third floor," she said later. A two- to three-mile system of tunnels connected various parts of the main building and the outlying buildings; back staircases led from various wards to the tunnels. Patients were marched to

145

the dining room through the tunnels since the hospital didn't want large groups of people from one ward trooping through the other wards. The tunnels were also well-known as places where two patients might steal a few intimate moments together—"bed parties," as they were called.

Each floor had six wards on each side that went off into the twisting wings, with the men's wards off to the left and women's wards to the right. About 20 patients were housed in each ward. Large oak rocking chairs stood in the corridors; they were made by inmates at Fort Madison prison and were purposefully large and heavy so that patients couldn't throw them. There were no televisions or radios since patients might throw these too.

Many of the wards had their own particular character. For instance, there was a ward for "persnickety" women. And in some wards, patients knew their own names but not much more. In the violent ward, also known as the "mean ward," the men would sit in the rocking chairs and rock for hours. Or they might spend half the day pushing huge floor polishers back and forth, as if in a hypnotic trance. And then, imperceptibly, a restlessness would take over. Suddenly, someone would "blow" (in mental hospital parlance), break up a rocking chair, and a tremendous fight would ensue. Sometimes when these men were taken down for shock treatments, they would blow, as well. Four or five attendants would be required to hold them down.

Some patients had grounds privileges and could sit on the benches along the drive at the front of the hospital and go to the canteen, located outside the main building. The canteen had a few booths, where patients or staff would sit. The man who ran the place, a patient named Lester, was tall, gray-haired, and rather handsome. Jackie found him charming. Later, she learned that he had beheaded his wife.

It was the patients, above all, who astonished and fascinated the newly arrived Yamahiros. These were the days before tranquilizers and antipsychotic drugs were in widespread use; the hospital was filled with bizarre characters. There was the "cop," named Bob, who would stand in the hospital parking lot on weekends when visitors arrived, directing traffic. Short and bowlegged, Bob wore a black visored hat, a sheriff's badge, and big black shoes. He always carried a night watchman's clock, which made him look even more official. But Bob was a patient, not an employee.

Then there was the woman, nearly six feet tall, who carried a massive Bible with her every place she went and believed she was Queen Victoria. She was infatuated with Roy Yamahiro. When she spotted Roy—usually at Grand Central Station, where the two corridors met—she'd rush over to talk to him. But she didn't feel so warmly toward Jackie. Every time she saw her, she'd spit at her.

In those days, many patients stayed for years, if not for the rest of their lives; by and large they were poor folk with nowhere else to go. The hospital even had its own cemetery. When a patient went "to staff"—the obligatory appearance before the doctors and psychologists prior to release—it was such an event that the news spread through the hospital like wildfire. A woman who worked as ward attendant at Mount Pleasant for many years told the story of how a patient had cross-stitched a skirt for her. When the attendant asked the patient how much money she would like for it, the patient was dumbfounded. She had been in the hospital for so long that she had no idea of prices. Finally, the patient asked for a pair of cotton stockings as payment. But cotton stockings had gone out years before and weren't even made anymore.

Even in Roy and Jackie's time, some patients were not

mentally ill at all. Jackie became friendly with a woman whose family kept her at the hospital because she had polio; she had to wear a brace on her leg, and they wanted her out of sight. The woman was a talented musician, known for playing "Dizzy Fingers" on the piano at breakneck pace. Then there was a woman in her 50s who had been brought in for observation and diagnosed as a paranoid schizophrenic. She was very wealthy and kept insisting to Roy and Jackie that her family was trying to get her committed in order to get possession of her money. After several weeks in the hospital, she was released to her family's care. She pleaded not to go, but she had no choice. Two weeks later she died under suspicious circumstances.

At Mount Pleasant, patients' days were forever the same: Each morning they would eat breakfast and go to work—in the laundry or the cannery, say. It was as if they were on a payroll, except they were never paid for their labor. In the evening they would return to their rooms and perhaps read a magazine. Some of the women did embroidery; the men might play cards. Movies took place on Tuesday night, dances on Friday, and church on Sunday.

The most frequently used treatment was electroshock therapy. Three mornings a week, patients lined up on the first floor for electroshock, sometimes 12 or 14 in a group. One patient, a young man, was dubbed by the staff the "shockproof kid." He received shock treatments a few times a week for years and years. Afterward, he would walk around with a benign look on his face, but when the shock wore off, he would grow very violent, so the doctors would shock him again. Other patients received insulin or penicillin. For some of the more functional patients, there was occupational and group therapy. For many, though, there was no treatment, just the tedium of time passing.

As at the state mental hospital at Cherokee, the physicians at Mount Pleasant were almost entirely foreign-born, largely from Central and Eastern Europe. Although they were licensed in Europe and, in many cases, possessed medical specialties and years of experience, they were unable to become licensed in the United States, so they wound up working in state mental hospitals, which couldn't afford to pay salaries that American-born doctors demanded. Many of these Mount Pleasant physicians were getting on in years and couldn't speak English well. None had any background in mental health: One was an allergy specialist, another a specialist in liver disease. Ward attendants viewed them with contempt. "They were old foreigners who couldn't get a job anywhere else," one attendant said. "We had to stand up when they came onto the ward. It peed me off. It was a well-known fact that they couldn't work anywhere else. You couldn't understand them. I don't know how the patients could understand them. You couldn't read their instructions on a chart."

In the small staff dining room, everyone had assigned seats. Across from Jackie sat Dr. Koff, who was said to have married the same woman seven times. He was also the best bridge player at Mount Pleasant—he played "for blood," Jackie said. Dr. Gipp, who rarely spoke, had a large German wife who ordered him about. Dr. Sampter went on vacation to Mackinaw Island in Michigan where motorized vehicles were not allowed; when he returned, he announced his intention to write a mystery novel set on an island where a gangster made his getaway on a lawn mower. Dr. Milke was a Polish refugee—younger, serious, seemingly more professional than the others. And then there was Dr. Klodnycky, the physician in charge of the sexual psychopath ward. Rough and gruff and all business, he always had a frown on his face. That was Jackie's view anyway. One attendant who worked there at the time referred to Dr. Klodnycky as "a good egg."

For most of these physicians, Mount Pleasant was an easy posting. They had little contact with patients and left almost everything to the attendants. Doctors did give electroshock treatments and prescribed drugs (such as were available at the time), and they spent a lot of time doing paperwork. But that was all. For the doctors, it was a cozy arrangement. They received pleasant and commodious apartments and took their meals in the staff dining room. Patients cleaned the doctors' apartments, made their beds, did their laundry, starched their shirts, even starched their undershorts. They might have been colonial officials in British India or Malaya.

Roy and Jackie enjoyed many of these same privileges but didn't share the colonial mentality. They quickly became known as the "liberal kids." After all, they had spent four years at the University of Wisconsin in Madison, a bastion of political nonconformity where Sen. Joe McCarthy—Wisconsin's own—was roundly booed when he came to speak. Roy's rebellious nature—and youthful high spirits—sometimes got him into trouble. There was the time he went on an exercise regimen and got up early in the morning to jog around the hospital grounds. Someone spotted him, and, within minutes, a car carrying six attendants was bearing down upon him. They assumed he was a runaway patient. And when he wore Bermuda shorts and knee socks downtown during their first summer at Mount Pleasant, the hospital was in a near uproar. The attendants told the patients not to listen to anything that Dr. Yamahiro said; he was "crazy," they insisted, because he had gone into town in such undignified attire.

Still, Roy and Jackie were sociable and outgoing, and that

counted for a lot. By contrast, Dick Gundersen, the other psychology intern, was rather reserved; he would go back to his apartment at the end of the day and didn't interact much with the rest of the staff.

The Yamahiros were rebels in another way: They were an interracial couple, a rarity at the time, particularly in Mount Pleasant, Iowa. Roy was a Japanese-American from the West Coast, while Jackie was a white woman from a state where non-Caucasians (except for American Indians) were few and far between. Roy was tall, and at Mount Pleasant, he got a crew cut, which resulted in no end of teasing. Jackie was dark and petite and pretty and didn't hesitate to speak her mind. Roy had grown up in foster homes on the West Coast and was interned during World War II in Idaho at a camp for Japanese-Americans. He spent the period from age 11 until his junior year in high school at the camp, and when the war ended did his senior year at a high school in Madison. After the war, he joined the U.S. Marines. His fellow marines called him "Murphy"—it was easier to pronounce than Yamahiro.

Although they were well-liked at Mount Pleasant—and Roy was highly respected as a psychologist—the couple experienced slights, especially at the beginning, which Jackie attributed to racial prejudice. "People were really appalled to have an interracial couple in their midst," she said. When the young psychology interns first arrived, they went to see the superintendent on the women's side whose job it was to assign apartments to the staff. The superintendent assigned blond-haired Dick Gundersen—who was unmarried—an apartment with a double bed; the Yamahiros received one with twin beds.

Toward the end of July 1955, after they had been at Mount Pleasant less than two months, Roy, Jackie, and Dick Gundersen were called to a meeting in the office of Dr. Brown,

151

the hospital superintendent. "We are going to be opening a ward for sexual psychopaths," he told them. Would the three of them be willing to stay on another year, until the following September, to work with the new group? Roy and Dick's responsibilities would include the entire hospital, but they'd have particular responsibility for the special ward. A new chief psychologist would soon be arriving, so they wouldn't be completely on their own. Meanwhile, Jackie would be promoted from the reception desk to the hospital's social services department, where she would have direct contact with patients and their families.

Roy and Jackie agreed in a flash. They didn't have much money, and a full year working at Mount Pleasant, with almost all their expenses covered, would enable them to put away some savings for when Roy began his Ph.D. Roy had been working with schizophrenic patients and planned to go into clinical psychology; the sexual psychopath ward presented an excellent opportunity for hands-on experience. In Jackie's case, a year at Mount Pleasant would allow her to get some training as a social worker and help her establish herself in a new career. For Dick Gundersen, it was an exciting proposition as well: his first real job after having been in school for years. For all of them, the new ward promised a corner of the hospital they could make their own, a channel for their idealism in a hidebound institution where anything new was suspect.

As for the sexual psychopaths themselves, they were simply an unknown quantity.

CHAPTER 12

The Men in the Pink Shirts

That unknown quantity began to alarm the townsfolk of Mount Pleasant almost from the moment that Governor Hoegh and the Board of Control announced plans for the new ward for sexual psychopaths. They had read in the newspaper about the Triplett case and the murder of Donna Sue Davis. They were unsure how dangerous this new group of patients might turn out to be; although prisoners from Fort Madison had been working at the hospital for years, the townspeople feared the worst. Just the term *sexual psychopath* made the citizens of Mount Pleasant want to lock their doors and hide their children in the basement, and one could hardly blame them.

Mount Pleasant was a proud and prosperous town of 8,000. An old town, founded in 1835, it was the county seat of Henry County and the home of Iowa Wesleyan College. Early on, it acquired a reputation as the "Athens of Iowa" (a name later appropriated by Iowa City); an 1875 Iowa atlas notes that it had "long enjoyed a reputation abroad for its liberal support for educational institutions and churches, and the high standard of morality maintained by its citizens generally." Sen. James Harlan, the father of Mary Todd Lincoln, hailed from Mount Pleasant. The town square was surrounded on three sides by two- and three-story brick commercial buildings. The residential area featured a number of fine Queen Anne–style homes, and the college buildings and shaded lawns gave the place a distinguished air. In many ways Mount Pleasant seemed more like a New England town than an Iowa one, well-mannered and Republican, with aspirations to culture.

Roy and Jackie Yamahiro, however, didn't view Mount Pleasant as some kind of latter-day Athens. To them, it was stuffy and small-minded. There was a tavern on the square with a large front window that was never washed. Inside, florescent lights gaudily illuminated anyone who had the temerity to come in for a beer; students from Iowa Wesleyan were not allowed on that side of the square, presumably because they might be subject to the temptations of alcohol. This was a town in the shadow of a Methodist college, after all, in a state where the sale of liquor by the drink remained illegal, and many people didn't approve of a tavern on the main square. One day, Roy and Jackie went downtown to Penney's to buy a shirt for Roy. "What church do you go to?" the salesman asked them. Although the question was intended as neighborly, Roy was offended. To him, religion was a private matter; in Mount Pleasant it was the subject that followed after you learned someone's name and occupation.

On August 3, less than two weeks after the governor's announcement, the editorial page of the daily *Mt. Pleasant News* noted that "some local persons" expressed concern about the new ward to be established in their midst. They wondered whether the hospital was properly equipped to ensure the confinement of the sexual deviates. Was it adequately staffed? Could the inmates escape? "We suspect that state officials have also thought of that, but to be sure, it's a good idea to remind them," continued the editorialist. "They would be negligent, it seems to us, if they do not handle the deviates with restrictions similar to those placed upon men sentenced to [the state prisons at] Ft. Madison or Anamosa."

As a matter of fact, the town's anxiety was increasing by the day. The school board passed a resolution urging the Board of Control to provide for "proper restraint" of the sexual psy-

chopaths and sent a letter to state officials. The Chamber of
Commerce wrote its own letter to the Board of Control,
expressing similar concerns and calling for a meeting. People
talked about building a 10-foot-high wall around the Mental
Health Institute.

Hospital officials moved to calm local opinion. Dr. Milke,
the Polish refugee physician, addressed a meeting of the
Kiwanis Club. The hospital was making provisions for proper
handling of the deviates, he assured the Kiwanians. And it was
unlikely that Mount Pleasant would receive any of what he
called the "sex-murderer type of criminal" anyway. Instead, he
anticipated that many of the sexual deviates sent to the hospital would merely be homosexuals. Interestingly, Dr. Milke's
comments came on August 22, well over a week before the
Sioux City roundup began.

On the following day, Governor Hoegh also attempted to
reassure the public. Speaking at the dedication of a $2 million
addition to the state mental hospital at Independence, near
Cedar Rapids, the governor assured the residents of Mount
Pleasant "they should have no fear" of the residents of the new
ward. "We have assured the citizens they will be kept confined
within the institution," the governor said. Security was the
first thing he had made sure of, he promised. Four men had
already been committed to the special ward, and Dr. Charles
Graves, director of state mental hospitals, stated that none
were dangerous. They were "cooperative" patients who "want
something done about their problem," said Dr. Graves.
"They're nice guys: They're just sick. They're in a jam because
they have a peculiar makeup."

Nonetheless, on Tuesday, September 6, five members of the
Mount Pleasant Chamber of Commerce drove to Des Moines
to meet with the governor and the Board of Control. The

group included a lawyer, an osteopath, the manager of the local JCPenney, and two other businessmen. Afterward, Henry Burma, head of the Board of Control, announced that they had had a "nice meeting" and "we believe that we sent the Mount Pleasant people home satisfied. They were a little upset, and they came in to see us about it." The businessmen, he said, were laboring under a misconception: They thought that "the fellows we will send to the institute are tougher than they really are. They were afraid of escapes and trouble in the Mount Pleasant community. They thought about the recent killing of a child at Sioux City and thought every one these fellows is a killer. That, of course, is not true."

But the meeting was not quite as amicable as the head of the Board of Control wanted to portray it. For one thing, the Mount Pleasant businessmen demanded that bars be placed on the windows of the special ward. Board of Control members resisted that demand; it might hinder rehabilitation, they argued. Governor Hoegh, whose idea it had been to set up the ward in the first place, tried to mediate between the two sides. "Let's just be certain that we don't have any slip [up] down there," he told the Board. The *Mt. Pleasant News* reported that while the businessmen expressed appreciation for the Board's attention, they were still unsure whether the state officials were "fully sympathetic with the local feeling on the question of restraints."

The local businessmen were "good people who just got carried away," in the view of Tom Bell, a Mount Pleasant lawyer who knew them all. Many years later, Bell, a distinguished-looking man in his 80s who still came into his office everyday in a tweed suit, would recall the whole affair as "such small-town Iowa." They were "righteous bastards," he said. "Their wives were proud of them. They were afraid that those guys at the hospital would take over the town. They were all Rotarians. It just makes me laugh." Homosexuals were nothing new in Mount Pleasant, anyway, Bell pointed out. He recalled the time back in the 1930s when the school nurse at Iowa Wesleyan was caught in a compromising position with another woman. In those days, there were three or four gay faculty members at the college. "We just coped with them," said Bell. "They are all God's children."

What the lawyer and the osteopath and the manager of JCPenney just couldn't understand was that the men being sent down to Mount Pleasant as sexual psychopaths were mostly the hairdressers and window dressers of Sioux City.

The citizenry of Mount Pleasant were not the only ones who were apprehensive about the impending arrival of the so-called sexual psychopaths. Many of the employees at the hospital were concerned as well. The ward attendants feared problems. It soon turned out, however, that the sexual psychopath ward was easy, even desirable duty for the attendants. Patients were cooperative; there were no fights, no chairs broken, no need to wrestle anyone to the floor. All that was needed was just a little extra watchfulness in the dormitory when the lights went out.

Among the nonprofessional staff, there was anxiety too. Jackie Yamahiro was the only person in the social services department who would have anything to do with the new arrivals. Everyone else was disapproving or just plain scared. A woman who worked as the hospital's bookkeeper at the time summed up these feelings. "To this day, I can't stand the sight of a man in a pink shirt," she said, her distaste still palpable in her voice years later.

Did the men in the sexual psychopath ward wear pink shirts? she was asked.

"A lot of them did!"

The doctors at Mount Pleasant were distinctly unenthusiastic as well, but for different reasons. Most didn't think they could do anything for the men—short of castration (a course of action recommended by one of the doctors, perhaps only half-seriously, over lunch in the staff dining room). Dr. Brown, the superintendent, had had misgivings about the passage of the sexual psychopath law and had argued against the opening of a special ward at Mount Pleasant. "There is no specific cure or treatment for that condition," Dr. Brown told *The Des Moines Register*. "The law requires me to report to the court once a year. What can I say? I can't say they are cured. I can't say they'll not resort to sexual deviation again. They can be put on probation. But if the court asks me if they are cured, I can only say I don't know. It's part of their personality makeup."

These feelings aside, the hospital readied itself for the new arrivals. Monroe Fairchild, a psychologist who had previously worked at a Texas prison, came on board as the new head of the psychology department. Patients were moved around to create an empty ward. Nonetheless, when the men first began to arrive in large numbers, the general attitude was confusion. "We didn't know what was happening or why they were coming to us in a batch like that," psychologist Dick Gundersen would say. "In some ways, at least from my vantage point, we weren't prepared. We were just told, 'Do what you can with these patients because they are gradually going to be coming over here.' And we worked like beavers, Roy and I."

By the time the governor had made his reassuring statements on August 23, Ward 15 East was receiving its first patients. One was Lloyd Madsen, a musician sent from down Fort Dodge after being charged with sodomy. He arrived at Mount Pleasant on August 15. There was another man from Fort Dodge as well—Gary Morgan, who was sentenced to

Mount Pleasant for exposing himself to a young girl. On September 1 came Clayton Lee Smith, a Dakota City, Nebraska, man, arrested in Sioux City and charged with the possession of obscene books and pictures. And then, in the last 10 days of September, following the roundup, they began arriving in large numbers from Sioux City. Among them were, on September 20, Leo Vandermeer, Henry Jensen and Elmer Myers; on September 23, Karl Schmidt; on September 24, Frank Hildebrandt and Gregg Phillips; Harold McBride on September 26; Harold Cooper on September 27; and on September 29, Doug Thorson and Duane Wheeler.

Dancing With Greta Garbo

There is a photograph of Roy Yamahiro and Harold McBride outdoors on the grounds of Mount Pleasant on a warm late fall day. In pleated pants, a white T-shirt, and a V-neck sweater, Roy looks unexpectedly stylish. His hair is parted on the side—he hadn't gotten his trademark 1955 crew cut yet. Harold is dressed in pleated pants and a white shirt; his wife was coming to visit that day so he was permitted to wear his street clothes. He is trying to smile for the camera but just can't bring it off. There's another photo, taken at the same time, of the therapy group that Roy led. All six patients in the photo are dressed in state-issue jeans and work shirts, except for Lloyd Madsen (the musician sent down from Fort Dodge) and Harold. Everyone is smiling this time, except for Harold, who looks serious, almost grim. It's late in the day, toward the end of October or early November; the shadows are long, and the trees are already bare of leaves.

For Harold McBride, perhaps more than any of the rest of the 20 men, incarceration was extremely difficult. He worried about Glenda and the children. He had lost his license to cut hair, a consequence of pleading guilty to a felony. He watched despairingly as his wife was forced to sell his business, put their furniture in storage, and moved herself and the three children out of their Kingsley apartment to stay with his family in Woodward. And in his darkest moments he was convinced he would never get out of Mount Pleasant. "My life was shattered," Harold said 40 years later. "It was gone. I was devastated and scared to death. I didn't know what was going to happen."

His medical records bear this out. After Harold's first

physical examination on October 3, Dr. Koff noted that the patient's mood indicated "somewhat of a depression, however, he is not suicidal." In a psychological evaluation a month later, Roy Yamahiro found Harold "congenial, cooperative but very tense and nervous." He added, "This whole experience has been a rather frightening one for him and quite difficult to accept."

And, then, as if things weren't bad enough, barely a week after his arrival at Mount Pleasant, Harold was informed that he was to leave at 6 A.M. the following morning for Sioux City to give evidence before the grand jury in the case of his friend Vern Peterson. Vern, a hairdresser in a small northwest Iowa town, had been brought in about the time of the roundup and kept in jail in Sioux City. Assistant county attorney John Clemens had already telephoned Harold at Mount Pleasant on October 3 to inquire whether he and Vern had had sexual contacts. Clemens wasn't permitted to speak with Harold directly since that was against hospital policy. According to Harold's medical records, Dr. Klodnycky relayed his patient's response: Yes, Harold had had sexual relations with Vern—"69," as Dr. Klodnycky referred to it—three or four times between 1952 and '54. But Harold insists that once he got to Sioux City, he changed his story. He and Vern had just been good friends, he told the prosecutor. Did he know that Vern was homosexual? Yes, he said. That answer alone provided some corroborating evidence for the county attorney.

Vern was a nice guy, and Harold hated to involve him. But Vern was involved as it was, Harold rationalized. Someone else had to have turned him in to begin with, after all. Vern was never sent to Mount Pleasant, and no records in the Woodbury County Clerk's office indicate that he was convicted of any crime during this period. Harold stayed overnight at

161

the Sioux City jail and was brought back to the mental hospital the following morning. Giving evidence against Vern was "the hardest thing I had to do," he said.

In his November 25, 1955, interview with *The Des Moines Register*, county attorney Don O'Brien appears to allude to the incident. In the interview, O'Brien mentions that one of the men had returned to Sioux City briefly from the hospital to testify before the grand jury. "He looked to me like he had improved 100%," O'Brien told the newspaper. "His whole attitude seemed changed. He was very pleased with his treatment at the hospital."

As time passed, even Harold McBride began to adapt to Mount Pleasant. Once the doors locked behind the men and the immediate shock of being there passed, more than anything, life at the hospital was boring. Like the regular mental patients, they would march through the tunnels to breakfast every morning. They'd clean their ward and do some assigned work. On some days, there would be group therapy. They'd go to lunch. In the afternoon, there would be more work to do or, for some, a couple of hours of occupational therapy—leather craft or woodworking. Evenings were mostly given over to writing letters or playing cards or reading two-year-old magazines.

Harold and his friend Gene Bergstrom passed the hours discussing what they would do once they got out, conversations that cemented a friendship that would endure until Gene's death many years later. Gene talked about moving to California. Harold indulged him in this idea but really wasn't sure about it for himself. Glenda and the kids had just moved to Woodward, and he was reluctant to uproot them yet again. And the question remained, hovering over every conversation: Would they ever get out of Mount Pleasant at all? Unlike most of the prisoners at Fort Madison, just down the road, they didn't have a release date to look forward to. And, for the moment, Harold and Gene didn't even have their driver's licenses, since those had been revoked when they were sentenced.

In the day room, Doug Thorson and Duane Wheeler played bridge. For Doug, bridge playing was partly a matter of pride; he thought that it "threw the attendants clear off" that men labeled as sexual psychopaths had the intelligence to play such a cerebral and complicated game. It was a small consolation, but then all the consolations at Mount Pleasant were small ones.

At mealtimes, the men from 15 East ate with the regular mental patients at large round oak tables in the first-floor dining room. Everyone stood in line waiting for their portions, cafeteria style. Some of the patients threw food or had fits or convulsions; sometimes fights broke out. One day, while waiting in line for his lunch, one of the mental patients unzipped his trousers and began to masturbate; the attendants took him away. Except for the occasional argument, there was little conversation in the dining room.

One morning after breakfast, the men in 15 East were marched to a ward on another floor, where the hospital had a special work assignment for them. They were given buckets and paint brushes. Their job, they were told, was to paint the wards on the men's side of the hospital. So began their major task at Mount Pleasant. Each day they would paint a different ward until they had completed them all. They'd start at one end and proceed down the ward, room by room, leaving the corridor for last. The color was an institutional beige or gray. In the "untidy" ward, prep work consisted of scraping feces off the walls. While each ward was being painted, the patients who lived there were removed for the day. The painting was very much in line with Mount Pleasant's policy of using patients to perform menial tasks; it also reflected the hospital's uncertainty about what to do with the men from the special ward. There was another motive too: It kept the men in 15 East isolated and away from the other patients.

Some of the men were happy for the occupation. In Harold's case, the painting helped take his mind off his worries and it made time pass. Others felt exploited. "Therapy, they called it," sneered Doug. "It was cheap labor."

The attendants watched them closely. The men were never alone; they couldn't go anywhere in the hospital without an attendant to accompany them. The head of the painting crew never left two of them alone in a room. In later years, Doug was surprised to see a photograph of Roy Yamahiro's therapy group outdoors on the grounds; Doug and the others who weren't in Roy's group never had the opportunity to go out of the main building. In particular, pains were taken to make sure the men from the sexual psychopath ward had no contact with the female mental patients—apparently out of fear that they might molest them. This may have been an attempt to address the concerns of the townspeople of Mount Pleasant, but it made little sense.

Despite initial misgivings, most of the ward attendants treated them decently. There was one exception, however: Jim Blackwell, a former prison guard whom patients remembered as a man with steel-gray hair, wire-rimmed spectacles, beady eyes, and a rough manner; he was particularly nasty, even sadistic. Years later Doug would shudder at the thought of him. "He was a real SOB," Doug said. "He would try and catch you on any small detail to get you in trouble. You would be playing cards and you would put a card down and your hand might fall on someone else's—purely innocent—and he'd report it. 'I'll make you men even if you aren't men,' he'd say."

At the end of the ward was a seclusion room with padded walls, but it was rarely used. Mostly, the men in 15 East were model patients. One day, though, Harold's friend Gene Bergstrom decided to see what seclusion was all about. Perhaps boredom drove him to it. That's what Harold thought, anyway. So Gene began pounding his fists against the wall in his room. When Blackwell and another attendant threw him in seclusion, Gene made no attempt to resist. He was let out after a few hours. Afterward, Gene had a good laugh: "It wasn't too bad. It wasn't too bad."

The only break in the monotony came with the movies every Tuesday night and the dances every Friday. These took place at the gym on the second floor. A balcony overlooked the gym; the staff could sit there and watch the entertainment as well. The movies were generally of high quality and relatively current. There was Frank Sinatra and Doris Day in *Young at Heart*, the 1954 musical remake of a Fannie Hurst novel about the romantic entanglements of four small-town sisters. Another was *Hondo*, a Western starring John Wayne, James Arness, and Ward Bond. The men in 15 East found that there was nothing quite like watching a movie in a mental hospital. Toward the middle of *Young at Heart*, a perky Doris Day tells a morose and self-pitying musician, played by Frank Sinatra, "All I know is that there is a straightjacket waiting with your number on it!" And the patients at Mount Pleasant just roared with laughter.

But the Friday night dances were the true highlight of the week. The dances, bringing together patients and staff, also attracted townspeople from Mount Pleasant who watched from the balcony. Everyone looked forward to them. For these occasions, patients were permitted to wear their own clothes, not state issue, and this was a big deal: It gave the impression of normal life. On Friday afternoon, the men in 15 East were handed their street clothes; they wrapped them around the steam pipes to make sure they were neatly pressed by the time the dance started. Female patients put on makeup. Then the much awaited moment arrived. The male patients stood on one side of the gym, and the women on the other; attendants and their wives sat on the stage. It was easy to pick out the men from 15 East—they dressed more stylishly than everyone else. (This may be the origin of the story about the pink shirts.) Everybody mixed in; doctors' wives danced with male patients and male ward attendants with female patients.

That year they danced to songs like "Blue Moon," "Lullaby of Birdland," "Shine on Harvest Moon," and the "Hesitation Waltz," Harold remembers. The music was mostly waltzes and two-steps. There were a few jitterbugs but not many. It was believed that faster music, more frenetic rhythms, might get the patients too riled up.

Harold, a good dancer, had a regular dance partner—the wife of a ward attendant who was on duty when the dances took place. The expectation was that the men from the sexual psychopath ward would ask some of the female mental patients to dance; in fact, they were told to do so. Doug was never sure whether a dance partner was going to fall down in the middle of "Blue Moon" or throw up all over him or kick him in the stomach. The Sioux City group gave the female patients special names, usually after showbiz personalities. There was one they called Greta Garbo; she looked and behaved just like her—remote, mysterious, somehow alluring. It was said she had killed her mother. Another was dubbed

Betty Hutton—foul-mouthed but otherwise pleasant. Then there was Tillie, a middle-aged, heavy-set woman whose hair was chopped off and who always showed up at the dances in a house dress. She was charmed by Billy Ivers, the youngest of the patients in 15 East. As soon as the music started, she would make a beeline for Billy, who did his best to be gracious.

Everyone did his best, really. It was a good tactic—to show that you were cooperative and helpful and doing all you could toward rehabilitation. "We thought we were doing more good than what they expected of us by talking and dancing with the women patients," said Doug. "You would get to be friends with them for a half an hour or five minutes maybe and they would go off their rocker again. The next time you saw them, they wouldn't know you."

During this period, the dances at Mount Pleasant began to be much talked about, both at the hospital and in the town, particularly because of the musical abilities of the men from 15 East who made up the patient dance band. "They were our orchestra," a woman who worked as a transcriptionist at the time said of the men in the special ward. "They were as good an orchestra as you could find today." The band was led by Lloyd Madsen, who had played the organ professionally before being sent to Mount Pleasant. There was a violin, a trumpet, an accordion, a piano, and always, Lloyd on the organ.

The story went that Lloyd had been arrested in the middle of a performance at the Cobblestone Ballroom at Lake Okoboji, a popular resort in northern Iowa. It was just like a movie: The police entered the ballroom, the music stopped, and he was taken away to jail in Fort Dodge and sentenced to Mount Pleasant as a sexual psychopath. Lloyd had been involved with a young doctor in Fort Dodge who subsequently left town. (A Fort Dodge dentist recalled that the doctor had a "gorgeous convertible" and that he let Lloyd borrow it. That's when the dentist said he knew "something was up.") Lloyd, 23, was tall and stocky and very talented musically. He had a number of privileges that the other men on the sexual psychopath ward didn't have. He was frequently allowed out of the ward to practice and often permitted to dress in street clothes. Although Lloyd successfully avoided most of the painting details, the other men in 15 East didn't resent him, since his success reflected well on everyone in the ward. Lloyd was the favorite of Harold Craig, the music therapist, and, above all, of Dr. Monroe Fairchild, the recently arrived chief psychologist, who was Roy Yamahiro and Dick Gundersen's boss.

Fairchild was a man so obese that the only way to keep his trousers from falling down was to hitch them up over his stomach. He was always puffing and sweating and could barely fit into the chair in his tiny office. He had worked at a prison in Texas and was never serious for a moment; he was always cracking jokes, many of which had to do with homosexuals. He and Harold Craig, the music therapist, and Lloyd were constantly together. Rumors circulated among the staff that Fairchild and the music therapist were both gay. On one occasion an attendant went to Fairchild's office to escort a patient back to the ward; afterward, he told people that Fairchild had had his pants down. There was a lot of talk about this.

Fairchild and Craig concocted a scheme to have Lloyd play the organ at lunch and dinner. They had a speaker system installed in the patient dining room. The idea was therapeutic—to soothe the patients, especially at a time of day when some tended to act out and get into trouble. But it may also have been a way to make Lloyd's life easier, to get him out of the ward so he could practice and perform every day.

It was also a way they could spend more time with him.

Whatever their motives, Mount Pleasant must have been among the few state mental institutions in the country where the patients enjoyed live piped-in music at mealtimes. Later, after Lloyd left and the sexual psychopath ward was shut down, not only did the music at lunch and dinner come to an end, but the dances stopped too. The orchestra had made the dances so good that once the men in 15 East were gone, no one was interested anymore.

By late October, the ward was becoming overcrowded. There were 35 people in a space intended for 20. And there was only one bathtub. The Sioux City contingent made up the majority, but there were others too: homosexual men from other parts of the state, a couple of pedophiles, a cross-dresser, and a prisoner sent over from nearby Fort Madison.

Jackie Yamahiro, who saw the Sioux City men when they were first admitted and took their medical and family histories, began to see changes in them. Initially they were depressed, scared, anxious. They didn't know what was going to happen to them or how long they would have to remain at the hospital. Once they settled down and realized what life was going to be like at Mount Pleasant, they began to express varying degrees of anger and resentment. But overall, Jackie never saw as much anger as she had expected. There was a certain passivity about the men, a passivity that may have had to do in part with being gay in the 1950s. By and large, they seemed to accept their fates, and somewhere in the back of their minds, perhaps they thought they deserved them.

One of the people Jackie looked out for was Billy Ivers, the youngest in the ward. Billy had arrived at Mount Pleasant, driven by his aunt, on October 21, more than three weeks later than most of the other men from Sioux City. To a certain extent he had been lucky. He hadn't gone to jail even after his arrest. And he avoided having to go to the hospital under guard in a car with the door handles removed; he had even brought a suitcase with him. Maybe it was because he was just a kid, only 18 at the time. But once he got to the hospital, his luck had clearly run out.

The first week, he hardly spoke, although he had been friends with some of the men in the ward: Duane Wheeler, who was his fellow student at hairdressing school and whom he absolutely adored, and Doug Thorson, who had given him a love bite on the neck that night at the drive-in restaurant in Riverside. At Mount Pleasant, Billy felt he was "in the middle of a menagerie," and his imagination ran wild. He was scared of some of the patients on the sexual psychopath ward and of the ordinary mental patients. He was terrified he would be given shock treatments. After a week Jackie Yamahiro sat him down and told him the hospital was very concerned about him. He knew he had to shape up.

Billy had grown up in a Nebraska town just across the river from Sioux City, raised by his mother and aunt, who both doted on him. At hairdressing school, Duane had taken him under his wing. People were always taking Billy Ivers under their wing or trying to get him into bed, and he was always on the verge of inheriting a large sum of money. That was Billy. He was chubby and cute, with dyed, coal-black hair, horn-rimmed glasses, and bright, darting eyes. He had gone into hairdressing because a girlfriend was in beauty school, and Billy decided it was "fascinating, clean-cut work."

Billy was a tease with both men and women. But when the teasing began to seem as if it was really going to lead some-where, he would feign an attack of appendicitis. That worked well until Billy let one of Sioux City's best known physicians take him to a hotel room late at night. He tried the old ruse, but the doctor saw the scar (Billy really had had appendicitis long before) and pressured him to have sex. After that he began to go "here and there," as he put it, and have sex with other men. Still, he didn't think of himself as homosexual. He was young, and in those days a sense of homosexual identity was weak, and distinctions between gay and straight weren't so absolute; it was easier to fool others—and to fool yourself—about where you stood on Dr. Kinsey's sexual scale.

It was 2 o'clock on a September afternoon, and Billy was at home in the kitchen with his aunt when the police telephoned. They asked him to come down to the corner for a chat. Officers Burke and Verbeski were sitting in an unmarked car. They drove him across the state line to Sioux City. "Do you know Duane Wheeler?" they asked him in the car. Of course, he did, from hairdressing school, and he said so, but they didn't accuse him of anything until they got him to the police station. Then they told him they had proof that he had had relations with various men. He denied it. When they told him they would have to tell his uncle about his sexual activities, he broke down. The cops asked him something about Floyd Edwards's bedspread. He admitted to knowing that it was chenille. They told him that if he would sign a confession, he could go home. He signed, and in fact they did let him go home.

On his court papers, it was stated that Billy had admitted to having sex with Gary Paul Marsh, the high school student, in a car in Riverside Park. Billy would later emphatically deny he had ever met Gary, insist he didn't have a car or access to one, and furthermore that "I wasn't interested in 15-year-olds." He assumed that Floyd Edwards had given his name, and it may have been convenient for the authorities to link him with Gary instead: Floyd may have simply named too many people. Anyway, the greater number of men linked to an underage high school student, the better, from point of view of the authorities.

A little more than a month later he found himself at Mount Pleasant. Ironically he was put in a room with Floyd Edwards, the owner of the chenille bedspread. As the youngest on the ward, he received special attention. A lot of the guys on the ward were interested in him, and not merely the other patients. When he went to take a bath on his second day there, Blackwell, the sadistic ward attendant, accompanied him, leering at him the entire time, he remembers. As Billy got out of the tub, the attendant grabbed his privates. Years later it would still give Billy the willies just to think about it. Then there was the smell of the place—a smell that felt like it had been there forever and seemed to go right through him. Billy was certainly not adjusting very well that first week at Mount Pleasant. After Jackie Yamahiro talked to him, though, he began to fare a little better. He was still scared and all he wanted was to get out, but at least he was talking and joking and had his own circle of friends, Duane and Doug and Frank Hildebrandt.

And then the odious Blackwell himself began to take Billy under his wing. They would play cribbage together, and the attendant would take Billy off to the canteen where Billy would buy Del Monte kosher pickles and Spam. Their relationship was beginning to take on a paternal character. "Stay out of the dormitory!" Blackwell would warn him. Billy would peek in, curious, but otherwise heeded Blackwell's advice.

By the time Billy arrived, the mood in the ward was lightening up a bit anyway. "It wasn't like college," said Billy, who had spent a year at the University of Nebraska before enrolling in beauty school. "But we made the most of it. When you went for therapy, people would ask you, 'How did it go?' " To Doug Thorson, being at Mount Pleasant reminded him of basic training—a situation to be endured but one that also brought out a sense of camaraderie. Everyone was in the same boat and had to get along, even if some suspected that the main reason why they were there in the first place was that the guy across the hall (or in the next bed) had given their names to the police.

When a patient on the ward was having a particularly bad time, the others helped him out as much as they could. For example, there was Dave Hoffman, a young Sioux City man with a penchant for cross-dressing and who had been turned over to the police by his parents, who wanted him cured. He had been sent down by the court and arrived later than the others. When he was told he had to bathe in bathwater that had been used by three or four other people, Hoffman made a scene. "I won't go in there! I won't!" he shouted. Doug and Duane took him aside and told him, "You have to get into that bathtub or they are going to throw you in there!" He went.

Then, after a while, Duane himself began to fall apart. He had been all right for the first couple of months, but suddenly he was on the verge of cracking. He couldn't take it anymore, he said. The uncertainty, the tedium, the sense of being watched and cooped up all the time—everything was getting to him. If he didn't leave, he'd really go crazy. Doug had some long talks with him, and in the end Duane emerged all right, but as Doug remembers, it was a "close call."

Family members came for visits, but Mount Pleasant was a long drive from Sioux City, especially in those days, and getting there and back often meant a two or three day expedition. Visits took place in the visitors' lounge on the first floor, just across from Dr. Brown's office. Doug's mother came, and so did Billy Ivers's. Billy's mother often brought food; on one occasion, Billy recalls, he was allowed out with her for a picnic. Harold McBride's wife came every couple of weeks, bringing the couple's three children. By that point she had moved in with Harold's family in Woodward so she could drive to Mount Pleasant and back on the same day.

Meanwhile, Roy and Jackie Yamahiro were doing their best to make life bearable for the men. As a Japanese-American during World War II, Roy had been rounded up and interned himself, much as the men at Mount Pleasant were interned. He knew something of what they were going through and tried to ease their burdens. Still, his authority was limited. He was just a psychologist; he didn't make the rules—or the laws of the state of Iowa, for that matter. But he could help in small ways. He often took his therapy group out to play baseball, as long as the warm weather lasted. In one game, a team of men from the sexual psychopath ward played against a team of ward attendants and their wives. On another day, Jackie took the highest functioning women's ward to play baseball against the men from 15 East, even though the sexual psychopaths weren't supposed to have any contact with female patients. All was going well until the middle of the game, when some of the women players began to hallucinate. One of the women who was the most enthusiastic about playing spent her time in the outfield talking to voices, instead of catching fly balls. The experiment was not repeated.

Even as the situation improved slightly, fear and anxiety hung over Ward 15 East. There was still no indication as to when the men might be released. All their outgoing mail was read by the social services department. (That was true of the regular mental patients too.) They remained at the mercy of ward attendants, psychologists and physicians, the state mental health bureaucrats, and the politicians in Des Moines.

"They could have done anything to us medically," Billy Ivers would realize later. "They could have turned us into vegetables, and there wasn't anything we could have done about it. I wasn't really aware of that at the time. Now that I think about it, I don't believe they knew what to do with us. We were very normal people, except for our sexuality. And in some cases, very talented people. They just didn't know what to do with us."

CHAPTER 14

Therapy

The electroshock therapy that Billy Ivers and Harold McBride feared so much never took place. Perhaps Dr. Brown, the Mount Pleasant superintendent, who was opposed to having the men there in the first place and believed little could be done to treat them, was opposed to it. The other horrors sometimes visited upon homosexuals in mental hospitals in the 1950s—lobotomies, hormone treatments, and aversion therapies—were absent as well. The notion of castrating the men never got beyond lunchtime chatter at the doctors' table. Nonetheless, whatever Dr. Brown's personal views, the homosexual men were at Mount Pleasant to be cured. And according to the provisions of the sexual psychopath law, until they were cured, they couldn't be released. So the hospital made at least a minimal effort at treatment, an effort that fell almost entirely on the psychologists—Roy Yamahiro, Dick Gundersen, and Monroe Fairchild.

During this period, the accepted dogma in the United States and in most of the English-speaking world was that homosexuality was a mental illness. Male homosexuality was believed to be rooted in an early childhood in which a close-binding, seductive mother and detached father distorted the boy's sexual identifications. (In female homosexuality, the dynamics were more or less reversed.) A leading exponent of this idea was Dr. Irving Bieber, a professor of psychiatry at New York Medical College. Under the sponsorship of the New York Society of Medical Psychoanalysts, Bieber undertook a comparative study of 200 male homosexual and heterosexual patients. The results showed an overly close mother-son relationship in 69% of the male homosexuals, more than twice the percentage of heterosexuals. Bieber's sample, however, was badly skewed. Of the 106 homosexual patients in his study, 26 had previously been diagnosed as schizophrenic, and all were in therapy of some sort. Bieber never attempted to corroborate his conclusions by examining gay men who were not in psychiatric treatment.

Nonetheless, Bieber's view of the causes of homosexuality was widely accepted among medical practitioners and the general public. Theories postulating a genetic basis for sexual orientation would become influential later; in the 1950s psychological explanations were dominant, and the overbearing mother figure was always close at hand. (*Momism* was a period buzz word.) And since the cause of homosexuality was to be found in early childhood experiences, the cure lay in psychoanalysis. "A heterosexual shift is a possibility for all homosexuals who are strongly motivated to change," Bieber writes in his book *Homosexuality: A Psychoanalytic Study of Male Homosexuals,* published in 1962. Bieber cited figures that claimed that slightly more than a quarter of patients who were homosexual at the start of treatment with him shifted to exclusive heterosexuality. Other psychoanalysts claimed a success rate of as high as one in two. The idea of homosexuality as an illness that could be cured was also embraced by many homosexuals as a possible way out of a hostile social environment and ensuing personal unhappiness.

Dick Gundersen, the young psychology intern, accepted the prevailing psychiatric thinking and was optimistic that a cure was possible. In his undergraduate and graduate training, Gundersen had been taught that an adult homosexual interested in becoming heterosexual could do so if he was able to gain insight into the psychological factors that had led him astray. All that was needed was motivation, time, and effort.

Yet there were those at Mount Pleasant who had their doubts. Dr. Brown was one of them. Another was Monroe Fairchild, Gundersen's superior, whose own sexuality was rumored about at the hospital. Although Fairchild never directly expressed his views on the subject, it was evident to his colleagues how he felt. As Gundersen understood it, Fairchild's attitude went something like this: "Well, we're stuck with these guys, and they are probably unlikely or unwilling to change, so we'll go through the motions and do what we can do."

Roy Yamahiro stood somewhere in between. Like Fairchild, he doubted whether a cure was possible. But, like Gundersen, he was determined to do something. He didn't want to just go through the motions and give in to the usual Mount Pleasant inertia. He was young and energetic, and the sexual psychopaths were the channel for his idealism. Unlike Gundersen, however, he believed that the men should learn to adjust to their homosexuality and feel comfortable about it. Jackie Yamahiro remembers the two psychologists spending many evenings arguing about the subject.

But whatever Roy Yamahiro thought in private, in public he had to reflect the hospital's mission that the men were there to be cured. This is reflected in his notes on Harold McBride, written on November 3, after Harold had been in the hospital for more than a month. Roy found him "immature in handling many of his needs," and concluded that his "sexual deviation is symptomatic of a more extensive syndrome." He went on, "perhaps his strongest need is that of affection, approval, and dependency. Being fully aware of this need and not being able to adequately satisfy it, he reverts to a more sensuous level of infantile craving for physical contact. In adults, this type of contact craving is often manifested in the area of sexual behavior. It is this examiner's opinion that this patient's homosexual behavior is a symptom of a complex inner conflict which is not centered solely in the area of sex."

In a later note, on December 15, Roy continued along the same line. For Harold, homosexuality represented "an infantile method of satisfying his need for dependency. Like an infant, this need is expressed in a craving for physical contact. As a consequence this maladaptive mode of adjustment brought him to this hospital."

Roy was unable to see Harold's homosexual inclinations as anything other than a symptom of other problems. Why else would a married man who claimed to love his wife seek out sexual relations with other men? And certainly, at least in these medical notes, Roy never expressed the opinion that in fact Harold might simply have a homosexual or bisexual orientation that was integral to his makeup. Roy's public stance was that homosexuality was a maladaptation, and there had to be psychological causes to explain it.

One thing Roy and Dick Gundersen did agree upon was that shock treatments were inappropriate for these men. Gundersen viewed electroshock therapy as something useful for patients who were severely depressed or psychotic. The men in 15 East were neither. In fact, their spirits were generally congenial and jovial, he found; they were "halfway content." Giving them shock treatments, Gundersen was convinced, would be like giving medication for the wrong disease. As for aversion therapy—showing the patients pictures of naked men and then applying some negative stimulus (sometimes a shock)—none of the psychologists had enough experience to apply it.

So they fell back on what they knew—old-fashioned group and individual psychotherapy. The therapy groups, which met a couple of times a week, usually consisted of six or eight men and were not much different from the usual run of such groups. As Gundersen recalled it, in his group he would ask the participants to talk about what had happened in Sioux City. Someone might describe his pattern of homosexual relations. And the psychologist would lead the discussion, guide them and prod them with questions such as: What did the others in the group think motivated the speaker? How did he feel? Why did he do it? What could he do in the future to avoid this kind of behavior? Then someone would jump in and say, "I had those same feelings," and there would be more talk, more prodding in the direction of the world of heterosexuality that Gundersen was convinced lay almost within the men's grasp.

Doug Thorson, who was in Gundersen's group, was struck by how little Gundersen knew about homosexuals or gay life. From the moment the psychologist started asking questions, Doug could tell he didn't have a clue. So the men tried to educate Gundersen while playing along with him at same time. Whether the education was succeeding was doubtful: According to Doug, Gundersen kept asking the same naive questions every time.

Doug's recklessness and bravado were constantly getting him into trouble in these group sessions. He simply refused to provide Gundersen with the answers that he wanted to hear. And Doug knew—as everybody in the group knew—that getting out of Mount Pleasant depended on giving the right answers. But he just couldn't help himself.

There was the time in group therapy when Gundersen asked, "Do you plan to associate with anyone in this room when you get out?"

Doug spoke up. "Why not?" he demanded boldly. It was from the heart, all right—there was Duane and the life they planned together, a relationship that was becoming more and more solid by the day, despite the "cure"—but it was obviously not the answer the psychologist was seeking.

Another time Gundersen asked, "How many men have you guys had sex with?"

Doug couldn't resist the opportunity to show off. "Three hundred to 400, overseas," he volunteered, a big grin on his face.

The other men in the group listened with rapt attention, like a bunch of World War II vets swapping war stories about the battle of Guadalcanal. Actually, Doug was exaggerating wildly. The real number was probably 30 at the most, as he admitted that evening back at the ward. He may have gained the momentary admiration of his fellow patients, but once again Doug wasn't helping his situation. You didn't want to indicate that your homosexuality was too deeply rooted, or they'd never let you go home.

Only when Gundersen asked, "Did you ever have sex with a woman? Did you reach climax?" and Doug replied, "Yes—and I enjoyed it too!" did his bravado stand him in good stead. For once he had come up with the right answer.

To Doug, these therapy sessions were a farce. The men would laugh about it once group was over, he said.

Part of the difficulty in treating the men—whether the goal was cure or adjustment—was that they were prisoners who wanted to say the right thing so they could get out of the hospital. (In this, Doug seems to have been the exception.) This distorted the process, undermining the honesty and openness on which the therapeutic relationship depends. In individual psychotherapy with Roy Yamahiro, Harold McBride was afraid he might divulge something that could stand in the way of being released. He'd lie to Roy or tell him what he thought he wanted to hear. He'd play down his homosexual feelings, emphasize how much he loved his wife and was sexually aroused by her. He'd agree with him about certain things he didn't necessarily feel or believe. After a while he began to trust Roy more and open up to him. But that took time, and it complicated the doctor-patient relationship.

Harold had a good deal of individual therapy during his stay at Mount Pleasant. Perhaps he was seen as salvageable; after all, he was married and had a family. He was intelligent and worldly, and Roy Yamahiro was particularly drawn to him. But just how much actual psychotherapy took place over-all is questionable. The sexual psychopath ward was hardly the psychologists' only duty. Gundersen, Yamahiro and Fairchild divided up nearly 1,500 patients in the hospital among the three of them; there was therapy to be done and evaluations and paperwork, to say nothing of day-to-day problems. They were stretched thin. Consequently, although group therapy was supposed to take place a couple of times a week, that was not always the case.

Billy Ivers, for one, would in fact recall going to group therapy only once or twice during his entire stay and never to individual therapy. When he first arrived he thought there would be "some big thing, a cure!"—but in fact there was nothing. The only medication he got was a couple of aspirins. (In that he was fortunate.) Still, he thought, the whole experience was therapy of a sort: You had no alternative but to sit there and feel sorry for yourself and think.

Whatever occurred at Mount Pleasant in terms of therapy, it was clear that the medical doctors played little role in the whole process. Every morning, Dr. Klodnycky, who was officially assigned to the sexual psychopath ward, passed through 15 East on his rounds. He'd wave and call out to the men jocularly, "Good Morning, Hotel Imperial!" After his greeting, he'd move on to the next ward. It was virtually his only contact with the men in 15 East.

Matters of the Heart

Once his fears and wild imaginings abated, Billy Ivers was beginning to notice another patient on 15 East—a farmer from Homer, Nebraska, named Jim Kerns. Jim, was a clean-cut, all-American boy, "so masculine, so fresh, so good looking," Billy thought. "If you met him, you would be sure he was a minister." Jim had been leading a classic double life, working on the family farm in Homer and going across the river into Sioux City for sex with men. He was under pressure from his family to marry. Jim had been brought in the roundup, too, one of the first to be charged. Billy watched him from afar. Sex was the furthest thing from Billy's mind, but even at Mount Pleasant, his heart was still alive.

But if Billy's involvement with Jim Kerns primarily consisted of adoration, that wasn't true of many of the others. Thirty-five men, mostly homosexual, were crowded into tiny cubicles and a dormitory in one ward under very tense and trying circumstances, in which the need for affection was great. At night the lights were left on in the corridors, the doors to the rooms were open, and there was always an attendant on duty; nonetheless the possibilities for sex were very real. One evening Harold McBride was almost asleep when his roommate, Frank Hildebrandt, jumped into his bed and began to make love to him. It never happened again—there wasn't even much attraction there, at least on Harold's part—but it illustrated some of the need for release that the men experienced and its easy availability.

The staff and the ward attendants in particular, were not unaware of this. After a couple of weeks as roommates,

Doug and Duane were put in separate rooms. Someone had figured out that their friendship was something more than just platonic. Meanwhile Blackwell was warning Billy Ivers to stay out of the dormitory, which was quickly acquiring a notorious reputation. "I heard it was quite a chore keeping the boys apart in the evenings," one man who worked at the hospital at that time noted wryly. For his part, Dr. Klodyncky apparently believed it was an enviable situation—all those homosexual men crowded together. To him, it was the "Hotel Imperial."

In her tiny office in the social services department on the first floor, Jackie Yamahiro was becoming the confidante of the men in 15 East and the link with their families. She would interview their visitors, trying to get a picture of the men's lives; she'd pass phone messages from the men to their families and the families to the men. Sometimes the men would make appointments to see her just to get off the ward and talk to a sympathetic soul.

Increasingly, though, their main purpose in coming to her was to discuss their romantic problems. In the ward there were some established couples that predated Mount Pleasant—Doug and Duane, for example. But there were newer, less stable combinations too. Relationships were becoming more intense, more fraught by the day; jealousies and romantic rivalries grew, disrupting the sense of solidarity. One afternoon one of the Sioux City men came into her office, visibly upset. He had become sexually involved with another man on the ward, but now his new lover was losing interest; someone else had entered the picture. He had tears in his eyes as he talked to her. Until then Jackie had only had a superficial understanding of homosexuality. But at that moment in her office she began to comprehend that a relationship between two men could involve the same degree of feeling as that between a man and a woman. It was a lesson that stayed with her—one of those moments when her perception of the world was enlarged and changed forever.

Nonetheless, at age 23, Jackie hardly considered herself an authority on the subject of relationships and felt she really didn't know how to counsel anyone. The best she could do was be someone they could talk to. Although she had never before met any self-identified homosexual men, she said later, "I never had any feelings except acceptance for the people who were sentenced there. I had a lot of compassion for them. I'm not sure why."

Yet Jackie, like Roy, was a child of her time. She too had been taught that male homosexuality had its roots in early childhood, the consequence of an overbearing mother and a distant father. As she interviewed the men and their families and wrote up her accounts of their lives, she looked for common threads. If she interviewed someone whose mother was obviously dominant in the family, she'd say to herself, *Aha, found one!* But in real life, things weren't as consistent as they were in her psychology textbooks, and she wasn't finding the patterns she was supposed to find. There were some cases where the men had strong mother figures, but others where the father was the major influence. She learned over time that people couldn't be pigeonholed quite as neatly as Irving Bieber and the so-called experts at New York Medical College believed.

She was learning other things too. One day she was chatting in her office with a patient from 15 East who told her, "You can always tell when someone is homosexual."

"Oh, I don't believe that," she said. "If I met all of you guys somewhere else, I'd never suspect."

"You can tell!" the patient persisted. "I know about someone who will surprise you: Rock Hudson."

Jackie didn't believe him. Thirty years later, when it was revealed that the actor was gay and dying of AIDS, the moment came back to her.

Of course, getting close to the men sometimes had unintended consequences, as Jackie discovered when one of the patients in 15 East became infatuated with her. The patient, Wade Hammond, was a ruggedly handsome man of about 35 who had the toughness and vulnerability of an aging James Dean. He had spent most of his life in institutions and had been sent to Mount Pleasant from the penitentiary at Fort Madison after sexually assaulting another prisoner. Some of the men on the ward were afraid of him. He wrote romantic notes to Jackie and made a purse for her in occupational therapy. The infatuation went no further, but it was awkward for Jackie.

At the same time, as Jackie and Roy's involvement with the men deepened, they began to take risks on their behalf. At first that involved just bending the rules: taking them out to play baseball on a warm fall afternoon or downstairs to play Ping-Pong as the weather grew colder, or bringing them from the ward to the auditorium where Lloyd Madsen was practicing the organ on a Saturday afternoon. Some at the hospital may have disapproved—the men were supposed to be "restrained," after all—but these infractions weren't really too serious.

Then one evening, Roy and Jackie took a greater risk, which involved Harold McBride and his wife, Glenda. Once Harold was arrested and sent to Mount Pleasant, he had never really had a chance to talk to Glenda. Up until then, she had never known he had sex with men; certainly they had never discussed it. Their marriage was on shaky ground. Glenda would come and visit at the hospital—sometimes bringing the kids—but the couple had to meet in the visitor's lounge. Attendants were always lurking in the background, and other patients were receiving visitors there at the same time; it was impossible to have the kind of private and intimate conversation the couple obviously needed. So one Tuesday evening, when a movie was about to start and almost everyone else was distracted, Jackie led Harold's wife up to her and Roy's apartment on the third floor of the hospital. Roy asked an attendant to go to 15 East and get Harold off the ward. Roy then sneaked him into the apartment. It wasn't a conjugal visit as much as a chance for Harold and Glenda to sort out everything that had turned their lives upside down. Roy and Jackie stood guard in the hall the entire time. The couple was alone for an hour, and no one ever found out.

The Power and The Glory

Christmas, 1955, arrived at Mount Pleasant. The Donnellson Mennonite Missionary Circle and the Mount Pleasant Blue Ladies came to call, singing Christmas carols on the wards. The American Legion and the VFW served holiday luncheons to veterans who were patients at the hospital, giving them gifts and helping them wrap presents for their families. Young people from the Church of the Nazarene in Mount Pleasant presented a pageant and choral music. A large Christmas tree stood just inside the entrance to the main building, and each ward had its own tree, though no one remembers one in 15 East.

On the Friday evening before Christmas came the culmination of the holiday activities: a 12-act Christmas variety pageant featuring the best talent the hospital had to offer. Under Lloyd Madsen's direction, the patients rehearsed for days in advance. There were constant comings and goings from the wards, particularly 15 East. When the evening arrived, greenery covered the gymnasium stage. The patients wore their best clothes; the doctors and their wives were in attendance, bringing with them an Old World flavor; townspeople overflowed the balcony. Lloyd led the performance and played the organ and the piano. The woman who had polio—and whose family had put her in Mount Pleasant to keep her out of sight—sang "O Holy Night." Doug played the trumpet, which he hadn't done since high school. Harold sang in the choir, even though he could barely carry a note.

Roy and Jackie had planned to leave on the day of the pageant to return to Wisconsin for the holidays. But Wade

Hammond, the patient in 15 East who had been a prisoner at Fort Madison, pleaded with them to stay an extra day. He would be performing a solo of the vocal version of "The Lord's Prayer," and it would mean a lot to him if they were there. They agreed. It was toward the end of the program that Wade's moment arrived. He had never sung publicly and was obviously nervous, but he had a fine and very deep bass voice and soon relaxed. As the piece rose to its emotional peak, the entire gymnasium seemed to hold its breath: For Thine is the kingdom, and the power, and the glory / Forever and ever.

In her balcony seat, Jackie remembered a recording by Paul Robeson she had heard in her student days. That bass voice! Wade could have had a career as a singer, had things turned out differently, she thought. Roy, who was Wade's psychologist, was also taken completely by surprise. The depth of feeling was so unexpected, so contrary to the man they knew, the personality hardened by years in prison. Roy and Jackie suspected that the performance was one of the few accomplishments of Wade's life, and it seemed to give some meaning to what they were doing at Mount Pleasant.

Everyone agreed it was the best Christmas pageant the hospital had ever had. It had a polished, almost professional quality, which was largely due to the talents of the men in the sexual psychopath ward. Though they weren't the only performers, the men in 15 East were the heart and soul of the Christmas show. Lloyd's musical direction, Wade's solo, even the minor parts—Doug's trumpet playing and Harold's singing—seemed to demonstrate that despite all the men had gone through, there was something grander, loftier than the endless bad dream of days at the mental hospital. "For Thine is the kingdom, the power, and the glory"—even at Mount Pleasant.

Nonetheless, when the carolers came around to the various wards the next day, there was one ward that was considered too dangerous to enter: the sexual psychopath ward. And so Christmas, 1955, came and went in 15 East.

CHAPTER 17

Christmas in Sioux City

Just before Christmas that year, there came one of those periodic breaks in the Donna Sue Davis case, still unsolved after almost six months. Police in Reno, Nevada, arrested Virgil Vance Wilson, 31, on charges of intoxication and disorderly conduct. In the course of interrogation, Wilson admitted that some time in July, he had stolen a car and kidnapped a little girl in Onawa, Iowa, a town just south of Sioux City. Suspecting that the girl might be Donna Sue Davis, Reno police immediately telephoned their counterparts in Sioux City. But once Wilson sobered up, he recanted. On December 20, Sioux City Police Chief James O'Keefe announced that Wilson had been eliminated as a suspect. It had been established that Wilson had been in Des Moines in the company of friends as late as 7 P.M. on the night that Donna Sue was murdered. Since the little girl had been snatched from her crib at 9:30, it would have been impossible for Wilson to have arrived in Sioux City in time to commit the crime. The investigation into Donna Sue's death was continuing, the police chief said.

In its end-of-the-year survey, the executives of Associated Press newspapers and radio stations in Iowa voted the slaying of Donna Sue Davis as the "top news event in Iowa" in 1955. The Davis case won 265 votes, narrowly beating out the visit of a Russian farm delegation to Iowa, which garnered 257 votes. Third place went to falling farm prices.

Cured

Almost as precipitously as the start of the roundup itself, the men began to be released. Harold McBride got out on New Year's Day, 1956, the first man in the ward to gain his freedom. He had been at Mount Pleasant for a little more than three months, in addition to the month he had spent in jail in Sioux City.

Clearly there were people at the hospital pushing for his release. Two weeks before, in his note of December 15, Roy Yamahiro had praised Harold's "rapid progress." Perhaps the most favorable indicator, wrote the psychologist, was Harold's "enthusiasm, courage, and keen desire to understand himself and his problems." Dr. Klodnycky echoed this in his parole note of December 27: "During his stay here he has gained very much insight in his condition, and he believes he has learned very much here to understand his own condition, and he is sure he will never return to his habit."

Forces outside the hospital were helping him too—Harold's wife, his brother and sister-in-law, and family friends. In the petition for his release, his lawyer, Sioux City attorney Ervin Hutchison, said that if Harold were allowed to leave Mount Pleasant, he would promise to join his family in Woodward. The petition also stated that "at all times hereafter," Harold would undergo private psychiatric treatment with "Miss Seymour," a psychologist at Woodward State Hospital who was a personal friend. Miss Seymour expressed her willingness for the defendant to be paroled to her, according to the lawyer.

A month before, on November 25, *The Des Moines Register* had published an article headlined "Can't Tell If Sex

Deviate Really Cured" in which Mount Pleasant superintendent W.B. Brown expressed strong doubts about whether anything could be done to change the sexual proclivities of the incarcerated men. Dr. Brown's comments gave Harold's lawyer some ammunition, and he referred to them in his petition to the court: "The said Dr. W.B. Brown...has publicly stated...that he cannot say to this court that this defendant is cured, but can only state that he does not know, that it is part of the defendant's personality makeup; and further the said Dr. Brown has stated that he does not know what is going to happen to the defendant and other deviates now confined to the said Mount Pleasant Institute."

The *Register* article wasn't the only journalistic scrutiny that the sexual psychopath ward was receiving. A week earlier, on November 17, 1955, *The Sioux City Journal* published a story raising the issue of the expense of holding the men at Mount Pleasant. Under the headline "Deviates Cost County $1,500," the *Journal* revealed that Woodbury County was paying $1,500 a month per inmate to keep 15 of the 21 men who had been sentenced in Sioux City, at the mental hospital. (Two of the remaining men were from other Iowa counties, which were paying for them, while three were from Nebraska and one from South Dakota.) The newspaper noted that if the men had been incarcerated at the state penitentiaries at Fort Madison or Anamosa, the state, not the county, would have footed the bill. County attorney Don O'Brien would tell the *Register* the following week, "We think it's well worth the cost." With Woodbury County paying out a total of $22,500 a month to keep the men under lock and key, however, it was clearly in the county's interest that the situation not continue indefinitely.

At the same time, the Board of Control began to rethink its

policy of sending everyone arrested under the sexual psychopath law to Mount Pleasant. Ward 15 East could barely handle the patients already there. "The other state hospitals are going to start taking these people," announced board chairman Henry Burma in early December. "Mount Pleasant's facilities for this group are taxed to the limit." In the future, Burma announced, men classified as sexual psychopaths would be sent to the mental hospital serving the part of the state in which they lived. Thus, anyone sentenced in Sioux City would go to the state mental hospital at Cherokee, not to Mount Pleasant.

Meanwhile, Doug Thorson was close to being released. On January 13, 1956, Dr. Gundersen wrote in his notes that Doug was "slowly progressing in group therapy." He was still occasionally making use of "intellectualization" and "ego defense" to "qualify" and "rationalize" his homosexuality. While he was frequently moody and offered little to the group, other times he showed "great initiative and insight." Dr. Gundersen concluded that "individual psychotherapy for this man should be recommended upon his release from the hospital."

In a parole note dated January 25, Dr. Klodnycky was more positive. The doctor restated Doug's claim that at the time he had been sent to Mount Pleasant, he had been engaged to a woman with whom he was having "normal" heterosexual relations and who wanted to "straighten him up." Dr. Klodnycky went on, "While staying here he learned very much to understand himself better and to control himself. When he gets out of here, he will definitely stay away from his deviated practices. He is going to marry that girl who knows everything about his difficulties, and she is willing to marry him."

Hospital authorities apparently didn't bother to investigate whether such a young woman existed, or whether the facts were as Doug stated. At this point it was simply convenient to take Doug's word for it.

It became increasingly clear that the special ward, so enthusiastically embraced by Governor Hoegh and others the previous July and August, was not working out. 15 East was overcrowded, the authorities in Sioux City were worried about the expense, the newspapers were looking at the story more critically, and Dr. Brown grew increasingly vocal in expressing his doubts. The immediate panic of the weeks after the murder of Donna Sue had abated. It was time for the men to go.

On January 31, 1956, at 10:30 A.M., Doug was presented to staff. "Going to staff," the Mount Pleasant term for a discharge hearing, always took place in Dr. Brown's office on the first floor in the main entrance area. Usually, most of the clinical staff, including psychologists and social workers, were present. On some occasions, there could be up to 15 or 20 in the room. That morning, as Doug stood outside in the hall, Drs. Gundersen and Klodnycky gave a brief outline of the reasons that led to his commitment to the hospital in the first place, and what had been achieved. Then Doug was invited inside to answer questions.

"How do you feel about yourself now?" the doctors asked him. "Are you going to go back to the kind of life you led before? Do you still have desires toward men?"

Doug was on his best behavior this time. "Absolutely not," he replied. "You people taught me a lesson."

He repeated the story about the young woman who was willing to marry him. And he added that he was hopeful that Kresge's, his employer at the time of his arrest, would transfer him to another state. In Doug's view, the questions were stupid, just as Dr. Gundersen's questions in group therapy had been stupid, but he wasn't going to ruin his chance this time.

If he had learned one thing at Mount Pleasant, it was that sometimes it was smart to keep your opinions to yourself.

The staff recommended that he be sent home, and on February 4, Doug Thorson was released to the custody of his mother in Sioux City. He had been at Mount Pleasant more than four months and in jail in Sioux City for one month.

Most of the other men from Sioux City were released that winter—Karl Schmidt, the dance teacher, on January 27; Frank Hildebrandt, the roommate of Harold McBride, on February 2; Harold's friend, Gene Bergstrom, a few days later; Jim Kerns, the Nebraska farmer for whom Billy Ivers's heart beat during those long days and nights, on February 11; and Floyd Edwards, whom Billy thought had probably given his name to the police, on February 17. Billy himself was released on March 3. Before Billy went to staff, Roy Yamahiro coached him, rehearsing the kinds of questions he would be asked and the answers the doctors would be looking for. It was an advantage that Dick Gundersen's patients didn't have.

Lloyd Madsen, the organist, stayed longer. He had been one of the first to arrive at the ward—back on August 15—and he wasn't released until April 25, an eight-month stint altogether. Perhaps his musical ability was just too valuable for the hospital; he couldn't easily be replaced. Or perhaps certain people on staff had their own, more personal reasons, for wanting him to stay.

As for Duane Wheeler, he had been presented to staff in late January, just before Doug Thorson. A couple of days after that, at the Friday night dance, an attendant called Duane off the floor. His brother Bob had arrived to take him home. They got as far as Des Moines that night and had a couple of drinks at the bar of the hotel where they stayed. Bob hadn't been down to Mount Pleasant to visit while Duane was incarcerated—he was an engineer on the railroad and couldn't take time off from work—so there was a lot to catch up on. Conversation mostly concerned Bob's three kids, with whom Duane was very close. "He didn't talk about the hospital," Bob recalled in later years. "I was there to listen, but he didn't talk about it, and I didn't ask." One thing Duane apparently never bothered to mention to his brother was that his friend Doug had been at Mount Pleasant with him as well.

In petitions as to why their clients should be released, attorneys for the men made a variety of promises regarding their future behavior. Harold McBride would be taking therapy "at all times hereafter" with Miss Seymour; Jim Kerns was engaged to be married and would be taking a teaching job in Roswell, New Mexico; Gene Bergstrom had "employment lined up for himself" and was "ready, willing, and able to continue private psychiatric treatment"; Lloyd Madsen would be paroled to Monsignor Ernest Graham of St. Cecilia's Cathedral in Omaha.

The men were put on parole for a period of three years. All received a certificate of discharge from Mount Pleasant signed by Dr. Brown. The certificates stated that they were "Recovered (Cured)."

The sexual psychopath ward was shut down the following fall of 1956.

Upon his release from Mount Pleasant, Harold McBride went to work as a ward attendant at the Woodward State Hospital for Epileptics and the Feeble-Minded, where he had worked many years before. His brother and sister-in-law had jobs at the hospital, and Glenda had been hired there too while her husband was at Mount Pleasant. It was an odd choice, certainly, but Harold had lost his license to cut hair and he needed a job. Perhaps working at the state hospital served a psychological function for him as well. It was an opportunity to gain some degree of control over an experience that had come close to wrecking his life. He was on the other side now and could come home to his own bed at night. In any event, he knew the territory.

Miss Seymour, the psychologist who was supposed to be Harold's therapist, also worked at Woodward State Hospital. But Harold never did go into therapy with her. "Sure, I knew Dr. Seymour because I used to do her hair," he would say afterward. "But that was it. I never saw her as a patient. I never even knew that the lawyer had promised the judge that I would do that." Miss Seymour had apparently just lent her name to help get Harold released, one of the many kindnesses he received.

Years later Harold asked a hairdresser who was a friend in those days—and who knew some of the other men sent to Mount Pleasant, including Gene Bergstrom—to write something about the public reaction to what had happened. She wrote:

> Concerning the incident in Sioux City, Iowa, in 1955. The observance of friends in the area was mainly shock and disappointment to see the publicity of acquaintances. Not knowing what the laws were involving these acts it was mostly surprise there was a jail sentence, and thought that [it] was unnecessary. The incident was soon forgotten and no judgments made by close friends ,to my knowledge. It was an unfortunate circumstance, and hoped the arrests made would solve a problem for those involved.

Three months after his release from Mount Pleasant, Harold got his hairdressing license back. To do this, he had to appear before a judge in the courthouse in Adel, south of Woodward. Two women from the Kingsley area came down for the hearing. They told the judge they would continue to be Harold's clients. (This was required by law.) The judge asked Harold what he planned to do in the future. Harold said that he planned to leave the state. "That is probably in your best interest," said the judge, and granted him his license.

Despite the judge's encouragement, Harold didn't leave the state, at least not immediately. In April he got a job cutting hair in a salon in Des Moines. Then his mother died unexpectedly. Harold and Glenda took that as a sign that it was time to go. Glenda had grown up in Pomona, California, and she still had family there. So in June they loaded up the Pontiac; it was crammed so full that Harold's brother built a box on top of the roof for their belongings. Every time they went over a bump, the baggage seemed as if it were about to spill all over the highway. With the three children, they set out for California and a new life.

They pulled into Pomona at 3 o'clock on a Tuesday afternoon, just in time to see a beauty products salesman walking out the door of a hair salon. Harold approached the man and asked whether he knew of any available jobs. By the next day, Harold was back in the hair business, working at a local salon. On Friday the owners gave him the keys to the front door. "We're going to Vegas for a week," they announced. "Could you manage the shop?"

Perhaps the past could be forgotten, though there were still some lessons learned. "I didn't make any resolutions not to have sex with men anymore or anything like that," Harold said. "But I sure was more careful." A few months later Eugene Bergstrom followed Harold out to California. He went back into the hair business, and soon after married "Mrs. Eugene."

Doug Thorson and Duane Wheeler headed for California too. At his probation hearing, the judge told Doug not to have contact with anyone from the hospital, but Doug, characteristically, wasn't going to be told what to do. He and Duane were planning their future together. Duane had spent a lot of time in California, where his aunts and uncles lived, and Doug had heard about a company in Des Moines that hired people to drive cars to the West Coast. So a few weeks after their probation hearings, they were on their way to Southern California in a brand new Cadillac. They drove mostly along Route 66, through Oklahoma and Texas and New Mexico. The car was due at its destination in 10 days, and they made it to California in just four. That gave them almost a week to explore Southern California before the car had to be delivered. It was a terrific feeling: A month ago they had been locked up in a mental hospital, and now here they were driving along the beaches and through the mountains in a new Cadillac.

Doug and Duane settled in Santa Monica. They decided not to live together, however, at least until the end of their three-year period of probation. It didn't hurt to be extra cautious. If the probation officer found out they shared the same address, their parole might even be revoked. You could never be too sure. Each month they filled out their probation reports, telling the court back in Sioux City where they were living and working. A minister signed Doug's forms; a doctor signed Duane's. They were starting over, but they were looking backward too.

Duane went to finish his courses at beauty school in West Hollywood. Doug got a job at a five-and-dime store; he only had $100 to his name and needed a job immediately. He told the owners he had just gotten out of the service. But after a few months the store wanted to promote him to a managerial position and requested a full background check. Doug quit, concerned they might find out about what had taken place in Sioux City. Then he went to work for the Beneficial Finance Company, where he received two promotions in just a few months. The company proposed that he manage one of their offices and also asked for a background check. Doug quit that job too.

Once their probation was over and the last report had been sent in to the authorities, Doug received an official letter postmarked Sioux City. It was a bill from Woodbury County asking for $2,000, a portion of the amount the county had spent to keep him at Mount Pleasant. Assessing prisoners for the cost of their incarceration is perfectly legal in Iowa—the right of the authorities to do so is stated in a prisoner's pre-sentence report. But judges rarely exercise this privilege, except when a prisoner is wealthy or has large assets. In the case of Doug and the others, Woodbury County had paid out a lot of unanticipated money and wanted to get some of it back. Actually, the total amount for Doug's four months at Mount Pleasant should have come to $6,000. "Maybe they gave us a credit for all the painting we did," he joked bitterly. Doug tossed the bill out and never heard from the county again.

Meanwhile, Billy Ivers went back to living with his mother and aunt just outside of Sioux City and to attending beauty school. And then, soon after, he began seeing a lot of Jim Kerns, the "clean-cut, all-American" farmer whom he had first met at Mount Pleasant. They continued seeing each other for the next several years. It wasn't the perfect relationship, though. "Jim had one small problem," said Billy. "He didn't want to be gay." Jim eventually married. Many years later, when the relationship was long over, Billy's face would light up just at the mention of Jim's name. And it had all started during the days of the "cure" at Mount Pleasant.

That first summer that Doug and Duane were in California, they ran into Harold McBride in Laguna Beach. It was good to see a familiar face from Iowa, and they were glad that Harold and Glenda and the kids had made it to California and that Harold was cutting hair again. But none of them said a word about Mount Pleasant. The silence was beginning. If you didn't mention it, perhaps it had never happened. The shame was so great, and the sense of outrage was pushed deeper and deeper inside as the years went by.

But there was at least one of their number who didn't appear to share that sense of outrage. He was Leo Vandermeer, who had been a salesman at a Sioux City department store before he was brought in in the roundup. Leo, 31 at the time, was tall and gawky and lived with his brother. He "got mixed up with the wrong crowd," as he put it; the night he was arrested, he was "half lit" and "a kid propositioned me." He didn't remember much of what happened except that he found himself in the Sioux City jail, charged with lascivious acts with a child, and wound up at Mount Pleasant.

Leo had been in the same class at East High School with Dick Burke and Ed Verbeski, the two policemen who made most, if not all, of the arrests in the roundup, and he knew them both. (A fey-looking Leo, a cocky Verbeski, and a scowling Burke appear together on the same page of the 1942 *Arrow*, the East High yearbook, when they were sophomores; Leo and Verbeski were in the same homeroom.) Leo had been at the Warrior bar the night Doug was arrested. If he had been a little more aware—and a lot more sober, he told Doug—he might have alerted everyone as to who Burke and Verbeski really were and maybe have got himself out of a jam too. But that didn't happen. "I got what was coming to me, I guess," he said.

He tried to put the best face on Mount Pleasant. At first it was "really strange," but he was determined to get something positive out of his time there. There were "a lot of classes," as he referred to occupational and group therapy. Being at the hospital was "helpful." The therapists "knew pretty much what we were like. They cared about you." That was the end of the subject, as far as he was concerned. "I never wanted to think about it again."

Like so many of the men, once he was released, he moved to California. Then, seven months after he left Mount Pleasant, Leo got married.

Did his wife know about his past and Mount Pleasant? he was asked 40 years later. By then he was still married, retired after spending most of his life working in and managing department stores in small towns in Nebraska.

"That is a little personal," he said.

"She knew!" insisted Doug when Leo's reaction was recounted to him. Leo had called Doug on the phone back in 1956 when he was about to get married to tell him the news.

Was he "cured," as it said on his release certificate?

"I'm sure the doctors felt that way or they wouldn't have written that," said Leo.

"Ha!" Doug snorted.

CHAPTER 19 ──────────────────────────────

Closing the Books

On November 13, 1957, two years and four months after the slaying of Donna Sue Davis—and with no new developments in the investigation—*The Sioux City Journal* closed the books on its reward fund for information leading to the arrest and conviction of the little girl's killer. Individual contributions were returned to the donors, or in cases when the donors could not be located or the gifts were anonymous, to Donna Sue's family. A citizen's committee had managed the fund and had extended its life on two occasions—once for a year and the second time for four months. But there seemed little point anymore. The murderer might be caught someday; it was always possible, of course. But the committee and the *Journal* had concluded that continuing to hold on to the reward money would serve "no useful purpose." The newspaper wrote, "If any person or persons having knowledge of the slayer's identity desired to furnish such information to the authorities, he, she or they would have done so by this time."

Three months later, in January 1958, a closed inquest into the case was conducted at the Woodbury County courthouse in Sioux City. Nothing came of it.

PART 4: THE SECOND ROUNDUP

SIOUX CITY, IOWA, SEPTEMBER 1958

"Too many young Sioux Cityans are being given 'dangerous' freedom. They are allowed to come and go from such places as downtown movies at all hours of the night. Any of the unchaperoned are easy prey for the sexual pervert.... Our kids are carefree and happy, never realizing fear or doubting their safety. The parent must worry for them, for tragedy can strike at any time or place."

—*The Sioux City Press-Dispatch* editorial, October 9, 1958

CHAPTER 20

Fighting Back

Even as the books were closed on the Donna Sue Davis reward fund, even as the men arrested in the 1955 roundup moved on with their lives, and the sexual psychopath ward faded into a distant memory, the hysteria that had engulfed Sioux City continued to linger just below the surface of daily life. It could always be called upon, if necessary; it was just too useful for police and politicians.

And so in the fall of 1958, there was another roundup. This time, no sex crimes precipitated it; there seemed to be no obvious reason. Perhaps it was that county attorney Don O'Brien, who had played a major role in the 1955 incarcerations, was in an uphill battle in a race for Congress and thought the morals issue might win him some votes. Or perhaps it was that the Sheraton Corporation, which had purchased the Warrior Hotel two years before, was upset that the pay toilets in the men's room were becoming jammed with dimes, so the company complained to the police, who then put the bathroom under surveillance. (That was the story that went around.) Whatever the reason, the arrests and the naming of names began again.

The cops arrested Pete Reynolds in the Warrior men's room on the night of Monday, September 21. Pete, 22, was fresh out of Morningside College. A couple of weeks before, he had just begun his first year as an English teacher at East High School. Pete had gone to East himself, where he'd been a star debater, student council president, and a "king's attendant" at Homecoming. His passion was politics. In the 1954 high school yearbook *The Arrow*, there's a photo of Pete, in a sport coat and khakis, his hair in a crew cut, orating in a statewide debate competition, with the girls on the debate team on one side and the boys on the other, all watching admiringly.

At a teachers' meeting at school on the afternoon of his arrest, Pete had noticed that J.B. Kuhler, a longtime history teacher at East, was nowhere to be seen. "J.B. is gone," the principal, S.M. Hickman, announced vaguely. "I don't know when he'll be coming back." Pete found this strange because J.B. was the kind of teacher who never missed a day of school. But he didn't give the absence any further thought. Pete was living with his parents, and after school he went home to eat dinner and correct papers. It was a warm evening, and he was restless. He wrote a letter to a friend who was a graduate student at the University of Michigan in Ann Arbor and drove downtown to the post office to mail it. On the way, he stopped at the Warrior Hotel men's room.

Pete had discovered the Warrior the previous spring when he was finishing his senior year at Morningside. He'd sit in a stall and tap his feet, and soon enough someone's hand or leg would eventually find its way from the next stall; the two neighbors might pass notes to each other. Like Officer Dick Burke, Pete had stumbled upon the "international code of homosexuality." Occasionally he'd meet someone and they'd go elsewhere to have sex. The first person he met this way was a traveling salesman staying at the Warrior; they went up to his room. Pete didn't have too much trouble meeting men: He was personable and smart and good-looking in a solid, Midwestern sort of way. After Pete had sex with someone, he'd always go to confession.

That past summer, the summer he graduated from Morningside, he had gone to Europe on a college trip. In New York City, on the way, the group leader—a speech professor at

Morningside—had taken some of the students to a gay bar in Greenwich Village on a kind of an anthropological expedition. For Pete, a whole new world had opened up.

Still, Pete wasn't very well versed in sex or sex practices. He was aware that he liked men, but he was still convinced that he would get married by the time he was 25. He was attracted to older men, so he wasn't worried that his sexual activities might compromise his teaching job; he wouldn't end up involved with any students. He didn't think his homosexual dalliances would ever go beyond the Warrior men's room. Maybe the next summer he'd go to New York, find that bar again, and get the whole thing out of his system. But for the moment his main concern was his classes. When he was in Europe that summer, teaching was virtually all he thought about. On the boat over and back, he would stay in his cabin and draw up lesson plans. One of the books he was planning to teach was *The Scarlet Letter*, an interesting choice—one could say a prophetic one— considering what was to follow.

Going into the Warrior men's room that evening, Pete felt a mixture of excitement, guilt, and confusion—he always did— but that didn't stop him. He was dressed in his usual casual attire: a polo shirt, jeans, white socks, and penny loafers. His hair was short, but he no longer had a crew cut; as a teacher, you were expected to have a part in your hair—that signified maturity. He sat in one of the stalls, moved his feet, and eventually a leg made its way under the partition into Pete's stall. Pete touched the leg. The owner of the leg wrote a note asking, "What do you want?" Pete wrote back, "Nothing." Predictably, he was already having second thoughts. He got up, flushed the toilet, and went to wash his hands. As he stood in front of the sink, he felt a hand on his shoulder.

Pete Reynolds was pinched.

Pete knew the arresting officer, Robert Johnson, who lived down the block from Pete and refereed at neighborhood basketball games. He was in his 30s, blond and pleasant looking. Johnson took Pete down the corridor to the hotel barber shop and ordered him to sit in the barber chair. Two other cops—E.H. Anders and Arnie Nielsen—stood surrounding him. Nielsen was a friend of Pete's father; while not wealthy, the Reynoldses were a prominent family in Sioux City—Pete's father was a manager at a fertilizer company. It was a little after 8:45 in the evening. The lights in the barbershop were off, and everyone sat in the dark. The barbershop's windows offered a view of the corridor leading to the men's room; the cops were observing who was coming and going, and they didn't want to be seen. Pete inhaled the sweet and somewhat sickening smell of hair tonic. As he later remembered it, Dick Burke, scourge of Sioux City's homosexuals, wasn't present, although Burke's name—not Nielsen's—appeared on the court documents as one of the arresting officers. Perhaps because of his friendship with Pete's father, Nielsen didn't want to be associated with the case.

The cops questioned Pete for a couple of hours. Arnie Nielsen tried to coax Pete in friendly fashion. "Give us the name of somebody else, and then you can go home," Nielsen would say. "Your father doesn't have to know about this." As they talked, a blond, heavyset man of about Pete's age wandered down the corridor to the john every 10 minutes or so. But it was a slow night at the Warrior: The man would go back to the street and back to the john again. They had been trying to get him all weekend, the cops told Pete. Did he know him? "No," said Pete. That wasn't entirely true. Pete didn't know his name—it was Darrell Albertson—but he had had sex with him in a car in Stone Park and another time while just driving around. The cops again promised they'd let him go home and kept pressing: "Have you been with him?" The danger of the situation grew clearer to Pete with every passing moment. He sat in the dark in a barber's chair, clutching the letter to his friend in Ann Arbor as if it were a life preserver, being interrogated by three police officers who alternated between soothing and threatening words; he had to be at school first thing in the morning and hadn't finished correcting all his papers.

Finally, Pete admitted he had "been with" Albertson. ("Been with" was the police euphemism for sexual relations.) Could he go home now? No, said Johnson, the officer who had arrested him and who was playing "bad cop" to Nielsen's "good cop." They needed another name. Pete hesitated. Finally, after more cajoling, he offered up the name of William Schultz, a 28-year-old man from a small Nebraska town who had once followed Pete home and rang the doorbell. The two had sex, something Pete had never done in his parents' house before, and Pete blamed Schultz, though he was equally to blame. He thought Schultz was too pushy. If he had to name a name to get out of there, it might as well be Schultz's.

But the cops still wouldn't let him go home. They told him they were going to get him "some help." Pete had read in the newspaper about the Mount Pleasant incarcerations three years prior. He had been a sophomore at Morningside then. He knew Ralph Eckert—the man who had been arrested but avoided going to Mount Pleasant because of cancer of the blood and family connections; Pete had "been with" him. Pete was convinced he was probably going to be sent away to Mount Pleasant or maybe Cherokee. *Well, at least that will cure me,* he thought. He didn't want to be gay, fought against it, confessed it, made all sorts of resolutions and promises to himself and to God—none of which helped.

Pete was permitted to phone his parents, and then the police wagon came and took him to jail. It was getting close to 11 P.M. An hour or two later Pete saw Darrell Albertson being brought in and put in a nearby cell. Pete's own cellmate was the custodian at the church that Pete's family attended; Pete had known he was gay. In the next cell was J.B. Kuhler; that explained why he hadn't been at the teachers' meeting. On several occasions Pete had seen him leaving the Warrior, but they had never acknowledged their shared sexual proclivities.

In the morning Pete called out to him and asked how he was doing.

"Terrible," said J.B.

J.B., who was 52, had a wife and two children; his son was a student at East High. He was a man of many interests and talents: He had written a history textbook and his hobby was visiting Civil War battlefields; he also played the organ. J.B. had been entrapped by Dick Burke, passing notes in the Warrior bathroom. Burke had had J.B. as a teacher and didn't like him. Burke wasn't alone in his feelings; J.B. had a reputation for being nasty and sarcastic with students. Pete had seen that side of him when traveling in a car with Kuhler and some other teachers on the way to a faculty meeting before school began. Pete was appalled by the cynicism and the negativity of the teachers in the group; J.B. was the ringleader, the most cynical and negative of all of them. J.B. had a heavy beard and sweated a lot, which might explain the pungent men's cologne he was known for wearing.

Burke would later claim that S.M. Hickman, the principal of East, congratulated him for arresting J.B. At the time, Burke was studying for his high school equivalency diploma (he had left school to join the Navy during World War II), and Hickman supposedly told him, "You should get a certificate just for that"—for bringing in J.B. Kuhler. J.B.'s arrest was one of the things Burke was particularly proud of. "His first name was Bernice," Burke would say acidly in a conversation in later years, as if that explained everything. Actually his first name was not Bernice; it was Joyce. Joyce Benjamin Kuhler.

Pete's parents got him an attorney, who showed up the next morning. In the late afternoon, Pete and the others were brought to Judge George Prichard's courtroom. Judge Prichard had been one of the two judges who had sent the 1955 group to Mount Pleasant. But this time things were being handled differently. In most of the cases, the sexual psychopath law wouldn't be invoked. That would be too messy and expensive; anyway, the political pressures weren't the same as they'd been in 1955 in the aftermath of the Jimmy Bremmers and Donna Sue Davis murders. There would be a deal: The men would plead guilty to conspiracy to commit a felony, and in exchange they'd be paroled to their lawyers for two years. (Whether this decision originated in the county attorney's office or in the judge's chambers is unclear.) Pete would leave town, go off to graduate school somewhere—Colorado was mentioned—and put it all behind him. He glanced at the statement he was supposed to sign, which began that on such-and-such a date, "I conspired to commit a felony with Darrell Albertson." Pete was confused, particularly since he didn't know Albertson by name. "I don't know who Darrell Albertson is," he said. "I didn't do anything with him. All I did was rub this cop's leg." His attorney told him, "They're just matching up names for the court records." Pete signed the document.

Judge Prichard sentenced him to two year's probation as agreed. Pete was permitted to go home, where he composed his letter of resignation to the school and went over to get his files. The following day, *The Sioux City Journal* reported the story under the headline, "Sentence Six In Roundup," including Pete's name and street address. (This was a step backward for the *Journal*; during the 1955 roundup it published names and towns, but not street addresses. Pete blamed this on Fred Kelly, a reporter who covered the arrests. People went to Kelly on Pete's behalf and on the behalf of other arrested men, pleading with him not to publish names and addresses, but he wouldn't listen.)

That was when Pete Reynolds became a pariah in Sioux City, deserted by everyone—friends, associates, fraternity brothers—except his parents and his brother.

But he was fortunate compared to J.B. Kuhler. J.B. was in the midst of pleading guilty to a charge of conspiracy to commit a felony, when his lawyer urged him to sit down for a moment so he could explain to him the consequences of his plea. They were in a little room just off the sheriff's office. Mrs. Kuhler was there too. Then J.B. mentioned to his lawyer that there was another little matter he should know about: some money missing from the Sioux City Teachers' Credit Union. At that point the already overwrought Mrs. Kuhler appeared as if she might have a heart attack. The lawyer immediately dashed over to the county attorney's office to tell him that plea taking was off for the day. Then he returned to ask Kuhler some questions.

"Is more than $1,000 missing?" the lawyer asked.

"Yes," said J.B.

"More than $5,000?"

"Yes." At that point, as the lawyer recalls, Mrs. Kuhler's entire body began to shake.

"Is it over $25,000?" he finally asked.

"It is over $25,000," replied J.B. Kuhler.

A few minutes later the lawyer informed J.B. that he represented the credit union and therefore could not represent him.

The total amount embezzled by J.B. Kuhler was $35,957. A month later he was convicted of embezzlement and sentenced to five years at the state penitentiary in Fort Madison, to run concurrently with his sentence on the morals count. The story goes that when J.B. arrived at Fort Madison, the chaplain told him, "Another case of Providence intervening. Our organist left last week."

Altogether, 13 men were arrested in the second roundup. All but two were offered the same deal that Pete got: parole for two years on the condition that they undergo psychiatric treatment. J.B. Kuhler was an exception, in view of the other charge against him. So was a 24-year-old man, arrested in late July, who had been convicted of a previous felony; he was sent to the state mental hospital at Cherokee as a sexual psychopath. (A 16-year-old boy allegedly involved with one of the men was also declared a sexual psychopath and sent to Cherokee as well.) In an article headlined "Morals Roundup Shows Threat To City Youth," the weekly *Sioux City Press-Dispatch* listed the occupations (but not the names) of those arrested. They were as follows:

4 schoolteachers, two of whom were instructors in
    Sioux City schools
2 bank tellers
a Sioux City contractor
a jewelry store salesman
a clerk
a laundry employee
a photo technician
an antique dealer in a nearby city
an out-of-town newspaper publisher

The *Press-Dispatch* noted that "Each of the men is being questioned in connection with the unsolved slaying of Donna Sue Davis several years ago.... Investigators have long suspected that a sexual pervert committed the crime." Sioux City's most famous child murder case had suddenly emerged from near oblivion to justify the latest round of arrests.

In an editorial the following week, the *Press-Dispatch* warned that sexual deviates posed a definite threat to the "youngsters of Sioux City." The newspaper tried to stir up as much public feeling as possible, invoking the names of Sioux City's murdered children yet again: "Jimmy Bremmers was playing in his own neighborhood during the broad daylight. Little Donna Sue Davis had been safely tucked in her crib. If someone could find these two when they were seemingly safe, how many times has your son or daughter been a ready target?" In its October 30 issue, the *Press-Dispatch* featured a cartoon that showed a rat walking away from a garbage can overflowing with trash. The caption read: "A Bad Smell—In Sioux City...the Morals Problem."

The *Press-Dispatch* was a labor paper, and organized labor was supporting Don O'Brien in his run for Congress, which may have been a factor in the newspaper's enthusiasm for the subject. Ironically, the newspaper's new editor, John Beach, would be arrested six months later by none other than Dick Burke in a sting operation. The editor was the one whom Dick Burke entrapped trying to extort protection money from a tavern owner.

Meanwhile, county attorney and congressional candidate O'Brien assumed a statesmanlike pose, while at the same time seeming to take advantage of the issue. In a public statement on October 24, he attempted to dampen public hysteria, criticizing the circulation of "numerous and persistent rumors regarding men in various professions." Crimes "are not solved by the irresponsible circulation of malicious rumors," said the county attorney, "and I urge that any information be given to the proper authorities for investigation." Then, two days before the election, at a rally for Democratic Party leaders, O'Brien called for passage of a national sexual psychopath law.

If any or all of this was election year maneuvering, it failed. O'Brien ran well, giving eight-term Republican congressman Charlie Hoeven his toughest race in years, but still lost by 5,000 votes. In that same election, voters chose Assistant county attorney James R. Brodie to replace O'Brien as county attorney. O'Brien was finally out of office, but the damage had been done.

Pete Reynolds was not going to graduate school in Colorado, as had first been suggested. If he had to go into exile, it would be a nearby one. He was accepted at Creighton University in Omaha, 100 miles away, starting in the January term. In the meantime, Pete was increasingly isolated and miserable. He was unemployed, and his friends and fraternity brothers wouldn't have anything to do with him. Three teachers from Morningside, including the speech teacher who had taken him to the gay bar in Greenwich Village, paid him a visit and told him not to set foot on the campus again, a particularly bitter blow. (Pete had been a major Morningside booster.) He spent his days writing letters to his friend at Ann Arbor, his sole confidant, and brooding. He'd go to church and the movies, always by himself. His parents would make him go out to dinner with them. They would arrive at the Green Gables, where the family used to eat all the time (it was famous for its matzoh ball soup), and people would say hello to his parents but never acknowledge Pete. His parents were having a rough time too.

His father had suffered a heart attack shortly before Pete's arrest and, now, when Pete wasn't around, he would sit at the kitchen table weeping and asking, "What have I done wrong?" His mother received anonymous phone calls demanding to know why her son wasn't in jail.

Many people in Sioux City found the probation granted to Pete and the other arrested men far too lenient. An October 5 letter to the *Journal*, signed by an irate Sioux Cityan named Lois Brunson, summed up that point of view:

> The police department receives a call about a morals offense. They spend hours, days, and sometimes weeks collecting evidence, tracking these men down, and arrest them. What happens? A district judge paroles them to their lawyer for two or more years! No wonder there's this kind of crime going on in Sioux City. What do these men have to fear—being paroled to their lawyers for two years? When I read in the *Journal* about another morals offender being paroled, I wonder if the police department is as disgusted as I am.

A woman in the Morningside neighborhood circulated a petition demanding that men convicted of morals offenses serve prison time instead of receiving probation. She even came to Pete's parents' door with the petition. Mrs. Reynolds politely asked her to leave.

Pete's correspondence with his friend in Ann Arbor continued to be a source of solace for him. He would give his letters to his father, who would take them to work and post them with the business mail. It turned out, however, that the company foreman was taking the letters home and reading them first. In one letter, Pete wrote, "I did it with Albertson and

Schultz, but I'm never going to do it with anyone again." The foreman showed the letter to his wife, who called Pete's aunt and uncle and read it to them. Pete's father was beside himself; it was a complete betrayal on the foreman's part. He was upset for another reason: Pete had assured him that he had never had sex with Albertson or Schultz, in spite of what he had admitted to the police in the barbershop that night.

Shortly afterward, Pete's father drove him down to Omaha to sign up for housing at Creighton. On the way home they stopped for a cup of coffee in Onawa, south of Sioux City. Mr. Reynolds was reading *The Sioux City Journal* when Pete saw his face turn white. The day's paper had reported that William Schultz had pleaded guilty to conspiracy to commit a felony with John Peter Reynolds. It was the first time in any of these arrests that the newspaper mentioned the name not only of the convicted man but of the co-conspirator as well.

And then Pete Reynolds did something extraordinary, something no one had done during the roundup three years before. He decided to fight back. He asked the judge to permit him to go back on the agreement for two years' probation and to change his plea from guilty to innocent. To do so was risking prison; he knew that. But he was determined: He still believed in himself and his future, had won too many citizenship awards and high school debating competitions, to let this one pass without a challenge. He didn't feel his lawyer had given him a chance to think out his original decision—and the lawyer had taken advantage of his father too, first demanding Pete's Chevrolet as payment and then the monetary equivalent ($1,500). There were practical reasons too. He wanted to keep his teachers certificate and wanted an honorable discharge from the Air National Guard. He was intent on vindication in the eyes of his family. So he hired new lawyers—Wally Huff, the pugnacious, pipe-smoking, corruption-busting former county attorney whom O'Brien had defeated in the 1954 election, and Huff's partner, Richard Rhinehart, a friend of Pete's brother.

In late November, after much prodding, the judge permitted Pete to change his plea. Then the following March the grand jury brought two counts of sodomy against him. By this time O'Brien was out of office and there was a new county attorney, but the prosecutors weren't any more lenient. They really appeared to be out to get him now. Since sodomy was punishable by 10 years in prison (as opposed to three years for the lesser conspiracy to commit a felony charge, to which Pete had originally pleaded guilty), the two counts meant that Pete was facing 20 years at Fort Madison or Anamosa. It was very risky indeed. And there was one major problem. Pete Reynolds had committed sodomy, or at least had sex, with both Albertson and Schultz.

Pete Reynolds wasn't the only person who was determined to fight the charges against him. The men in the 1958 roundup were more middle class than those in the 1955 group, more educated, more aware of their rights—schoolteachers, as well as the town's leading pediatrician, Peirce D. Knott, a man whose name was a delight to generations of Sioux City children. A 16-and-a-half-year-old boy claimed he had met Dr. Knott in the men's room of the Warrior Hotel and had sex with him. On October 2, two weeks after Pete Reynolds was arrested, police detectives Dick Burke, E.H. Anders, and William Dennison (lately of the Triplett case), arrested Dr. Knott at his office in the Frances Building in downtown Sioux City. Dr. Knott was 56, married, and had two children. He was charged with lascivious acts with a child.

Dr. Knott had grown up in a Victorian mansion on Jackson Street. His father was a surgeon, and the father wanted his son to follow in his footsteps. But the younger Knott had a deformed hand and became a pediatrician instead. He had been a major in the Army Medical Corps during World War II. He was a proud man with a gruff voice whom some found arrogant; Dick Burke's wife Madeleine thought he looked like a bulldog. After his arrest, he told his lawyer, "Things like this happen in life. I am going to face it because I am a thoroughbred." His lawyer couldn't get over that. Not too many people in Sioux City compared themselves to a racehorse.

Dr. Knott was also well-known, if not notorious, for his interest in young men. Some suspected that the police regularly shook down Dr. Knott over the years. The cops would see him cruising, follow him, and demand money from him; they called this "fruit picking." When Dr. Knott was arrested, opinion in town was sharply divided. Half the people said, "I'd never take my child to him." The other half said, "I'd take my child to him even if he was in prison." If a child was seriously ill, Dr. Knott would spend days at his bedside. At the time of his arrest, rumors circulated that he had been responsible for the deaths of Jimmy Bremmers and Donna Sue Davis, for which there was absolutely no evidence. Dr. Knott had treated neither child, and no one had ever accused him of any untoward behavior in regards to his patients.

Dr. Knott's accuser was Kurt Kistenmacher. A month after Knott's arrest, Kistenmacher told the grand jury that on or about August 12, 1958, he was in the men's room at the Warrior Hotel where he "committed an act of masturbation on the person of Peirce D. Knott." Kistenmacher was brought to testify before the grand jury from the state hospital at Cherokee, where he had been confined as a sexual psychopath.

223

(The Mount Pleasant ward had been shut down for two years by then, following the Board of Control's revised policy that those individuals labeled as sexual psychopaths were to be sent to the state mental hospital nearest where they lived.)

Kistenmacher's commitment as a sexual psychopath gave Dr. Knott a weapon to use in his own defense. In an open letter to the general public, dated November 7—five days before the grand jury was to hear Kistenmacher's testimony—Dr. Knott asserted his innocence. Since no one would tell him the name of his accuser, he had made his own inquiries, he said, discovering him to be a young man who was receiving treatment at the mental hospital in Cherokee. Dr. Knott wrote:

> I wish to state that I have never met this young man. What prompted this young man, [whom] I have never met, in the moment of [delusion] to accuse me, I know not. I am sure that those skilled in the treatment of mental health can give us the answer. It is truly ironic that this young man, by his unfounded accusation, could cause much grief and pain to men of fine reputations, some of whom are now giving him the best treatment that my profession can give those of a sick mind.

Dr. Knott then turned from Kurt Kistenmacher to himself. His whole reputation was at stake, he pointed out:

> For too many, to be accused is to be guilty, when the crime charged involves young children. I have children of my own. I have attended many of you as children and your children in your homes, and my actions in my profession have been open to all. I know, as I sit here in my office writing this letter, that not one person can ever say

that I did not do my best in protecting their children from sickness, death, pain, or from any other harm which might befall them.

Dr. Knott's lawyer was W.L. "Bill" Forker, who had recently left Don O'Brien's office after serving as assistant county attorney for three years. When the grand jury indicted Dr. Knott on November 14, 1958, the charge was that of having sex "with a child of the age of 16 years or under." It was on this very point that Forker saw an opening. Kurt Kistenmacher, Knott's accuser, had been born on February 9, 1942, which meant he was 16 years, 6 months, and 3 days old on the August day when he claimed to have committed that act of masturbation on the person of Dr. Knott. In Forker's mind, the issue was whether 16 and a half meant Kistenmacher was "a child of the age of 16 or under" or was actually older than 16 years.

It was a technicality but not an unimportant one. Forker didn't have much luck with district court judge M.E. Rawlings, however. In a December 15 ruling rejecting Forker's argument, Rawlings stated that "this court cannot believe that the legislature of Iowa intended that a person was 16 years of age and over whenever that person passed the first day of the 16th anniversary of his or her birth." The judge noted that if someone asked a person of 50 years and six months what his age was, that person would always respond that he was 50. To say that a person was over 50 the day after he had turned 50 placed "a technical and strained interpretation upon the matter of age" in the judge's view.

Rawlings's ruling was a disappointment. By sheer coincidence, however, two days earlier the judge's colleague on the district court bench, George Prichard, had ruled exactly the other way in a very similar case. A 20-year-old Sioux City man had been accused of "lascivious acts with a child" in a case that involved a girl who was 16 years and 2 months of age at the time. Judge Prichard dismissed the indictment, stating that the girl was past 16 and therefore not a child.

Given the two diametrically opposed rulings, only the Iowa supreme court could decide the matter, and that is where Forker took Dr. Knott's case. On June 9, 1956, in a unanimous decision, the state's highest court ruled that a child was under the age of 16 before his 16th birthday and over the age of 16 after his 16th birthday. Thus, under Iowa law, Kurt Kistenmacher was too old to be considered a child. The court did not rule on whether an illegal sex act had been committed that August day in the Warrior Hotel men's room. But the indictment against Peirce D. Knott had been thrown out.

Dr. Knott returned to the practice of medicine and seemingly was not damaged too badly by the whole affair. Yet the doctor was humbled. During this period, Dr. Knott was seen at a certain country club at nearby Lake Okoboji, where he was a member. According to custom, the maître d' would announce people as they entered the dining room and, on that day, he announced Dr. and Mrs. Peirce D. Knott. The entire dining room fell quiet. But Dr. Knott, ever the thoroughbred, walked to his table, his wife at his side, his head held high.

As for Kurt Kistenmacher, he was later released from Cherokee and worked as a waiter and a cook at a number of Sioux City establishments—Mook's Cafe, Don's Cafe, Harry's Hamburger shop, and at the Gizmo. Whether or not his stay at Cherokee "cured" him is unknown.

Pete Reynolds's lawyers tried to delay his trial as long as possible. It was 1959, and Pete was beginning to make a new life for himself in Omaha. He was studying toward two master's degrees, one in English and one in business, and was starting to make friends. But the past continued to intrude. His legal problems were the first thing he thought about in the morning and the last thing he thought about at night. He rode the bus home on a Friday and looked at the other passengers and said to himself, *I wonder what they are going to do this weekend. I am going to have to go to Sioux City and talk to my attorneys.*

In January 1959, the same month he began school, Pete returned to Sioux City to testify before the grand jury. The first sitting of the grand jury came back with no indictment. Then the newly elected county attorney, James Brodie, was killed in a plane crash while taking a prisoner to Fort Madison. Edward Samore, whom Brodie had defeated in the November election, took his position. The grand jury returned for another sitting. Pete didn't testify this time around, but Albertson and Schultz did, along with the police officers who were at the Warrior that night.

The grand jury testimony appeared extremely damning, no doubt about it. Darrell Albertson told the grand jury that on December 30, 1957, he had met Pete while sitting in a car outside the Sioux Bowling Alley. They then drove in separate cars out to Stone Park where at about 11:30 P.M. "[John] Peter Reynolds and I engaged in a homosexual act by taking his penis into my mouth." William Schultz told the grand jury that on September 1, 1958, Reynolds had placed "his penis in my rectum. I have had two homosexual acts with Peter Reynolds." Meanwhile, E.H. Anders, one of the arresting officers, testified that while in the barber shop, Pete admitted he was homosexual and that he had committed homosexual acts with both Albertson and Schultz. On the basis of this information, Anders stated, Albertson and Schultz had been arrested. When the grand jury indicted Pete that spring on two counts of sodomy, it seemed to have sound basis for doing so.

Albertson's testimony was particularly worrisome to Pete. Albertson, 21, was a shy and quiet man who worked as a bank teller and lived with his parents. He had a beautiful car in which he took great pride. Although Pete had had sex with Albertson a couple of times in Albertson's car, they never exchanged names. That was typical of gay sexual encounters in Sioux City at the time, a way of protecting yourself and others. The night they had gone to Stone Park together, Pete's car got stuck in the mud, and he had to call a tow truck to pull it out. Pete had paid cash and was given a receipt, but he was afraid the prosecution might investigate the tow truck company records, which could prove a date when he and Albertson had been together. Albertson, however, never revealed this potentially dangerous bit of evidence.

The defense continued to opt for delay. In October 1959, several months after the indictment, Pete went to Chicago for a lie detector test. He denied everything. When asked about the dates that Albertson and Schultz claimed he had sex with them, Pete passed easily. The police had picked dates essentially out of the air for when these sexual encounters took place; in the case of Albertson, they even had the wrong season. But when Pete was asked, "Did you ever have sex with Albertson and Schultz?" and answered "No," the polygraph machine indicated he was lying.

Pete's trial on the first sodomy count—the one involving Darrell Albertson—began on December 14, 1959, more than a year after he had changed his original guilty plea. Juries were thought to be more lenient at Christmas time, but for a charge as terrible as sodomy, it probably didn't matter what time of year it was. Judge George Paradise presided. The judge was a Greek-American who had immigrated to the United States at age 13; in 1956 he was named Sioux City's Outstanding Foreign-Born Citizen. Judge Paradise was not exactly a champion of individual rights. Several years later he would incur the wrath of the Iowa Civil Liberties Union when he sentenced a group of teenagers to six months in jail for harassing him in front of his house; he later emerged as a harsh critic of anti–Vietnam War protests. But he had a reputation for fairness, and anyway, Pete Reynolds was a local boy from a good family and had gone to the local college—Morningside—just like Judge Paradise.

The trial went on for nine days. Defense attorneys Huff and Rhinehart tried to disallow the testimony of the police officers, but Judge Paradise overruled them. The defense requested that the prosecution witnesses be segregated, which the judge disallowed. The defense asked for the trial to be held behind closed doors, but Judge Paradise rejected this request as well. Darrell Albertson took the stand, telling essentially the same story he had told the grand jury. Robert Johnson, the policeman who had entrapped Pete, testified about the events in the Warrior Hotel men's room and barbershop on the night Pete was arrested. There were some witnesses whom the prosecution had intended to have testify but didn't. One of them was J.B. Kuhler, Pete's fellow teacher at East, who was brought from Fort Madison at the county attorney's request. But for reasons that are unknown, he never appeared in court. The prosecution also wanted Ralph Eckert, arrested in the 1955 roundup, to testify as a state witness. The defense objected vociferously, and Eckert never testified either. Eckert's testimony would have been bad for Pete, given that Pete had "been with" him too.

Pete had his own character witnesses: a monsignor from the church he and his family attended, four fraternity brothers (who otherwise wouldn't have anything to do with him), and S.M. Hickman, the principal of East High (the same principal who supposedly told Dick Burke he deserved a commendation for arresting J.B. Kuhler). William Schultz, the other co-conspirator, was a rebuttal character witness for the prosecution. He testified that Pete was not of "good character" but didn't elaborate, apparently saving his fire for when Pete would be tried on the second count of sodomy.

Pete took the stand in his own defense and denied everything. "I lied, I'll admit it," he would say afterward, referring to sex with Albertson. "But you know what? The arresting officer got up and testified first and he described what I had done. He said that I was on the other side of the stall and that I put my hand under the stall and told him to 'get down and slide under.' It was such a blatant lie that I thought, *This is survival of the fittest.* I went to confession afterward and talked it over with the priest and had to say a few Hail Marys, but that was all."

At 10 A.M. on December 22, the jury began its deliberations. Twenty-four hours later jurors sent a note to the judge informing him they were unable to reach a verdict. "The vote is the same now as it was on the first ballot after lunch yesterday and on every since, namely 7 to 5," the foreman told Judge Paradise. The judge dismissed the jury, and county attorney Samore announced he would present the case again at the next grand jury session.

Despite the "victory" of a hung jury, the stress of the trial was too much for Pete, and he suffered a kind of nervous collapse. He was typing a paper for one of his courses when he froze up and was virtually paralyzed for an entire week. He dropped out of school and applied for a job at a large Omaha company. The personnel department made him change his name from Pete to John. His given name was John, but Peter was his middle name and nickname, and he had always been known as Pete. For some reason the firm had a policy against nicknames. The fact it had such a policy may have altered the entire course of Pete's life. For on his application form, there was a question asking whether he had ever been arrested; Pete checked "No." The company made the usual check on Pete's background and found nothing to contradict this. Fortunately, in his file at the courthouse in Sioux City, he was listed as Peter Reynolds, not John Reynolds. And so "John" Reynolds went to work for one of Omaha's biggest employers.

Meanwhile Pete Reynolds was still facing 20 years at Fort Madison.

The second trial didn't take place until January 17, 1961, and was far shorter than the first. The jury was sworn in, and as the trial was about to begin, Pete's mother walked into the courtroom. One of the jurors let out a gasp. She was a member of Mrs. Reynolds's bridge club. She informed the judge, M.E. Rawlings, who immediately declared a mistrial. "Good old mom and her bridge club," Pete said. "She got me out of trouble."

And she had, for by now the county attorney's office was wearying of the case. Six months later, on June 3, John Peter Reynolds pleaded guilty to two counts of lewd behavior, a misdemeanor, and was fined $200. The sodomy charges were thrown out due to insufficient evidence. After two years and nine months, Pete's ordeal was over.

Shortly afterward, Pete ran into William Schultz, the second man he had turned in, outside a gay bar in Omaha. Needless to say, Schultz wasn't very happy to see him; he knew Pete had ratted on him. Pete apologized. "It was the times," Pete would say later. No one was really to blame—not himself, not the friends or fraternity brothers who wouldn't speak to him afterward, not those people who cut him dead when he went out to the Gables for dinner with his parents. If there were any bad guys, he felt, they were Don O'Brien and Fred Kelly, the reporter for the *Journal* who had insisted on publishing the names and addresses of the arrested men. Pete's lawyer Richard Rhinehart didn't blame O'Brien, though. In his view, the culprit was Dick Burke, who was "on a crusade." Dick Burke, however, wasn't even present the night that Pete was arrested, at least according to Pete's account. As for O'Brien, he would later claim no memory of the 1958 roundup. "I was still county attorney, and I was still in charge of the place, and I would be responsible for whatever happened there," he said. "But I probably had very little if any direct participation in that because I was campaigning pretty near full time."

That day in Omaha, Schultz told Pete he understood why Pete had done what he did. But it didn't ease Pete's conscience much. Then there was the matter of Darrell Albertson. Pete felt worse for Albertson than he did for Schultz. Schultz was a somewhat sleazy character, in Pete's view, but Albertson was a gentle soul who would never hurt anyone. They had never been friends, exactly, but Pete felt he had betrayed him. Confessing his sins to a priest didn't solve the problem. He wanted to make it up to Albertson somehow. Albertson remained in Sioux City, working for much of the next two decades as a bartender at various local establishments. But Pete, in exile in Omaha, never saw him again.

The long legal battle took its toll on Pete and his family. His parents spent a large portion of their savings in attorney's fees; they never built the new house on the north side of town that his father had dreamed of for so many years. His brother left

Sioux City largely to get away from the bitter aftertaste of the case. Pete never taught in a public school again and was deprived of that great love of his life—teaching. He had lost his hometown too; he would only come back for short visits to his parents—and for their funerals. For him, Sioux City would always remain frozen in time, on an autumn day in 1958.

Nonetheless, Pete Reynolds—and Dr. Knott too—showed that you could fight and exhaust the system and win. The second roundup and Pete's trials marked the last gasp of the 1950s in Sioux City. Don O'Brien was out of office. Dick Burke would soon quit the police force and go into the polygraph business. There would be no more roundups, certainly not on the scale of 1955 and 1958. But for everyone who had been touched by the sex-crime panics of the decade, the past still would not go away. There were accounts to be settled.

PART 5: THE RECKONING

<u>FORT MADISON, IOWA, MARCH 1970</u>
<u>LE MARS, IOWA, OCTOBER 1972</u>
<u>AND WASHINGTON, D.C., OCTOBER 1978</u>

"I deny categorically that I did anything to violate the rights of Ernest Triplett. I don't think I ever did anything to knowingly hurt him."
—Donald O'Brien, testifying before the U.S. Senate Judiciary Committee, October 4, 1973

CHAPTER 21

Crimes of the Past 1

The first account to be settled was that of Ernest Triplett, whose arrest and conviction years before had set the stage for the dreadful events that were to follow. At Fort Madison penitentiary, Triplett was writing letters to anyone who would listen, seeking a reconsideration of his case. Triplett had been at "The Fort" for almost 15 years, since that July day in 1955 when Plymouth County attorney Bill Sturges and Sheriff Frank Scholer drove him down from Le Mars in Scholer's old Nash. He had spent much of those years working in the prison furniture shop. Triplett was 50 when he entered Fort Madison, but he had never given up proclaiming his innocence and hoping that somehow he would gain his freedom. The Iowa supreme court had turned down his appeal in 1957; the U.S. Supreme Court rejected it the next year. He filed five separate applications for a writ of habeas corpus in federal and Iowa district courts right through 1965. They were all rejected too.

Still, Triplett continued to send petitions to courts all over the country, even to those in states that had no jurisdiction in his case. He'd bring his petitions to Bill Abel, the personnel counselor at Fort Madison, whose job was to assist prisoners in such matters. Abel would tell Triplett not to waste his time sending petitions to courts in places like Nebraska or Colorado. "You're not doing any good by sending this," he'd say. Triplett would reply sharply, "Don't tell me I can't do that!" So Abel mailed the petitions for him, and the results were always the same. To Abel he was "poor Ernie," a name he rarely mentioned without a chuckle.

At this time, students at the Clinical Legal Education program at the College of Law at the University of Iowa in nearby Iowa City were considering various requests for legal assistance from prisoners at Fort Madison. Assisting prisoners with difficult appeals was an opportunity for law students to hone their skills. Moreover, in the political and social climate of the late '60s and early '70s, prisoners were emerging as sympathetic, if not romantic figures, celebrated in Bob Dylan songs and taken up by the New Left. The legal pendulum was swinging toward greater consideration of the rights of the accused. Law professors and their students were always on the lookout for some case of past injustice to overturn.

In March 1970, Philip Mause, the law school professor who headed the Clinical Legal Education program, received the following piece of correspondence, printed in pencil. It began:

> Collage of Iowa: Government Case; I cant Talk
> on Murde as I am not "qualified." "qualification."
> I feail are the ons That wear thear at the seance
> of the crime. couald tell You "More."
> We cant Go on Evidence of No Value....
> Harry Gibison Cheif of Dests of Souix City
> Iowa. charged me with 1st Degree Murder.
> Was a sex Feine and dided in the insane
> Ward...
> I reserve that right as you Have No Licience
> to Pratice Law as such as Student Laywers
> Have Not past the Bar accossion Fore to pratice
> Law. as Crimminals Laywers. Pleas appoint
> a (Crimminal Laywer).

The letter was signed Ernest Triplett. Along with it was a note from Bill Abel expressing his belief that Triplett might have a basis for an appeal.

Professor Mause and one of his students drove down to Fort Madison to interview Triplett and get his version of events. Triplett told them that he had been arrested the day Jimmy Bremmers had disappeared; the Sioux City police threatened him with "a phony homosexual charge." He decided to "sit tight." The police took him to a doctor who "shot him full of alcohol," but Triplett still revealed nothing. Later, a Pinkerton Agent named Joe Navaha suggested he commit himself to Cherokee; Triplett went along with this, thinking it would be better than jail. Triplett claimed that the police used the state mental hospital at Cherokee as a "second police station" for interrogation purposes. At Cherokee, the doctors gave him "truth serums." He said he eventually made up a story about killing the boy and told Joe Navaha where the body could be found. (In actuality, there was no such person as Joe Navaha associated with the case; Triplett was probably referring to Joe Matousek, the private detective who interviewed him at the police station in Sioux City.)

In July 1971, a law professor named Robert Bartels became the new head of the legal clinic and inherited the Triplett case. Bartels, 27, was a newcomer to Iowa; he had worked with a poverty law program in Detroit, practiced criminal law in California, and done postgraduate work at Stanford Law School. Despite the many bizarre aspects of Triplett's file—from his spelling and syntax to some of his claims as to what had transpired—Bartels immediately realized that the case involved some serious legal issues.

One of the issues was Triplett's confession. When Thomas Tacy had originally appealed Triplett's conviction to the Iowa supreme court in 1956, he argued that his client's confession had been involuntary. The state court rejected the appeal, claiming Triplett "fully understood the nature of the confession." By 1971, however, the law had changed. In a seven-year-old decision, *Jackson v. Denno*, the U.S. Supreme Court ruled that it was the obligation of a trial judge to make a determination as to whether a confession was admissible in court before a jury was permitted to hear that confession. The U.S. Supreme Court also ruled that the requirements of *Jackson v. Denno* were retroactive. If a court determined that a defendant's rights had been violated in this manner, at the very least he could receive a new hearing.

To receive such a hearing, Bartels would have to prove that the procedures used in Triplett's trial had violated *Jackson v. Denno*. That seemed indisputable: The trial judge, R.G. Rodman, had allowed the jury to hear Triplett's confession without making a determination himself on whether it was valid. Although Rodman's action was perfectly legal at the time, it wasn't legal under *Jackson v. Denno*. The second thing Bartels would need to prove was that the confession was involuntary. If the state court ruled that was so, Triplett could obtain a new trial. At the original trial in 1955, two things weighed most heavily against Triplett: his tape-recorded confession and his seemingly incriminating behavior when he was taken to the field on Ridge Road to view the remains of Jimmy Bremmers. If the confession could be thrown out, there would be virtually no case left.

When Bartels drove from Iowa City to Fort Madison on a sweltering late October day in 1971 to meet him for the first time, Triplett was 67 years old. As Bartels recounted in *Benefit of Law,* his 1988 book about the case, on that first visit he found that Triplett still had most of his hair and seemed in good physical condition. Triplett's hands were toughened from years of work sanding furniture, and his fingertips were stained a dark amber. He rambled on incessantly, sometimes incoherently, responding to Bartels's questions with statements like "You can lead a horse to water, but you can't make it drink." That had always been his habit, but it was intensified by a decade and a half of inhaling varnish fumes in the prison furniture shop. ("For years I never drawed a sober breath," Triplett would say later, referring to the effect of the fumes.) He spoke in a halting, fumbling, uncertain delivery, most likely the result of his third-stage syphilis. Bartels found him difficult to understand and communicate with. Still Triplett was relaxed and amiable; his folksy charm had weathered the years at Fort Madison. Bartels was won over.

The law professor and his students began many months of complex legal maneuverings to obtain a special hearing on Triplett's confession. But they encountered resistance from Bill Sturges, the Plymouth County attorney who had originally prosecuted Triplett and was still in office 17 years later. After a number of delays, the Plymouth County district court in Le Mars scheduled a hearing on October 3, 1972. Once the date was finally set, Bartels had seven weeks to investigate the case as thoroughly as possible.

District court judge C.F. Stillwill was concerned that Bartels lacked sufficient courtroom experience to handle the case. The judge went to Sturges and informed him that he planned to appoint a lawyer to assist Bartels. Sturges, who would be defending the state's case, was unconcerned about the hearing; he thought it would be merely routine. "I've been thinking about Mike Dull," the judge said. That was agreeable to Sturges, who knew the young Le Mars attorney and thought highly of him. Dull became co-counsel to Ernest Triplett.

Bartels was wary, however, concerned that Dull might obstruct the case. After all, he was a local attorney who had a personal relationship with Sturges, and Sturges had done everything in his power over the past few months to block the hearing. But these concerns quickly proved unfounded. Dull was enthusiastic; Bartels found him to be "a big surprise" who viewed the case as "a kind of adventure." And one of the first things Mike Dull did was to persuade Triplett to sign a waiver granting his attorneys the right to see his medical records from 1954 and 1955 at the state mental hospital at Cherokee.

On September 11, 1972, Dull drove over to Cherokee, where he spent two hours examining the records. He was astounded. What he found was a catalog of drugs—amphetamines and barbiturates and hallucinogens—that seemed right out of Haight-Ashbury. He didn't know very much about these drugs but realized right away that they transformed the case. There in graphic detail and precise dosage were the Desoxyn, Seconal, and sodium amytol that Triplett had received the afternoon he had given his tape recorded confession to Dr. Azordegan; there as well was the LSD that Dr. Sainz had administered to Triplett on the day he had been taken to Ridge Road to see the body of Jimmy Bremmers. None of this had been mentioned at the original trial or at any of the subsequent appeals, of course, because Thomas Tacy, Triplett's lawyer, had never taken the trouble to look at the records. Now Triplett's new attorneys had all the evidence they needed to prove that their client's confession had not been voluntary. Dull and Bartels immediately began a crash course in pharmacology.

On October 3, two weeks before the scheduled hearing, Dull went to see Bill Sturges to tell him what he had found. Sturges was as shocked and surprised as Dull had been three weeks before. He insisted that they drive to Cherokee immediately to see the original records. They did so. While they were there, they conferred with Eugene Wiemers, the superintendent of the mental hospital, who explained the effects of such drugs. Afterward, Dull and Sturges repaired to the parking lot for a discussion. "I have two choices," the county attorney told Dull with characteristic directness. "One, I move to dismiss the case against Triplett. Two, I go ahead and hope you mess up. I'll let you know in the morning."

On his way home, Sturges stopped to visit Frank Scholer, the former Plymouth County sheriff, who had been in charge of Triplett at the Plymouth County jail during the period of the trial. He was a sheriff of the old school—tough, intimidating, but absolutely straightforward. Did the sheriff know anything about Triplett having been given drugs at Cherokee? Sturges asked.

"Yes," said the sheriff. "But they were just tranquilizers, weren't they?"

Sturges was still reeling. The Triplett case had been his first case, the most famous case he had ever prosecuted. He had believed firmly in Triplett's guilt; he still did, despite the evidence Dull had uncovered. And he realized, at that moment, that he had been had: He had never been informed by the Sioux City police or the Woodbury County attorney's office or by the superintendent at Cherokee—all of whom might have known, probably did know—that Triplett had been on drugs when he confessed. He also understood that the greatest triumph of his years as county attorney—the conviction of Ernest Triplett—was about to be overturned and, moreover, that it absolutely should be overturned.

From that point, matters moved swiftly. Mike Dull talked to Dr. Willard Brinegar, who had been the superintendent of

Cherokee in 1955. Brinegar knew about the drugs, but when he testified at the trial, Tacy hadn't asked him about them specifically, and he hadn't volunteered the information. Meanwhile, Bartels's students in Iowa City were tracking down information about Tacy to see if he had provided "adequate counsel" to Triplett. They looked into rumors about Tacy's alleged drinking and also discovered that in 1951 he voluntarily surrendered his law license for two years in the wake of charges that he had failed to follow through on responsibilities to clients. Although these were clearly not reasons in and of themselves to throw out the conviction, they raised troubling questions and offered at least some explanation as to why Tacy had neglected to do a simple thing like examine Triplett's medical records.

At the same time, Dull was finding some interesting reasons as to why Triplett had behaved so oddly when he was taken to view Jimmy Bremmers's body. It wasn't just the LSD that might have explained why Triplett headed directly for the spot where the body had been found. Wally Huff, the Woodbury County attorney at the time of the murder, and a photographer who had been at the scene both confirmed that the area leading to the site of the body had been trampled down. A number of people had been there before Triplett arrived and created the path that Triplett simply followed.

In short, the case against Ernest Triplett was disintegrating by the moment.

Sturges and Dull met again three days after their visit to Cherokee. In the meantime, Sturges had had a chance to mull over everything he had seen and heard, and he had come to a decision. Triplett's confession was tainted, he told Dull—no doubt about it; the conviction should be overturned. More than that, the remaining evidence was simply too weak to retry

Triplett. As much as he hated to do so, as painful a decision as it was, he was willing to let Triplett go free. He would do so even though he had no doubt that Ernest Triplett had murdered Jimmy Bremmers.

There was a public relations snag, however. Two days before the hearing was to take place, *The Des Moines Register* published an article on the case that included an interview with Jimmy Bremmers's mother. Mr. Bremmers had died in 1962, and Jimmy's mother had remarried (she was Mrs. Carl Jensen now); she was also a grandmother of 11. But the pain of losing her only son had not abated. "I hate to see it all come out again," she told the newspaper. "All I can say is I hope he [Triplett] doesn't get out. We went through so much. It's something you don't get over. We went through hell, literally. I agree with what the judge said at the time [that Triplett had no redeeming qualities]. I hope I don't get called as a witness, and I hope he doesn't get out."

Mrs. Jensen's feelings, however, were not enough to stop the inevitable. On Monday, October 16, 1972, at 10 A.M., Ernest Triplett and his lawyers arrived at the Plymouth County courthouse in Le Mars. The hearing before Judge Lawrence J. McCormick took place in the same courtroom where Triplett had been tried and convicted 17 years before. Dr. Eugene Wiemers, the current Cherokee superintendent, testified about the effects of the drugs that Triplett had received in 1954. When Sturges asked Wiemers if any statement made after the administration of such massive doses of amphetamines and barbiturates could be considered voluntary, Wiemers responded, "No, absolutely not." Dr. Richard Leander, a Sioux Falls neuropsychiatry practitioner, concurred. The 80 milligrams of Desoxyn (six to eight times the usual dosage) that Triplett had received on the morning of his confession would have resulted in confusion and slurred speech, causing someone "to respond without too much conscious control," he said. In fact, a dose of that magnitude could have killed him.

Sturges waived oral argument, and the state's evidence was joined in and adopted as the evidence for the defendant. The state and the defense were operating virtually in lockstep.

At 2:45 in the afternoon Judge McCormick adjourned the hearing to write up his opinion. Triplett sat in the courtroom with his lawyers and law students, regaling them with stories of life at Fort Madison. He was back in the limelight and relishing every minute of it. Two hours later Judge McCormick returned to the bench. The courtroom was totally quiet, even though the results were a foregone conclusion. Reading from his opinion, the judge stated that Triplett's confession had taken place at a time when he was under the influence of a massive dosage of Desoxyn. "Confessions are admissible only if freely and voluntarily given," the judge stated. "The court now finds that the admissions made [in the 1955 trial] could not have been freely and voluntarily made." Saying that, Judge McCormick set aside Triplett's 1955 conviction.

Now it was Bill Sturges's turn. He had reviewed the files and checked police reports and all other evidence, he told the court. "Based on all these facts, as well as my experience as a county attorney," he said, "I must conclude that the state lacks evidence for a retrial." It was an emotional moment for Sturges, who had only recently announced he would not seek reelection as county attorney. The Triplett case was the first he had ever tried—and now, ironically, it was to be the last. He was trying to be stoic, but his voice was cracking. The judge sustained Sturges's motion for dismissal, and Ernest Triplett was a free man.

"I feel like bawling," said Triplett as he walked out of the courthouse, with a big smile on his face and his hand raised in a salute. He immediately went to enjoy his first glass of beer in 18 years. He would spend the night in the jail in Le Mars and then be driven back to Fort Madison where the warden would receive the judge's order for his release. Still, it was a bitter-sweet moment. The night before he had left Fort Madison for the Le Mars hearing, his guitar—his prize possession and the only thing he owned of consequence—had been stolen.

The next day's *Sioux City Journal* featured an interview with Raymond Flood, owner of the Flood Music Company, where Triplett had been employed when the police first brought him in as a suspect back in 1954. "What did they do, give him 50 bucks and a suit of clothes?" Flood asked sarcastically when a reporter called him for reaction to the judge's decision. Although he and his wife Mary had corresponded with Triplett during Triplett's first five years at Fort Madison, they hadn't heard from him since, he told the reporter. "He would always maintain his innocence," said Flood. "He was so simple and direct. But he had faith in our system of justice too. He seemed to know that everything would turn out all right eventually.... I don't suppose he has anybody left. He had a couple of brothers, but they were much older. I don't know what will become of him now. But at least he's a free man."

Ernest Triplett went to Iowa City to live on his Social Security. The day after his release, Dorothy Jensen, Jimmy Bremmers's mother, suffered a heart attack. She died three years later.

CHAPTER 22

Crimes of the Past 2

But what happened two decades before wouldn't fade away. The Triplett case bedeviled at least one person who at first glance seemed to have only peripheral involvement with it. That was Don O'Brien, the man who had been instrumental in sending Doug Thorson, Duane Wheeler, and Harold McBride to Mount Pleasant, and who had presided, at least officially, over the roundup that netted Pete Reynolds. Since stepping down from the county attorney's office to run unsuccessfully for Congress in 1958, O'Brien had been making his way in the political world. Massachusetts senator John F. Kennedy was putting together a political organization for his run for the White House the following year and was recruiting political figures from around the country. O'Brien signed on. When Kennedy made an appearance in Sioux City during the 1960 presidential campaign, it was O'Brien who escorted JFK and his sister Eunice Shriver from the airport to address a crowd at the Sioux City auditorium. (Kennedy even stopped for a 10-minute audience with O'Brien's mother, the ultimate political compliment.) The two men had a natural affinity: They were young, Irish Catholic, and Democrats. After his election as president, Kennedy named O'Brien to be U.S. attorney for the Northern District of Iowa.

On the day in 1961 that O'Brien walked to the federal building to be sworn in as U.S. attorney, something rather inauspicious happened, however. A flock of birds was flying overhead, and a mulberry-colored glop, the size of a quarter, fell on O'Brien's suit coat collar. He didn't have time to go home and change his suit before the swearing-in ceremony. "I wasn't exactly pure when I became a United States attorney," O'Brien would joke in later years. "I figured God was trying to tell me something."

After he left the U.S. attorney's post in 1967, he returned to the practice of law, developing a lucrative personal injury practice in Sioux City. At the same time, O'Brien continued to earn his stripes in Democratic Party politics. He managed Robert Kennedy's presidential campaigns in Nebraska and South Dakota during Kennedy's ill-starred 1968 presidential bid. He worked for George McGovern in the 1972 election and earned the South Dakota senator's praises: "One of the least pretentious people I have ever known." In the 1976 race he was in charge of Jimmy Carter's Michigan campaign. He was a member of the Democratic National Committee. But it was in September 1978, when Carter named him to be federal district judge for the Northern and Southern Districts of Iowa, that the impurities of his past returned to haunt him.

O'Brien's problems began several months earlier when it was revealed that he had the inside track for the judicial nomination. Michael Gartner, editor of *The Des Moines Register*, wrote a letter criticizing the nomination to the American Bar Association's Standing Committee on the Federal Judiciary. The newspaper followed up with a poll of 411 Iowa lawyers, which rated O'Brien a poor third out of five potential nominees. On the same day, a *Register* editorial suggested that politics, rather than merit, seemed to be the key factor in the expected choice of O'Brien.

Once he was nominated, the American Bar Association investigated O'Brien's qualifications to be a federal judge. That wasn't unusual; the ABA's Standing Committee on the Federal Judiciary had traditionally played a semiofficial role in screening candidates for the federal bench. But the committee unanimously found O'Brien to be "not qualified," and such a rating was unusual. In 10 years of evaluating candidates for the federal bench, the ABA had found only 28 out of 474 nominees to be not qualified.

And the primary reason for the ABA's opposition to O'Brien was what it called his "lack of professional sensitivity" in the case of Ernest Triplett.

When O'Brien became the county attorney in Sioux City back in January 1955, Jimmy Bremmers had been dead for four months, and Triplett was languishing at Cherokee, still not charged with any crime. By March, O'Brien turned the case over to Plymouth County attorney Bill Sturges for prosecution, the stated reason being that Jimmy's body had been found just over the county line, outside of O'Brien's jurisdiction. The ABA contended that it was likely that O'Brien had knowledge that Triplett's confession was tainted by drugs and that he had failed to tell anyone about it.

This conclusion was based on the January 31, 1955, letter to O'Brien from Dr. Willard Brinegar, then superintendent of Cherokee, replying to O'Brien's request for the record of Triplett's confession. In the letter, not only did Brinegar demand that O'Brien obtain a court order before he would hand over the tape recording—an unusual request in such a circumstance—but he stated, "I think there is question as to whether or not the patient's legal rights were violated in making the recording, since he did not know that it was made and was under drugs at the time of its making." Eight days later, O'Brien went ahead and got the court order. Since he had followed Brinegar's instructions regarding the tape, the ABA concluded that it was logical to assume he had read the letter and therefore knew about the drug-induced confession and decided he didn't want anything to do with the case. According to this scenario, when the opportunity presented itself, he passed the case over to an unsuspecting Bill Sturges in Plymouth County without informing him about the circumstances under which the confession was made. Sturges then went on to prosecute Triplett, relying upon tainted evidence.

The ABA's "not qualified" rating of O'Brien caused a firestorm. O'Brien was enormously well-connected politically, with important supporters both in the legal community and in the Democratic Party. The Iowa Bar Association immediately rushed to his defense, as did a number of liberal Democratic senators close to the Kennedys—James Abourezk of South Dakota, John Culver of Iowa (who had originally recommended O'Brien to President Carter), and Ted Kennedy himself. As a result, the ABA conducted a rare second investigation into his fitness. This follow-up investigation confirmed the findings of the first.

A heated five-hour confirmation hearing on the nomination took place before the Senate Judiciary Committee in Washington, D.C., on October 4, 1978. Kansas City attorney Thomas E. Deacy Jr. and Chicago attorney Don Reuben testified for the ABA. Both were prominent lawyers and members of the organization's Standing Committee on the Judiciary; Deacy had headed up the first investigation, and Reuben the second. The lawyers made a number of accusations against O'Brien: that he was often "poorly prepared" for trial appearances and that he responded to criticism by fellow members of the bar with "tactics and conduct that might possibly be appropriate to a highly charged political campaign" rather than "customary and accepted behavior towards fellow professionals." His nomination overall suggested nothing less than "political favoritism and politics," they stated.

The centerpiece of their case against O'Brien, however, was that when members of the ABA screening committee had quizzed him about Dr. Brineger's letter regarding Triplett's confession, O'Brien would "neither admit nor deny" that he received it. The ABA regarded this position as "evasive." To the ABA, his behavior in the entire Triplett matter was "the antithesis of the professional behavior expected of those who seek appointment to the federal judiciary."

O'Brien's difficulty was that he was unable to prove he had not read Dr. Brinegar's letter. According to one of his associates, O'Brien's habit throughout his legal career was that after reading a piece of correspondence, he would mark it mark it with his initials in red ink. During his tenure as Woodbury County attorney, all his files were kept in the county attorney's office, not in the county clerk's office as was customary. This associate says that when O'Brien departed in 1958, the new county attorney, Edward Samore, had these files destroyed; Samore assumed the files in the county attorney's office were merely copies of what was in the clerk's office. Actually, they were the sole records. More than 20 years later, O'Brien could be seen rummaging through his old office, searching fruitlessly for the original letter in hopes that it wasn't marked with his telltale red initials. But the letter was nowhere to be found. O'Brien couldn't refresh his own memory—or defend himself.

As a result, in his appearance before the Senate Judiciary Committee, all he could say was that he had never done anything to violate Triplett's rights. O'Brien described the matter to the senators as follows: "The Sioux City police department came to me and said there was a tape recording at a hospital in another jurisdiction. So I went to a judge and asked him what I had to do, and he told me I needed the court order. He told me what to say in it and signed it when I took in." In short,

O'Brien's defense was that he had learned that he needed a court order not from Brinegar's letter—which mentioned the matter of the drug-induced confession—but from a judge. He added that he never knew about the tainted nature of the confession until this was revealed at the hearing in Le Mars in October 1972.

It was a weak defense, but it turned out not to matter very much. The majority of the senators had their minds on other things. Of the 15 members of the committee, only two—South Dakota senator James Abourezk and Iowa senator John Culver, both strong O'Brien supporters—were present throughout most of the hearing. Three other senators made brief appearances. And one person who might have been an effective witness against O'Brien—former Plymouth County attorney Bill Sturges—declined to appear. Years later, Sturges blamed O'Brien for not originally informing him of the cloud over Triplett's confession. In his view, O'Brien had been elected county attorney by promising to "crack down on queers"; he knew that the confession had been drug-induced, and for that reason passed the case on to Sturges. With Triplett on trial, even in a neighboring county, O'Brien could still look "strong on queers" without having to prosecute a case in which he knew the evidence had been compromised. But Sturges's views were never made known to the Judiciary Committee.

What was most memorable about the hearing was the tongue-lashing of the ABA witnesses by Iowa senator John Culver, O'Brien's sponsor. Sen. James Abourezk, who chaired the hearing, had hoped to prevent Culver from engaging in polemics with the bar association witnesses. When Abourezk went off to lunch, Culver was just starting to harangue them. When the South Dakota senator returned an hour later, Culver was still in the midst of his fulmination, banging his fists on the table. "Out of all that, out of a perfect six-year career as a U.S. attorney," he thundered, "all you can come up with is...this case that occurred 23 years ago." (The following day, one ABA official accused Culver of acting like a "mad dog" during the hearing.)

The Judiciary Committee never took a formal vote on the nomination. An informal poll showed a majority of committee members in favor of sending the nomination to the Senate floor. The hearing ended at 3 P.M., with Culver and committee staffers telling reporters that a vote on the nomination would take place in a few days. But that was a feint. Senate majority leader Robert Byrd brought O'Brien's nomination for a vote on the Senate floor at 8 P.M. that same evening, even though it wasn't on the calendar of the day's Senate business and only a half dozen senators were present. O'Brien was confirmed by a voice vote.

Pushing through O'Brien's nomination was "a study in raw, brute Democratic Party politics," in the view of the ABA's Don Reuben. The other ABA investigator, Thomas Deacy, charged that he and Reuben were deliberately kept in front of the committee for several hours so they couldn't lobby other senators against O'Brien prior to the vote by the full Senate. "It was a pretty shabby performance," Deacy said. Some ABA officials were so furious at the way they were treated by the committee that there was talk that the ABA might stop screening judicial nominees altogether. In this atmosphere, U.S. attorney general Griffin Bell held a "peace lunch" with Deacy, Reuben, and other ABA officials to attempt to smooth things over. But by then the Carter administration had gotten what it wanted.

O'Brien's supporters had their own views of why the ABA opposed his nomination so vehemently. In his memoir, *Advise*

& Dissent, published in 1989, Senator Abourezk insisted that the bar association's motives were purely political. Abourezk had known O'Brien for many years, he wrote, and believed him to be a "decent person and a competent lawyer." O'Brien, however, "had been a partisan Democrat and he was what attorneys call a plaintiff's lawyer, that is, someone who represents little people who sue the establishment, the insurance companies, and other corporate interests," wrote Abourezk. "It was obvious...that the ABA wanted judges in place who sympathized with the establishment, rather than someone who might decide against it if the facts warranted it."

The ABA's Deacy had a succinct reply to Abourezk's accusations: "Just bullshit."

Revealingly, the one matter that might have conclusively demonstrated O'Brien's lack of fitness for the federal bench and given pause to his liberal supporters—his role in the Mount Pleasant incarcerations of 1955—was never mentioned by the American Bar Association or the Senate Judiciary Committee. The ABA investigators apparently never knew anything about it and never inquired into it.

In a curious twist, O'Brien's first major decision as a federal judge came in the case of a male-to-female transsexual named Verna (formerly Vern) Pinneke. Pinneke had asked the state of Iowa to pay for a sex-change operation, and the state refused. Pinneke then sued the state for $10,000. The case went before the recently appointed judge. In a May 15, 1979, decision, O'Brien sided with the plaintiff, ordering the Iowa Department of Social Services to pay Pinneke $3,024 for two operations, plus another $500 in damages. The Iowa Medicaid program had a legal responsibility to pay for sex-change operations when the procedure was "medically necessary," he ruled. O'Brien had been persuaded by a psychiatrist who told him that Pinneke was a male on the outside but a female on the inside, resulting in an intolerable situation. "I didn't have to argue with myself over that decision," O'Brien said. "Once I heard the psychiatrist's testimony, I knew that was the way I was going to rule." It was a landmark decision, the biggest step forward in Iowa's history for transgendered people, and they had Don O'Brien to thank.

PART 6: SEX-CRIME PANIC: LEGACY OF A TROUBLED PAST

CHAPTER 23

Sex-Crime Panic

In summer 1995, on the first evening of my arrival in Sioux City, I went for dinner at the home of Jean Mayberry and Aleta Fenceroy. The two women were virtually the only openly gay people in Sioux City at the time; their participation in the mass wedding on the steps of the U.S. Capitol during the 1993 Lesbian and Gay March on Washington made the front page of *The Sioux City Journal*. Jean and Aleta lived in a modest bungalow on the city's west side. It was an uncomfortably hot July night—the temperature would hit 107 by the end of the week and stay there—but a pot roast, that staple of Iowa hospitality no matter what the season, was warming on the stove.

Aleta led me to the kitchen window and pointed to the two-story frame house next door, just across the yard. "That's where Donna Sue Davis lived," she told me. "And look, there is the window where she was taken!" Actually, there wasn't a window any longer. Instead, a small addition—a closet or an alcove, probably—had been added on to first floor where the little girl's bedroom window once had been, covering up the scene of the crime. Someone, whether it was the Davises or a family who lived there later on, was determined to "wall up" the memory of what had taken place in 1955.

I didn't know that Jean and Aleta lived next door to Davises' old house; I had no expectation that on my first night in Sioux City I would be thrust so intimately into the events of 1955. But that was Sioux City: Everything was intimate, everyone knew everyone else. At a party a few months afterward, I met the high school girlfriend of Donna Sue's brother;

another woman I became friendly with worked with Donna Sue's first cousin.

It was only later that I realized that my arrival in Sioux City and my visit to Jean and Aleta's house coincided by 40 years exactly with the day that Donna Sue Davis's body was found in the cornfield in South Sioux City.

The Sioux City of 1995 was very different from the Sioux City of 1955. The downtown, once so vibrant, was struggling to survive. The malls on the outskirts had taken the business—and much of the life—out of it. Much of Lower Fourth Street, the old entertainment area that used to attract packinghouse workers and visiting Kiwanians, had been bulldozed for a new convention center. The Warrior Hotel still stood but was abandoned; its interior was covered with dust and falling plaster, home to hundreds of pigeons. Still, there was a new effort to revitalize downtown. What remained of Lower Fourth Street was being spruced up, and shops and restaurants were returning. Plans were afoot to reopen the Orpheum Theater, the last of the city's great movie palaces. Some of the most architecturally distinguished buildings—the Prairie style courthouse, for example—remained. The stockyards had all but departed, but computer giant Gateway 2000, located just across the Missouri River in South Dakota, was bringing high tech employment to Siouxland. And International Beef Products, located on the Nebraska side of the river, was importing a new kind of packinghouse worker: Mexicans, Nigerians, and Vietnamese.

In other ways Sioux City hadn't changed at all. It remained a family town, conservative, dominated by church and sporting events. Sure, you could buy liquor legally in a bar now; and a riverboat called the *Belle of Sioux City*, featuring slot machines and roulette tables, was anchored a stone's throw from downtown; and there was a gambling casino on an Indian reservation near Onawa, about 30 miles south. But there had always been drinking and gambling in Sioux City.

Like the rest of the town, Sioux City's gay community was very different from what it had been in the 1950s—and very much the same. There were a couple of gay bars and a fledgling organization called the Community Alliance (started by my hosts Jean Mayberry and Aleta Fenceroy) that published a newsletter and was lobbying reluctant city officials to add sexual orientation to the Sioux City's antidiscrimination protections. (The city council narrowly defeated a gay rights ordinance in the spring of 1998.) There was a small gay and lesbian student group at Morningside College, the school from which Pete Reynolds had been banished.

Sioux City even had a gay pride week every July. I attended one of the gay pride activities—a picnic held in an obscure corner of Stone Park. A softball game between a team of drag queens and a team of lesbians was in progress. It was an intriguing spectacle: the men in varieties of female and androgynous garb (and in various stages of intoxication), the women serious and determined. Three male cheerleaders wore large sun hats and dresses made out of layers of flip-flops and shouted humorously obscene chants. It was a hard-fought game, and in the end the men prevailed 19 to 18. The women were devastated. "We'll never live it down," two female players could be heard saying in distressed tones as they left the field. A rematch was promised for Labor Day.

The softball game was probably the most interesting activity taking place in Sioux City that July evening, but no one outside of a few people "in the know" ever heard about it. *The Sioux City Journal* didn't cover it, nor did the two local TV stations. And if they had covered it, most likely no one would have shown up to play.

In many respects, Sioux City's gay community was almost as closeted and hidden as in 1955. Large numbers of gay and lesbian Sioux Cityans moved away or socialized elsewhere—in Omaha or the Twin Cities. Others hid out in heterosexual marriages. Very few gay people in Sioux City were out to their families, friends, and employers. A survey by Community Alliance found a surprisingly high percentage of Sioux Cityans who believed they had lost jobs because their employers suspected they were gay. With so few opportunities for employment in Siouxland, people were afraid to be open about their homosexuality. The fact that their parents and uncles and cousins probably lived down the block or at best on the other side of town, and that in the course of a day they were likely to run into half a dozen of their former high school classmates, complicated matters further. So Sioux City's gay population continued to live secret lives, and amidst the invisibility, anti-gay attitudes and stereotypes flourished. There were plenty of towns of similar size around the country where the same situation prevailed, of course. Yet, I couldn't help wonder if the legacy of the town's troubled history didn't make things worse.

During my visits to Sioux City over the next year and a half, I often thought of that first evening when I looked across Jean and Aleta's yard to the house where Donna Sue Davis had been asleep the night she was abducted. The walling off of her bedroom window seemed an apt metaphor for the silence that continued to hang over the events of the 1950s. And while at least some people in Sioux City were willing to talk about the murders of Donna Sue and Jimmy Bremmers—these were, after all, the two most sensational crimes of the period—the silence surrounding the roundup of the 20 men in the aftermath of the two tragedies was particularly striking. To be sure, newspaper articles about the arrests and incarcerations could be found on microfilm in the Sioux City and Des Moines public libraries, but the events themselves seemed to have vanished almost entirely from collective memory. What had taken place was at odds with Sioux City's image of itself—the image of a family town filled with "nice" people, who, even if there were a few homosexuals in their midst, certainly wouldn't use them as scapegoats in an unsolved murder case and lock them up in a mental hospital. With a few exceptions, no one seemed to remember anything about what had happened in 1955 or claimed that they didn't remember. This included some of the men who had been sent to Mount Pleasant.

Researching the subject was no easy task. The names and the hometowns of the men charged in the 1955 roundup had been published in *The Des Moines Register* and in *The Sioux City Journal*, but many were dead by now. Duane Wheeler had died of cancer in the 1970s. Gene Bergstrom ("Mr. Eugene") was dead; so were Maynard Post and Ralph Eckert, the two men whose well-connected families saved them from being sent to the mental hospital. I found an address in another state for Jim Kerns, who had been Billy Ivers's heartthrob at Mount Pleasant. I wrote Jim a letter, alluding only vaguely to the events of 1955. His wife replied with a Christmas card featuring a recipe for snowman buns taken from *Betty Crocker's Christmas Cookbook*. "I am Jim Kerns's wife," she wrote. "Yes, he did live in Sioux City, Iowa. Jim died in 1980 of cancer. I don't know if I could help you with any news."

Not surprisingly, almost all of those who were still alive had long ago left town. One of the original 20, Floyd Edwards, was living in Sioux City, however. Floyd had tried to pick up

263

Doug Thorson that night at the Warrior bar, and it was Floyd's chenille bedspread that Billy Ivers had made the mistake of identifying. A lot of people knew Floyd, including Aleta Fenceroy. A few days before my first visit, Aleta sought out Floyd to ask what he remembered about the roundup. At that point she had no idea that he was one of the men sent to Mount Pleasant. He told her he didn't know anything at all. Some months later, another friend of Floyd's approached him on my behalf. "It wasn't me," he insisted. "I wasn't one of them." Floyd may have had his particular reasons for keeping silent. Court records and conversations with people involved in the case left little doubt in my mind that he had named names—two, almost certainly, probably three, perhaps more.

In the meantime, I did manage to get in touch by telephone with Leo Vandermeer, the former department store window dresser who assured me he had been "cured" at Mount Pleasant and had been married for 41 years. Leo informed me that he had ripped a letter I had written him into little pieces. He was 71, suffered from a heart condition, and was hard of hearing. Could I pay a visit to him in the Nebraska town where he and his wife had retired, I inquired? Leo was horrified at the prospect. "I've wiped the whole thing out of my mind," he said. And that was that.

I tracked down Frank Hildebrandt, the hairdresser who had been involved with the Arthur Murray dance instructor and shared a room (and a brief moment of sexual bliss) at Mount Pleasant with Harold McBride. Frank, who was living in Las Vegas, wrote me a letter saying, "I see no purpose in living in the past. I don't want to have anything to do with this issue. I try to forget the past and live for today." Still, I went to visit the South Dakota farm town where Frank had grown up. It was a thriving place in the middle of rolling hills and rich farmland, a throwback to an earlier America, and I was curious about a life that had led from there to Sioux City and then to Los Angeles (where Frank had cut hair for many years) and to retirement in Las Vegas. But Frank would always remain a mystery.

I wanted to do these men a good turn, or so I thought, to expose an injustice, to bring an era's prejudice and paranoia to light. But that was not how many of them saw it. I felt sometimes as if I was up against the habits of mind of an entire generation—and of an entire region of the country as well.

There was another man who had been sent to Mount Pleasant who was well-known in Sioux City: Billy Ivers, the youngest of the bunch. Billy had been famous for his parties, I was told, and was "very talented with the hair"; women would "fight" to get into the salon that he had owned for many years.

Tracking down Billy proved an adventure. I telephoned a number of gay men in Sioux City who were about Billy's age and might know his whereabouts. Half of them hung up on me; the other half didn't know where he was—maybe California or Nevada, they said. I toured the local beauty shops, places with names like Stylette and Smart Set and Partners in Style. People who worked there remembered Billy—he had made quite an impression during his days in Sioux City—but they insisted that they hadn't seen him in years and had no idea where he might be.

It was months before I located Billy Ivers, through a cousin of his who ran poker games at a Las Vegas casino. And it turned out that Billy had been in Sioux City all along, lying low for various reasons, none of which I completely understood.

While I was continuing my search for Billy, I found Doug Thorson. He was back in Iowa too, having returned to a depressed farm town to take care of his aged mother. In Los Angeles, Doug had had his own faintly glamorous business—raising circus animals to rent for movies and TV commercials. At one point he had 60 animals in his backyard, including lions, leopards, and bears. Each year he would throw a huge birthday bash for his oldest lion; celebrities like Joan Crawford and Barbara Stanwyck would put in an appearance, he said. But that was all in the past. Duane Wheeler, with whom he had spent 15 years, was long dead; so was the lover who followed Duane. Doug was bored and lonely and spent his time watching TV and listening to right-wing radio talk shows. His bluntness and outspokenness, however, had not been dulled by the years. He was an angry white guy (railing against liberals and welfare), but one of the things he was angry about was Mount Pleasant and how "unfair" it all was. Doug was suspicious, but he was willing to talk.

When I eventually did spend time with some of the men who had gone to Mount Pleasant—Doug Thorson and Harold McBride and finally Billy Ivers—they usually wanted to discuss something other than the events of 1955. Billy spent hours going on about his successful career in hair. Doug was mostly interested in discussing how much he hated his small town: how the people were a bunch of narrow-minded hypocrites; everyone was having an affair with everyone else and incest was rampant. It was always an effort on my part to tug them back to the subject at hand: "Now, when you were at Mount Pleasant, do you remember when...?"

Like Leo Vandermeer, they too had tried to wipe Mount Pleasant out of their minds. After all, Doug Thorson and Duane Wheeler had been so secretive that Duane's brother Bob, who had driven Duane home from Mount Pleasant, had

had no idea that his brother's friend Doug had been sent to the mental hospital too. Once Billy Ivers was home, his mother and aunt never brought up the subject again. And Harold McBride had never told the man he had been involved with for 21 years after the death of his wife, Glenda, in 1965. Harold had shared every intimate aspect of his life with him except one: Mount Pleasant.

Pete Reynolds, who had been arrested in the 1958 roundup, was an exception. He was eager to talk, to recall every memory of that grim time, including memories that didn't show him in a particularly flattering light. But his circumstances were different from those of Doug and Harold and Billy. He had fought the charges, and unlike the men arrested three years earlier, he hadn't experienced the trauma of being locked up in a mental hospital. He tended to see the world in political terms: His car was plastered with bumper stickers urging people to FLUSH RUSH and BOOT NEWT. He lived in Omaha, where the gay community was relatively open and politically active.

The reticence of the others was understandable. Who wanted to admit he had once been committed to a state mental hospital for inviting a police officer back to his apartment to have sex or for knowing the material of someone's bedspread? It wasn't only shameful; it was embarrassing, it was stupid. And in later years when the social climate started to change, it began to sound strange and even suspect. What? Committed to a mental hospital just because you were gay? Surely there must have been some other reason.

When these men did begin to confront their pasts, the results were sometimes cathartic. After our first conversation, Doug Thorson had nightmares for two weeks running. Before long he was calling me with facts he'd overlooked and suggestions of various aspects of the case to investigate; he started having squabbles on the telephone with one of the antigay radio talk show hosts he listened to regularly.

It was on a trip to Denver that I met Harold McBride. Jackie Yamahiro, the former Mount Pleasant social worker, was retired and living in a Denver suburb. (Her husband Roy had died some years before.) I had interviewed Jackie by phone and wanted to meet her in person. She and Roy appeared to be the only heroes in the entire squalid affair. These days Jackie was volunteering at the Colorado AIDS Project in Denver. She hadn't worked with gay men before coming to Mount Pleasant nor in the intervening years, but now she was answering phones, doing intake interviews, and becoming involved in the lives of some of her clients just as she had in 1955. Jackie encouraged me to track down Harold, who was still living in Southern California; he agreed to come to Denver for a "reunion." I would join them for the weekend.

Harold, 76 by then, was still cutting hair (although his customers were dying off and he was having trouble making ends meet). He was hard of hearing but still vigorous. He remained active in community theater and the state cosmetology association, just as he had been in Iowa in the 1950s; he was out of the closet and involved with the Names Project, the organization that put together the AIDS memorial quilt. On the surface at least, he seemed to have surmounted his ordeal of 1955. Still, talking about Mount Pleasant was difficult for Harold, and he had large gaps in his memory.

On Saturday of the reunion weekend, Jackie, Harold, and I drove up to the old Victorian town of Leadville, high in the Rockies. It was a beautiful early spring day; the sun blazed on the snow-covered landscape, throwing everything into sharp relief. But once we arrived in Leadville, Harold complained of severe stomach cramps; he slept the entire way back to Denver.

Perhaps the altitude made him ill, but Harold admitted later it was probably nerves. When we got back to Jackie's house, his memories returned in a flood.

"I feel strongly about this," he said when it was all over. "I want you to use my real name in the book. I don't want you to use a pseudonym." As publication neared, however, Harold expressed reservations, and, as I'd done for the other men sent to Mount Pleasant, I ended up changing his name.

The last of men I met was Lloyd Madsen, the leader of the patient dance band at Mount Pleasant. I had gotten his address from the National Guild of Organists and wrote to him a few times, with no response. I was particularly disappointed. I was sure that Lloyd could shed a great deal of light on what had happened at Mount Pleasant—the dances, the Christmas pageant, his seemingly mysterious relationship with the chief psychologist and the music therapist.

Toward the end of my research, I happened to be in Los Angeles, so I drove out to the address the Guild of Organists had given me. In a pleasant middle-class neighborhood of Santa Monica, I found Lloyd's name on the mailbox. I rang the bell, and a nice-looking man in his 60s answered. Yes, he had gotten my letters, but he wanted to let the past remain the past. He invited me inside. There was a large and very ornate organ in his living room and framed musical and theatrical posters and programs on the walls. He was a sweet and gentle man, we talked amiably, and he asked me if I would like to go and have "dinner" with him. (It was 3 o'clock in the afternoon.) Then he sat down and played a Chopin nocturne on the organ. There was a certain enchantment about it all.

We drove to Denny's, where Lloyd told me all sorts of personal things—about his former wife, his kids, and his health—but almost nothing about Mount Pleasant. He made it clear that was off-limits. At assorted moments, I would throw in a question about those days, hoping he might tell me something, anything. Was it was true that he was arrested playing at the Cobblestone Ballroom at Lake Okoboji? He had played at a place called Tony's in Fort Dodge and at the Orpheum Theater in Cedar Rapids, he said. But Lake Okoboji? He'd never even heard of it. Did he play the organ at meal times at Mount Pleasant? He might have.

"It was all politics," he told me in the car on the way home. As we pulled up in front of his house, I asked him if he remembered a psychologist at the mental hospital named Monroe Fairchild. Lloyd suddenly came alive: "Oh, God, that guy! After I left Mount Pleasant, he followed me to Denver. I had to call the police on him. He was in love with me." And then he shook my hand, shut the car door, and was gone.

I paid two visits to Don O'Brien in his office in the federal building in Sioux City. By then in his early 70s, the former county attorney who had been instrumental in sending the 20 men to Mount Pleasant was a federal judge with senior status. Senior status meant that he filled in for other judges but really worked as hard as ever, he explained. Don O'Brien was an important man. When you got out of the elevator on the third floor of the federal building, you were greeted by an oil painting of O'Brien, clad in his judicial robes. (In May 2000, a courtroom in the U.S. courthouse in Sioux City was dedicated in his honor.) His person was virtually indistinguishable from the high position he held.

O'Brien was white-haired and wore glasses, cordial, and not imposing. His manner was calm and deliberate, his style casual. On one occasion when I went to his office to pick up an article he had written, the door was wide open and he was alone, going over some legal materials, without a secretary or law clerk in sight. He was known to answer his own phone. These were qualities that made him admired by many people.

At our first meeting, he was a little defensive. Then again, who wouldn't be defensive, given the circumstances?

"You probably think this is a low point in the history of gays in the United States," Don O'Brien said to me.

O'Brien was unrepentant about what had happened in Sioux City in 1955. Still, he was concerned about his reputation. After all, he was one of the most liberal federal judges in the Midwest—a "bleeding heart liberal," in the view of one prominent Sioux City police officer. ("The U.S. attorneys think I am hotter on them than on the prisoners," O'Brien told me proudly.) He tried to clarify his 1955 statement in *The Des Moines Register* in which he had said, "The word is out they're not welcome in Sioux City anymore." He hadn't meant to imply that gay men weren't welcome in Sioux City, he explained; the men who were unwelcome were "men who were charged with sexual acts or charged with sex with minors." He added, "No one was ever run out of town that I know of. If they had roots here, they came back."

The judge told me he had seen television coverage of gay parades in San Francisco. "Do you think homosexuals have a propensity to recruit others more than heterosexuals do?" he wanted to know. And he was interested in numbers: What percentage of gays recruited, did I think? He actually used to word "recruited," which surprised me. He believed "You can get someone started on this." And to prove it, he told a story about one of his former law clerks, who had only been in Sioux City a short while. Late one afternoon the phone rang, and since no one else was in the office, O'Brien answered it. On the line was a local hairdresser calling for the law clerk.

The law clerk later explained to O'Brien that he had met the hairdresser at a bar and that the guy had been pestering him. "He was one of the aggressive ones," suggested the judge.

Several months after our first meeting, I went to see Judge O'Brien again. When I arrived at his office, he asked if it would be all right if another lawyer sat in on the conversation. He also wanted to tape record it. He was cordial as the first time we met, but clearly he took this meeting more seriously. At points, he behaved as if he were giving a deposition in a legal case, weighing his words cautiously and being careful not to say anything that might be used against him. If our first conversation had been relatively informal (I had taken notes), on this occasion there would be no anecdotes about law clerks and hairdressers.

This time he didn't seem to remember very much. For example, he had "no independent recollection" of the September 1958 roundup that exiled Pete Reynolds from Sioux City. He even tried to convince me that there had been no roundup that year at all. Some of the cases of the 13 men involved might have been left over from previous judicial terms and had been decided in one swoop by Judge Prichard, he suggested. But the proof—from court records, news articles, and personal accounts—was indisputable. In any event, O'Brien insisted he probably had little, if any, direct participation in the 1958 arrests because he had been busy running for Congress. (Reading *The Sioux City Journal* gave a different impression, however. In its September 25, 1958 news story, headlined "Sentence Six in Roundup," the newspaper wrote, "Donald E. O'Brien, Woodbury County attorney, who signed the information against the six men, said the felony which the men conspired to commit involved immoral acts.")

When he did remember things, his memory was, in his

words, "imperfect." For example, he recalled the day when the Sioux City police came to the county attorney's office and told him that Jimmy Bremmers's remains had finally been found. "We drove over there and saw the body," he said. I gently told him that he hadn't been elected county attorney yet when Jimmy Bremmers was killed, that he had not taken office until three months later. (As a city prosecutor, it is possible that he was taken to view Jimmy's remains, however.)

Sometimes I felt sorry for O'Brien. Here he was being challenged on things that happened 40 years ago that he couldn't recall clearly and thus couldn't really defend himself properly. At other times, I wondered if some of this memory loss was a matter of convenience. In his confusion over whether he was in office when Jimmy Bremmers was murdered, for example, was he just testing me, or trying to mislead me in some way, making such a major error to prove to me that he really couldn't remember things very well, thus making his lack of recollection of other smaller matters more credible? Perhaps I was being overly suspicious, too tough on him. He seemed a nice man who was trying to be helpful.

Many of his responses were somewhat contorted, and you could read into them almost anything you liked. For example, I asked him whether today he would approve of the kind of "naming names" that went on in the police interrogations of the men who were sent down to Mount Pleasant. "I wouldn't deny that those guys [the police] may have said, 'If you give me another name, I'll help you out,' " he noted. "I was never present when that happened, I don't think. But I probably wasn't present when they interrogated any of them. I would say to you that I can't say I didn't know that they were doing that. On the other hand, I can say I don't believe I was ever around when they interviewed anybody so I don't know that I knew it directly. If

273

they did do that, I would say to you that I'm not any more in favor of doing that than what the Whitewater prosecutor [investigating Bill and Hillary Clinton] is doing right now."

The first time we met I had asked him if it was all an over-reaction—the mass arrests, the incarcerations at Mount Pleasant. I asked him the second time too, wanting to give him an opportunity to change or clarify his position. But he wouldn't budge. "If you went down the street and talked to anybody in Sioux City at this time, they would say, 'We want this place straightened up,' " he insisted. "And I don't know it helped any to straighten it out in the long run by sending those guys there [to Mount Pleasant]. But it probably helped a little bit in that it got those folks and everybody else who had any kind of a problem—I'm not talking about gays particularly, but I'm talking about people who might be trying to grab kids or girls or whatever. It was all part of trying to get Sioux City in a better situation. That would be my crime!"

All right, but why round up 20 gay men in the aftermath of the killing of a little girl? "I can't give you an exact answer," he said. "But it is still a sex crime, so to speak. Now, you take the ordinary person on the street. They aren't going to draw much difference between that and two guys up in the library or in the Warrior Hotel. Now, there is a lot of difference. I understand that. The urges are different. I understand that. But the populace of Sioux City, I'm sure, didn't draw too many lines like that."

His attitudes toward homosexuality appeared to have changed somewhat over the years. These days, he thought the cause was probably genetic. (This seemed to contradict his statement that "You can get someone started on this," however.) In his view, the genetic explanation was "a much better, fairer, and closer explanation than what most people used to think 20 years ago—that homosexuals were bad people who were doing this intentionally and were lucky not to be treated worse than they were." A "hell of a lot" of people thought that way over the years, he noted. He himself didn't feel "near that tough," but he considered homosexuality a problem he wasn't smart enough to understand. "That is one of the reasons why I probably wanted to send them to some psychiatrists to see what they would say," he said. "If I had the same problem today, I would probably find the best testimony I could find."

He added that he had spent part of the winter in Key West, Florida, for the past 22 years, and the town probably had "more gay folks per capita than anyplace else. You can go down there and ask them how much trouble I've caused them!"

That was that. On the one hand there was the Don O'Brien, who as a judge made the state of Iowa pay for a transgendered person's sex change operation; ruled that a youngster in Council Bluffs had to be allowed to go to school even though he had herpes and the town was in an uproar; blocked prayers at two high school graduations in small towns east of Sioux City, although everyone in those towns was furious at him and the decision was eventually overturned. On the bench, Don O'Brien had proven on many occasions that he was willing to stand up for principle. But when it came to his role in locking up 20 men in a mental hospital back in 1955, in many cases solely because they were gay, O'Brien wasn't even willing to say, 'Well, maybe we went just a little too far during a very bad time." Mostly, he just said, "I don't remember."

Dick Burke had a much better memory and no need to hide or to repress anything. He was proud of everything he'd done. The minute I walked into his Sioux City apartment, the former police officer began to tell me, with no prompting on my part, about entrapping homosexuals at the Warrior Hotel, about learning the "international code of homosexuality," about the card files on gay men he used to keep in his locker down at headquarters. Madeleine, his wife of 49 years, wandered in and out doing the laundry, hearing snatches of conversation, apparently unfazed. Of course, everything was designed to make Dick Burke look important. But no matter, he was a marvelous source of information. It was from his scrapbooks that I first became aware of the 1958 roundup. Dick Burke had charisma, even though in the aftermath of back surgery, he walked with a cane, couldn't drive, and could barely get out of a chair. I couldn't help liking him just a little bit in spite of myself.

Still, Dick Burke was no one to tangle with, even in his old age and declining health. (He died in February 1997 at age 71.) He was tough and aggressive. His wife described how he had been in a boating accident and was in a near coma for 28 days, his brain all swollen, and then emerged from the ordeal "sharper than ever." "Commodore Burke," they called him. Dick related how a lawyer in Fort Dodge owed him money. Dick called him up at 3:30 A.M. to harass him. The lawyer paid up.

Dick and Madeleine Burke lived in an apartment in the shadow the Floyd Monument—the sandstone obelisk overlooking the Missouri that honored Sergeant Charles Floyd, who died on the Lewis and Clark expedition. There was a certain irony to this since the monument was Sioux City's outdoor gay cruising spot, with a bathroom that was the scene of some of the same activities that used to take place in the Warrior Hotel. I figured Dick Burke wanted to keep an eye on what was going on, in case he was ever called out of retirement.

Dick Burke didn't show any remorse. When I asked him if he thought it was right to send the 20 men to Mount Pleasant, his only reply was, "It was probably better than sending them to Anamosa or Fort Madison."

Wendell Pendleton also didn't show much remorse. He was the former state representative from Storm Lake who was one of the co-sponsors of the sexual psychopath bill when it was introduced the Iowa legislature in 1955. (The legislature repealed the law in 1976.) Now in his late 70s, Pendleton had retired to Florida's Gulf Coast, where I reached him by phone. "I don't apologize for that bill," he told me. The concept of "screening" (his euphemism for detaining) minor sex criminals to make sure they wouldn't commit major sex crimes was a perfectly reasonable one, he maintained. The law was an honest attempt to address the problem of people who commit "these unconscionable crimes that are inexplicable." Pendleton did concede that sending the men to Mount Pleasant had represented an improper application of the original law; the men had been "screened" for too long, he said. (He hadn't argued that at the time, however.) "I think there was nothing wrong with the sex psychopath law," he went on. "The psychiatrists jumped all over us. They claimed there was no such thing as a criminal sexual psychopath. But I think they might have been a little beyond the times."

And even if the law was improperly applied, the consequences weren't really that bad, he added. "They gathered up a great many of the homosexuals and sent them to the state hospital and they just kind of had a good time," Wendell Pendleton said. He laughed heartily at that.

To Doug and Duane and Harold and the others, it was no laughing matter, of course. Overall, though, it is hard to calculate the long-term effects of what occurred, to determine to what extent the traumas of the men arrested in the two roundups affected the rest of their lives. I only met them when they were in their late 50s, 60s, and 70s. They were proud Midwesterners of a generation who refused to see themselves as victims; they wanted to impress you with how much they'd overcome adversity, not how much they had been brought down by it. At the same time, they were gay (or bisexual) in an era when it was difficult and often dangerous to be so, when you learned how to conceal your real self and your real feelings simply to survive.

Thus, Gary Paul Marsh, the high school student whom Don O'Brien was trying to protect from something "worse" than murder, claimed that his arrest and ensuing ordeal "didn't stunt my growth. It didn't put a dent in me." By the time I met him, he was a bank teller in Florida and had been involved with the same man for 35 years. Billy Ivers also wouldn't accept the idea that being locked up in mental hospital, as awful as that was, might have been decisive in forming his character. "Maybe it made me more cautious," he said. "Maybe it slowed me down. But I was raised to believe there wasn't anything I couldn't accomplish. It didn't affect my life. I wouldn't let it." In part, this may have been the case because Billy was so young at the time, just as Gary Paul Marsh was young. Both were resilient; they hadn't really begun life yet.

At the same time, however, Billy was elusive, hard to track down and to pin down, and deliberately cultivated an air of mystique and mystery. When I finally located him, he was virtually hiding out, avoiding old friends, waiting to come into some family money, he said. I wondered if his elusiveness had anything to do with what had happened in 1955— when he had been tracked down and pinned down, when he had been called by the police one afternoon from his aunt's kitchen and locked up because he knew the material of some-one's bedspread.

Doug Thorson, for one, wouldn't attribute Billy's elusive-ness to Mount Pleasant. I had brought Doug and Billy togeth-er at Billy's apartment in Sioux City for the first time since they had been in the mental hospital together. Like the reunion of Jackie Yamahiro and Harold McBride, it was a little uneasy—it was great to see an old friend after all that time but it also brought back unpleasant memories. To Doug, Billy hadn't changed a bit. "He was always like that," Doug said. "He was always mysterious. He was like that at 18." For his part, Billy didn't think Doug had changed very much either—crusty, a lit-tle wild in his way, but still a good sort basically.

Harold McBride was quite different. At the time he was sent to Mount Pleasant, he was married with his own business and public standing. His arrest and incarceration caused a crisis in his marriage, although it took time for that crisis to manifest itself. If he hadn't been arrested and sent away, he might have gone on with his secret gay life unbeknownst to Glenda, and their marriage might have continued unaffected. As it was, the marriage fell under a strain that only ended when Glenda died. As for the rest of Harold's life, once he got to California, it seemed to pick up once again almost as if nothing had hap-pened. He was older than Billy Ivers, steadier and more stable—a married man, after all; his life had well-developed patterns that were relatively easy to return to after Mount Pleasant.

It was Pete Reynolds, arrested in 1958, whose life had been thrown off track more than anyone. He was never able to teach again, although he held a good job at a major Omaha corpo-ration until he retired. Throughout the years in his exile in Omaha, he remained very closeted about his homosexuality. He never had any long-term relationships; it was hard for him to get close to people, he admitted. How much of this was the result of what happened back in Sioux City in 1958? Would his life had been much different otherwise? Pete wondered too.

"You put an experience like this in a corner of your mind," Pete said. "It changed my life so much. And the scars, I'm sure, are not far below the surface. I would have been very happy to have remained a schoolteacher. I loved the kids; I loved teaching. You never get over that. I'm not angry or bitter. I was in the wrong place. I didn't have to be there. The experience taught me, as I got older, to be on the side of the underdog, on the side of the person who is in trouble. You come away with some habits you are glad you have.

"Even if I say that I put it in the back of my mind, there are times when I think about it. You never get over it, even though you can come down here to Omaha and make a new life. I hope that everyone who was involved was able to make a life. I hope they didn't have to go through life without having some sort of success or pleasure. That would be awful if you had to carry that through until the day you died. Imagine how bad that would be!"

But the murder of a brother is a different thing entirely. You carry that with you until the day you die. Karen Bremmers Hayden was 14 when her brother Jimmy was killed; her parents had left her in charge of him on the night he disappeared. Now she was 56, with eight children of her own; she was a great-grandmother, just as her mother had been at her age. Karen had a life marred by tragedy: Her first husband had been crushed between a truck and a loading dock in a work accident, leaving Karen a widow with two children at age 19; she had lived through the deaths of her father and mother. She blamed her mother's death on Ernest Triplett's release from prison. The heart attack her mother had suffered on the day he was let out of Fort Madison was the beginning of the end. To Karen, Ernest Triplett "got two of them—Jimmy and my mother."

Her mother, Karen told me, had kept all of Jimmy's possessions until she died—for 20 years. She even kept the clothes they had found him in. After her mother passed away, Karen and her sister got rid of the clothes. Clearly, her mother had never really accepted Jimmy's death. "Even after they found the body, any time we went anywhere, my mother would look for my brother," she said. "She thought maybe they were wrong; maybe it wasn't his body that they found. She'd look at kids all the time, thinking, 'Maybe it's him, Maybe it's Jimmy.' "

Karen had no doubt that Ernest Triplett had murdered her brother. He had first gone after the little Osborn boy, she said. When he didn't succeed, he took Jimmy. He had been hanging around the neighborhood for a couple of weeks, she insisted. The night of Jimmy's abduction, he had parked his car in an alley near their house, but everyone thought it was the boyfriend of a girl in the neighborhood. His release from Fort Madison was "really unfair."

The murder of her brother had followed her always. After his death, she and her younger sister Patty would walk into a room and suddenly all conversation would stop. "You knew they were talking about you," she said. The whole thing had wrecked her life. "I wouldn't go where people were," she said. "I wasn't like that before my brother died. I wouldn't go to a Tupperware party. I'd just order on the phone." Even years later, people would ask her maiden name, and when she said Bremmers, they would frown and say, "That sounds so familiar." Her sister moved out of town because of all the notoriety. "You couldn't get away from it," Karen said.

For a number of years, Karen and her husband lived in a bungalow a block away from the Cottage Avenue house where she and her sister and brother had lived as kids. Initially, she had hoped that moving back to the old neighborhood would help her to get over the whole thing. But she didn't get over it. The neighborhood had stayed the same; so many of the same people were still living there; it was as if time had stood still. Then, the year before I spoke with her, she and her husband put the house on the market and moved to a town about half an hour south of Sioux City. Putting just that short distance between herself and her past lifted "5,000 pounds" off her. "There was so much pressure," she said. "So many bad things happened back in Sioux City." Now she hated it when she had to go into Sioux City for shopping or an errand. "I get sick when I get to the city limits," she said.

I went and saw the house where Karen and her husband had lived in the old neighborhood. It was a blue shingled bungalow with a peaked roof and a red garage that looked like a little barn. There was a FOR SALE sign on the front lawn; Karen and her husband were having trouble finding a buyer. The house stood on a hill on the corner of Edmunds Avenue and Prescott Street. Just below the house lay the spot where Steve Counterman had glimpsed Jimmy Bremmers for the last time, standing next to the fir tree in the waning August light. It was as if Karen had moved into that blue shingled bungalow to stand guard over the spot from which her brother had been last seen. Like her mother, she had been waiting all those years for Jimmy to return.

On July 22, 1995, Ernest Triplett, age 90, died at the Iowa Care Center in Iowa City. On his death certificate, his place of birth was listed as Wittman, Iowa, a town that no longer exists. His occupation was described as "barber," and his business as "cosmetology," although, as far as I know,

Triplett had never worked in that profession. Cause of death was respiratory failure due to pneumonia, with lung cancer as the underlying cause. The body was unclaimed.

Karen Bremmers wasn't aware that Triplett had died. When I told her, she said, "He'll pay for it now!"

People in Sioux City would ask me if I thought that Ernest Triplett killed Jimmy Bremmers. And I had to answer that I honestly didn't know. A lot of things pointed to Triplett. I followed his route on the night of Jimmy's death—from the Meisches back up to the Osborns and then to the Bremmers house. He was definitely in the neighborhood, a logical suspect. Following his route was creepy. And then there were all those contradictory stories he had told the police: about talking to Jimmy Bremmers, letting him up on the running board of his car, seeing him hitchhiking on the road. Why would he tell the police these things if he were innocent?

But Triplett was a strange person, very strange. And so much about the case was questionable: the police tactics, the effort to portray him as a "sex fiend," the drug-induced confession, the court testimony about "striations" in the dashboard of Triplett's car. There was a need to find a suspect: any suspect. Triplett, the itinerant music salesman with few roots and an interest in marijuana and sex beyond the missionary position, fit the bill almost too well.

One person who firmly believed in Triplett's innocence was Robert Bartels, the law professor who was his co-counsel at the 1972 hearing and looked after him for many years following his release. Part of the reason he believed in Triplett was the lack of evidence—once you tossed out that tainted confession, there just wasn't much of a case against him. Bartels had spent a great deal of time with Triplett, both before the hearing and after Triplett left prison; he didn't believe that a guilty man "could have gotten by for that length of time without slipping up with me in our discussions about it." In the end, he said, those 17 years in prison were less important to Triplett than being labeled a child killer. "What Ernie wanted, more than the years back or monetary compensation, was some official statement that he did not do it," said Bartels. It was his vehemence in pursuing vindication and "his general demeanor in talking to me about it" that convinced Bartels he was innocent.

These days, Bartels, a professor at the Arizona State University College of Law, still had a lot of affection for Triplett. His 1988 book about the case, *Benefit of Law*, is clearly written from the point of view of a defense attorney who believed his client had been wronged. (The book was indispensable for the Triplett sections of this narrative.)

"What was Triplett really like?" I asked him. "Was he intelligent?"

"He was not a nuclear physicist," Bartels admitted. "But he was not unintelligent. He just wasn't very well educated."

Was he cunning?

"He thought himself as cunning," Bartels said. "He had these insights that seemed completely goofy at first but actually had a certain logic to them. Like I asked him, 'Why did you confess to these guys?' And Triplett said, 'They were after me to do it. That was part of it. The other part of it was that I figured after a while, since I didn't do it, what was the harm?' " His logic, Bartels noted, was "If you did commit the crime, then you certainly wouldn't want to admit it. If you didn't do it and you admitted it, then they would figure that out, and no harm would come to you and it would get them off your back."

What most impressed Bartels about Triplett was his toughness. You had to be tough—very tough—to survive at Fort Madison if you were sent up on a child murder rap. "It may have just been that he seemed harmless," Bartels said. "Or if he was as 'off' and as illogical when he went in as when I got to know him, that may have persuaded people not to do anything to him."

After Triplett's release from prison, Bartels and his law students arranged for him to live at a nursing home in Iowa City. It was the only accommodation that wouldn't cost anything. Triplett hated being there, Bartels recalls; it felt like prison all over again. At the nursing home, he met a woman named Clara; they both left there and got married. But Clara was in poor health, and Triplett wound up spending most of his time looking after her. When she died a year later, he inherited her house.

Soon after, Triplett came into some money. He sued the state of Iowa and filed a federal civil rights action against the principals in his case and those responsible for his improperly obtained confession: Cherokee state hospital physicians Asa Azordegan and Anthony Sainz; prosecutors Bill Sturges and Bob Beebe; Don O'Brien; Sioux City police officers Bill Dennison and Russell White; and Cherokee orderly Bill Sangwin. (All but Dennison, White, and Sangwin were eventually dropped from the suit.) In 1978 he settled out of court, with the state of Iowa paying Triplett $50,000 and the federal government settling for $3,000 in the civil rights case.

In those first years after his release, Triplett spent much of his time riding around Iowa City on a three-wheeled bicycle. He played the slide guitar—more Hank Williams than Liberace—made his own home brew, and invited the teenage boys in the neighborhood to sample it. They would stop by and visit him on days when they skipped school. "You'll learn more from me than you will in school," he'd tell them.

The times had finally caught up with Ernest Triplett, and people were intrigued by him. He loved to tell stories, and he

285

had a lot of them to tell—about the Depression and drugs and sex and the drifter's life, all related in that colorful, distinctive "Triplett-speak." He was the real thing. All those years at Fort Madison made him even more exotic. He had been locked up in an age of sex-crime panic and set free in an age of sex, drugs, and rock 'n' roll.

In 1980, eight years after he left Fort Madison, Triplett suffered a severe stroke that left him paralyzed on one side. During this period, University of Iowa students boarded with him and took care of him, and he was able to live at home for several years. By the end, though, he returned to the same nursing home he had entered when he first came to Iowa City.

I never got to meet Ernest Triplett. He died two weeks after I started working on the book. I did talk to a man who, as a law student, spent eight or 10 hours in conversation with Triplett at various Iowa City pubs. Needless to say, it didn't take much to get the gregarious Triplett to reminisce about his arrest and trial. He explained to the law student how, by spinning his web of tales about his supposed encounters with Jimmy Bremmers, he had managed to "put one over" on the Sioux City police. "He thought he was being smart, really," the law student said. "He liked the accommodations at the jail and the police station. They gave him all the food and cigarettes he wanted. He would tell me how clever he was. He would say, 'I gave them just enough to keep me there and not enough to hang me.'" Triplett took great pleasure in relating all this, even though his strategy had helped land him in Fort Madison. "In a lot of people, a story like that would make you suspicious," said the law student. "But with Ernie, anything was possible."

On another occasion, the student tried to get Triplett as drunk as possible to get him to tell what had really happened in Sioux City on that August night in 1954. This time it would be beer that would function as truth serum. But when he finally asked Triplett outright if he had killed Jimmy Bremmers, Triplett just became indignant.

"I assume you believe that Triplett was innocent," I said to the law student, who was by now a highly respected law professor.

He hesitated for a moment.

"Not at all," he said. "In fact, I always had a hunch that he was guilty."

The sequence of events that made up a sex-crime panic was clear: the murder of Jimmy Bremmers leading to the conviction of Ernest Triplett and the enactment of the sexual psychopath law; the murder of Donna Sue Davis, followed by the opening of the special ward and then the roundup necessary to fill that ward. Yet there remained frustrating, tantalizing questions: Did Triplett kill Jimmy Bremmers? And if not, then who did? Who gave the order for the roundup of Sioux City's gay men? Was it Don O'Brien? Or could the whole thing be blamed on an overzealous Dick Burke on a crusade? Documentation was missing: transcripts of police interrogations, back issues of *The Sioux City Press-Dispatch*, tapes of the TV coverage of Triplett's trial—all gone. Files had been thrown out, mislaid, lost forever. Too many people were dead; too many of those alive didn't remember or want to remember.

And there was still another mystery, perhaps the most disturbing of all: Who abducted a little Sioux City girl from her crib on a hot summer night, raped and sodomized her, covered her with cigarette burns, and dumped her body in a cornfield across the Missouri?

Forty years after the death of Donna Sue Davis, the case remains unsolved. No one was ever arrested or brought to trial. "The FBI under J. Edgar Hoover would always claim there wasn't a case they hadn't solved," said Don O'Brien. "I always knew there was one, and it was this one."

When I first came to Sioux City I had the fantasy that somehow I was going to find the missing clues to Donna Sue's murder, to succeed where J. Edgar Hoover's G-men and the Sioux City police had failed. But I realized this was a vain and silly idea, and I was quickly disabused of it. Various people in Sioux City would tell me they were convinced they knew who committed the crime; in the end it always turned out to be someone different, and nothing ever panned out.

Today, Harry Gibbons's meticulously detailed and cross-indexed notebooks of investigative reports still lie moldering in the basement of the police headquarters downtown, closed to the public. I tried my best to get access to them, but to no avail; the city attorney refused to grant me permission. Technically, Donna Sue's murder remains an open case. Gibbons, the ex-boxer who became chief of detectives, was said to have become completely obsessed with it. Years afterward he spent his spare moments poring over the handwritten pages of his investigative reports, trying to figure out some new lead, some unexplored angle. But the case remained a labyrinth, a trail of alibis and dead ends. Later, I was told, Gibbons went "goofy" and spent his last days in a mental hospital cutting out paper dolls.

Forty years after the murders of Jimmy Bremmers and Donna Sue Davis, far away from Sioux City, another child murder captured public attention. In the case of 7-year-old Megan Kanka, there was no doubt as to who had raped and killed her. The perpetrator was a twice-convicted sex criminal named Jesse Timmendequas who lived down the street from her Hamilton Township, New Jersey, home. Just as Iowa had passed its sexual psychopath law after the murder of Jimmy Bremmers, the New Jersey legislature moved swiftly to make sure a similar crime wouldn't happen again. The state enacted what came to be known as Megan's Law, requiring all convicted sex offenders to register with their local police departments once they were released from prison; the law also authorized that their names and addresses be available to the public. The U.S. Congress followed with a law mandating that every state establish a sex-offender registry or lose 10% of federal law enforcement assistance grants. Soon all 50 states had some version of Megan's Law.

The state of Kansas went further. After the murder of a 20-year-old woman by a paroled rapist in 1993, the legislature approved a bill that enabled the state to keep violent and dangerous sex offenders confined in mental hospitals after they had completed their prison sentences. In 1997, the U.S. Supreme Court narrowly upheld the Kansas law. In 2000, the Massachusetts supreme judicial court upheld a similar law, enacted a year before. In other states as well there was a growing trend to use commitment laws to send sex offenders to mental hospitals.

The impulses and arguments behind the 1990s laws were identical to those behind the sexual psychopath laws of the 1950s. Sex offenders had a high recidivism rate. Once released from prison, they often committed the same crime again. (The defendant in the Kansas case, 62-year-old Leroy Hendricks, had once told authorities that the only way he could stop molesting children was to die.) What could be done? How could more Jimmy Bremmerses or Donna Sue Davises or Megan Kankas be prevented? In the 1950s the idea was to classify people as sexual psychopaths and keep them in mental hospitals until "cured." In the 1990s and into the new millennium, the approach was not dissimilar: keep tabs on sex offenders long after they had served their time, watch their every move, put their picture up on every lamp post (in spring 2001, a judge in Corpus Christi, Texas, stopped just short of requiring that), and if necessary, lock them up in a state hospital till the end of their days.

As with the sexual psychopath laws, the 1990s approach was intended to reassure an anxious public. There was a strong case to be made that parents of small children had the right to know if a convicted child molester moved in around the corner. But both Megan's Law and the Kansas and Massachusetts laws also raised troubling questions about violation of civil liberties, about whether mental hospitals could serve as substitutes for prisons, about whether the state could lock someone up indefinitely once he had served his sentence.

There are, of course, major differences between the sex offender registration laws of the 1990s and what happened in Iowa in the 1950s. Despite the many questions raised by the current laws, at least they do target people who have committed violent sex offenses. Today, the legal distinctions between violent sexual predators and gay men are clearer than in the 1950s when all were lumped together under the catch-all category of sexual deviate. Mental hospitals are not used as warehouses for homosexuals; sodomy laws have been repealed in more than half the states, including Iowa, and are rarely enforced in jurisdictions where they are still on the books. If something similar happened today, gay political and legal organizations—to say nothing of the American Civil Liberties Union—would jump into the fray.

Nonetheless, what happened in Sioux City in 1955 remains a cautionary tale. After all, the Iowa sexual psychopath law was supposed to lock up serious sex offenders, not the hairdressers and window dressers of Sioux City. As we know, the law was used quite differently from the way it was originally intended. When political pressures demanded action, it was easier to round up homosexuals than violent sexual predators in an era when a "sexual deviate" was a vague and elastic concept and gay men were considered liable to commit acts of violence anyway.

In the 1950s, the paranoia of an often ugly decade made the situation worse. Ambitious politicians and unscrupulous police officers made things worse. Ignorance about sexuality and homosexuality made things worse too. Don O'Brien was right: The Mount Pleasant incarcerations, like the Boise arrests and the other antigay persecutions of the 1950s, do represent a "low point" in the history of gay people in the United States. But sex-crime panics—and panics of all sorts—are very much in the American grain, from the Salem witch trials right down to our own time. Prejudice against homosexuals is very much in the American grain too, as much as the social and legal situation of gay men and lesbians has improved in many parts of the country. Public fears and anxieties can lead to the enactment of bad laws, and laws enacted in an atmosphere of fear and anxiety can lead to even worse consequences. No one can say for sure that what happened in Sioux City in the 1950s couldn't happen again, in a different form, perhaps to a different group of people.

Who really can blame the men who survived Mount Pleasant for always looking behind them?

It was an early October day when I drove down to the town of Mount Pleasant, Iowa. The weather was still warm, and Mount Pleasant was unexpectedly charming—the town square green and leafy, with new benches and a bubbling fountain, and a big red-and-green threshing machine to advertise the Old

291

Thresher's Reunion that the town hosts every fall. There are shops on three sides of the square, giving the effect of an arcade, and brick sidewalks and old-style street lamps. The tavern with the dirty windows that so offended Jackie Yamahiro is long gone. It is a new day in Mount Pleasant. At the Take-a-Break café, a Roman Catholic priest, dressed in jeans and a polo shirt, sits reading *The New Yorker*. Just a few miles away lies Fairfield, the home of Maharishi International University, where the disciples of the Indian-born guru are said to levitate under airy domes.

Out on the highway, a sign points to the Mount Pleasant Mental Health Institute. You head up the long and impressive drive, and there stands the same forbidding building that had greeted Doug Thorson, Duane Wheeler, Billy Ivers, and Harold McBride 40 years before. Things have changed in one respect: The main hospital building is now a prison, as it has been since 1976. The twisting wings have been torn down, replaced by two-story brick additions; there is barbed wire all around. Something remains of the old state hospital, though: a 20-bed psychiatric unit and a 60-bed substance-abuse unit, located in a three-story brick structure just off to the side of the main building. With its barred windows and general air of neglect, the building looks like a middle school in a decaying inner-city neighborhood. It is hard to believe that this was once a grand institution with 1,410 acres, vegetable gardens, vineyards, a greenhouse, and poinsettias at Christmas.

Some of the "old bughousers" live nearby, and they like nothing better than to reminisce about the hospital in its halcyon days. They are good country people who spent their lives emptying bedpans and breaking up fights and holding patients down as they received their shock treatments. They have seen everything; they long ago gave up judging anyone. They don't remember too much about the men locked up in the sexual psychopath ward 40 years before. The ward was just one of many episodes at Mount Pleasant, dimly recalled, and since the men in the ward didn't give them much trouble, they don't stand out in their minds. What the old bughousers remember mostly, what they associate with the sexual psychopaths, is the patient dance band and the Friday night dances: "They were our orchestra." "They were good dressers; their shoes were always polished." "They were nice looking—you'd be surprised!" "They were all musicians, weren't they?" "They were pretty good dancers, that's for sure."

That's the way I see them too—Doug Thorson and crazy Greta Garbo sweeping across the dance floor to "Blue Moon," and Harold McBride two-stepping to "Lullaby of Birdland" with a glowing Betty Hutton on his arm. Tillie, with her hair chopped off, comes up to Billy Ivers as the music starts, and Billy gives her a sweet smile, thinking of his Nebraska farmer, standing a few feet away, so fresh, so clean-cut, so all-American, but completely oblivious. *Dear God, please, please, make him notice me.* Jackie Yamahiro looks down from the spectator's balcony, asking herself, How can I get them out of this? But for the moment, it almost doesn't matter. The orchestra breaks into "Shine on Harvest Moon" and the "Hesitation Waltz." Then the music fades. The dancers file out. The door of Ward 15 East slams shut.

Sex-Crime Panic Timeline

August 31, 1954: Jimmy Bremmers disappears in Sioux City.

September 2, 1954: Ernest Triplett detained in Jimmy Bremmers case.

September 16, 1954: Triplett commits himself to state mental hospital at Cherokee.

September 29, 1954: Body of Jimmy Bremmers found.

January 31, 1955: Sexual psychopath bill introduced in Iowa legislature.

March 3, 1955: Triplett charged in Bremmers case.

April 14, 1955: Iowa sexual psychopath law goes into effect.

June 13, 1955: Triplett found guilty and sentenced to life imprisonment.

July 8, 1955: Triplett enters Fort Madison prison.

July 10, 1955: Donna Sue Davis abducted from crib in Sioux City home.

July 11, 1955: Donna Sue Davis's body found.

July 16, 1955: First petition for incarceration under sexual psychopath law filed in Des Moines.

July 23, 1955: Announcement that Mount Pleasant hospital will set up special ward for those sentenced under sexual psychopath law.

September 1–8, 1955: Twenty men arrested in Sioux City for variety of charges related to "sexual deviation."

September 15–29, 1955: The men are sent to Mount Pleasant hospital as sexual psychopaths.

February–March 1956: Men released from Mount Pleasant and pronounced "cured."

Fall 1956: Sexual psychopath ward shut down.

October 1958: Fourteen men arrested in Sioux City on morals charges; paroled to lawyers.

October 17, 1972: Ernest Triplett conviction overturned in Bremmers murder.

October 18, 1972: Triplett released.

January 1, 1976: Iowa sexual psychopath law repealed.

October 4, 1978: U.S. Senate confirms Don O'Brien as federal judge.

July 22, 1995: Ernest Triplett dies in Iowa City, Iowa.

Today: Donna Sue Davis case remains unsolved.

People Interviewed

Robert Bartels
Tom Bell
Richard Burke
Thomas Deacy
Don Doyle
Kay Dull
Tom Fennell
Richard Gundersen
Bob Gunsolley
Bob Hansen
Karen Bremmers Hayden
Margaret Heumann
Billy Ivers (pseudonym)
Glada Koerselman
Lloyd Madsen (pseudonym)
Gary Paul Marsh (pseudonym)
Harold McBride (pseudonym)
Jack Milroy
Donald O'Brien
Donald Pendleton

Wendell Pendleton
Donald Reuben
John Peter Reynolds (pseudonym)
Richard Rhinehart
Jackie and John Rygh
Jackie Sangwin
Rita Starzl
William Sturges
George Thomas
Doug Thorson (pseudonym)
Henry Trysla
Leo Vandermeer (pseudonym)
Bob Wheeler (pseudonym)
Jackie Yamahiro
Louise Zershling

Bibliography

NEWSPAPERS AND MAGAZINES CONSULTED
The Sioux City Journal, The Sioux City Press-Dispatch, The Dakota County Star, The Des Moines Register, Des Moines Tribune, Mt. Pleasant News, The Le Mars Globe-Post, Le Mars Daily Sentinel, The Storm Lake Register, Storm Lake Pilot-Tribune, Council Bluffs Non-Pareil, Los Angeles Times, One, Time, Newsweek.

BOOKS AND JOURNAL ARTICLES USED
Abourezk, James G. (1989). *Advise & Dissent: Memoirs of South Dakota and the U.S. Senate.* Chicago: Lawrence Hill Books.

Bartels, Robert. (1988). *Benefit of Law: The Murder Case of Ernest Triplett*. Ames, Iowa: Iowa State University Press.

Berube, Allan. (1990). *Coming Out Under Fire*. New York: The Free Press.

Chauncey, George. (1993). "The Post-War Sex Crime Panics." In *True Stories From the American Past,* edited by William Graebner. New York: McGraw-Hill.

Cook, Fred J. (1971). *The Nightmare Decade: The Life and Times of Senator Joe McCarthy*. New York: Random House.

D'Emilio, John. (1992). *Making Trouble*. New York: Routledge.

D'Emilio, John. (1983). *Sexual Politics, Sexual Communities: The Making of a Homosexual Minority in the United States, 1940-1970*. Chicago: University of Chicago Press.

de River, J. Paul. (1949). *The Sexual Criminal: A Psychoanalytical Study*. Charles C. Thomas.

Freedman, Estelle B. " 'Uncontrolled Desires': The Response to the Sexual Psychopath, 1920-60." *The Journal of American History*, Vol. 74, June 1987.

Gerassi, John. (1966). *The Boys of Boise*. New York: The Macmillan Company.

Lee, Martin A. and Shlain, Bruce. (1985). *Acid Dreams: The CIA, LSD, and the Sixties Rebellion*. New York: Grove Press.

MacNama, Donal E.J. and Sagarin, Edward. (1977). *Sex, Crime, and the Law*. New York: The Free Press.

Miller, Neil. (1995). *Out of the Past*. New York: Vintage Books.

Ploscowe, Morris. (1951). *Sex and the Law*. New York: Prentice Hall.

Sorensen, Scott Alan. (1976). "Law Enforcement During the 1930s in Sioux City, Iowa." Master's Thesis. Department of History, University of South Dakota.

Sorensen, Scott Alan and Chicoine, B. Paul. (1982). *Sioux

City: A Pictorial History. Norfolk, Virginia: Donning
Company.

Sutherland, Edwin H. "The Sexual Psychopath Laws." *Journal
of Criminal Law and Criminology*, Vol. 40, No. 5, January-
February 1950.

Source Notes

PROLOGUE
Arrival: author's interviews with Doug Thorson (pseudonym)
and Jackie Yamahiro, 1995–1996.

CHAPTER 1: A BOY IS MISSING
Bremmers family and night of Jimmy disappearance: The
Sioux City Journal, September 1, 1954 and after; *State of
Iowa v. Ernest Triplett* transcript, Plymouth County district
court; author's interview with Karen Bremmers Hayden,
September 1996.
Sioux City background: Scott Alan Sorensen and B. Paul
Chicoine, *Sioux City: A Pictorial History*, p. 67 and follow-
ing, and pp. 191-199.

Bremmers search: *The Sioux City Journal*, week of September 1,
1954, and days following.

CHAPTER 2: ENTER ERNEST TRIPLETT
Triplett on the morning of Jimmy's disappearance: report of a
conversation with Triplett by Thomas L. Coriden, Woodbury
County corner on October 13, 1954, recorded in Triplett trial
transcript.
Triplett description: author's interviews with William Sturges,

1995–1996, Glada Koerselman, and various knowledgeable sources.

Triplett background and biography: Robert Bartels, *Benefit of Law: The Murder Case of Ernest Triplett*, pp. 77-79; life history of Ernest Triplett, courtesy of George Thomas.

Triplett in Sioux City: trial transcript; Bartels, pp. 1-6; *The Sioux City Journal*, September 1, 1954, and days following.

Triplett in custody: Triplett trial transcript; Bartels, pp. 5-7.

Sioux City background: Sorensen, "Law Enforcement During the 1930's in Sioux City Iowa"; various knowledgeable sources.

Police officers' descriptions: confidential sources.

Matousek recollections: Triplett trial transcript.

Triplett interrogation: Triplett statement to Sioux City police, September 15, 1954.

Kinsey findings: *Sexual Behavior in the Human Male*, Alfred Kinsey et al, quoted in Neil Miller, *Out of the Past*, pp. 250-51.

Triplett voluntary commitment: *The Sioux City Journal*, September 16, 1954.

CHAPTER 3: TRUTH SERUM

Background of Cherokee: *The Sioux City Journal*, November 21 and 22, 1988. Also Willard Brinegar deposition, February 10, 1978.

"He left in a straight jacket": author's interview with Jackie Sangwin, April 1996.

Dr. Sainz's past: interview with confidential source; Brinegar deposition.

LSD background: Martin A. Lee and Bruce Shlain, *Acid Dreams*, pp. 3-26.

Triplett hallucination: Bartels, p. 101.

Last search and discovery of Jimmy Bremmers's body: *The Sioux City Journal*, September 28 and 30, 1954.

Triplett and drugs: Bartels, pp. 99-103.

Triplett taken to view body: Triplett trial transcript.

Family reaction: *The Sioux City Journal*, September 30; personal interview with Karen Bremmers Hayden.

46 missing children: *The Sioux City Journal*, October 8, 1954.

Boy's fears of being next victim: confidential interview.

Triplett in custody: Triplett trial transcript; interview with confidential sources.

Triplett confession: Triplett trial transcript; Bartels, p. 102.

CHAPTER 4: "A LOVER OF LIBERACE" ON TRIAL

Triplett at Cherokee: Bartels, pp. 109-110.

Lyle Palmer confession: *The Sioux City Journal*, November 9 and 11, 1954.

O'Brien tape-recording episode: Bartels, p. 114.

O'Brien election campaign: *The Sioux City Journal*, October 31, 1954.

Turning over the tape: Bartels, p. 114

Preparations for Triplett release: Bartels, pp. 111-112.

Triplett arrest: *The Sioux City Journal*, April 13, 1955.

Le Mars history: *Le Mars Daily Sentinel*, "Pride in Our Past" supplement, February 29, 1996.

Trying Triplett in Plymouth County and Sturges background: author's interviews with Bill Sturges, 1995–96.

Beebe background: *The Sioux City Journal* obituary, November 17, 1988.

Thomas Tacy: Bartels, pp. 116-117; Sturges interview.

Judge Rodman description: Sturges interview.

Jury selection: *Sioux City Journal*, June 6, 1955.

Trial description: Triplett trial transcript; *The Sioux City Journal* and *The Le Mars Globe-Post*, June 6–18, 1955; author's interviews of Glada Koerselman and Bill Sturges.

Triplett confession: Bartels, pp. 24-25.

Liberace connection: *The Le Mars Globe-Post*, June 16, 1955.

Verdict: *The Sioux City Journal*, June 18, 1955.

Triplett sentenced: *The Sioux City Journal*, July 8, 1955.

Triplett sings: *The Le Mars Globe-Post*, June 23, 1955.

Triplett taken to Fort Madison: author's interview with Sturges.

CHAPTER 5: THE BODY IN THE CORNFIELD

Flood: *The Sioux City Journal*, July 10 and 11, 1955.

Disappearance of Donna Sue: *The Sioux City Journal*, July 11, 1955, and days following; *The Dakota County Star*, July 14, 1955.

Discovery of body: Bob Gunsolley, personal interview; author's personal interview with Judge Donald O'Brien, July 21, 1995.

Donna Sue's burial: *The Sioux City Journal* and *The Des Moines Register*, July 14, 1955.

"Get him!" and FBI-police cooperation: knowledgeable source.

Investigation: O'Brien, personal interview, July 21, 1995; Don Doyle, phone interview, December 1995.

Anxiety: *The Sioux City Journal*, *The Des Moines Register*, and *The Dakota County Star*, July 1955; personal interview with Henry Trysla.

Bremmers hysteria: *The Sioux City Journal*, August 1 and 7, 1955.

CHAPTER 6: NEEDED: 25 SEXUAL PSYCHOPATHS

The law: *Iowa Laws of 56th General Assembly*, chapter 121, sections 1-17.

Background on sexual psychopath concept and description of other moral panics: Estelle Freedman, " 'Uncontrolled

Desires': The Response to the Sexual Psychopath, 1920-1960," pp. 83-106; George Chauncey, "The Post-War Sex Crime Panics," pp. 161-178.

Newspaper headlines: *The Sioux City Journal*, September 1954–September 1955; *The Des Moines Register*, same period.

Arguments in favor of sexual psychopath laws: Sturges interview; Freedman essay.

Vagueness of laws: Edwin Sutherland, "The Sexual Psychopath Laws," pp. 543-554.

Ploscowe criticisms: Morris Ploscowe, *Sex and the Law*, pp. 216-241.

Passage of Iowa law: author's telephone interviews with Wendell Pendleton and Jack Milroy, 1996.

Newspaper letters and editorials: "Editorial Comment on Donna Sue Davis Case," *The Sioux City Journal*, July 23, 1955; "Letters," *The Sioux City Journal,* July 24, 1955. *Register* editorial: July 15, 1955.

Comments on background of Governor Hoegh: *The Sioux City Journal*, October 9, 1954, August 2, 1955, and September 5, 1955; Iowa *Official Register*, 1955–1956.

Establishment of special ward: *The Des Moines Register*, July 23 and 24, 1955.

CHAPTER 7: PINCHED

Doug and Duane background: author's interviews with Doug Thorson, 1995–1996; interview with Billy Ivers (pseudonym), 1996.

Sioux City movies: *The Sioux City Journal*, September 5, 1955.

Holiday on Ice: *The Sioux City Journal*, September 2, 1955; personal interview with Doug Thorson.

Warrior Hotel background: author's interview with Jackie and John Rygh, September 17, 1996; *The Sioux City Journal*, December 13, 1930 and February 22, 1931.

Doug's entrapment and arrest: author's interviews with Doug Thorson.

Dick Burke background and his version of arrest of Doug: author's interviews with Dick Burke, December 1 and 12, 1995.

CHAPTER 8: ENEMIES WITHIN

1950s antigay background: Miller, pp. 258-273 and 333-359; D'Emilio, *Sexual Politics, Sexual Communities*, pp. 40-53.

"Crush the Monster" in Boise: John Gerassi, *The Boys of Boise*, pp. 3-4.

"Sexual psychopath" as code word: Freedman, p. 103.

Homosexuals called psychopaths: de River, *The Sexual Criminal*.

CHAPTER 9: NAMING NAMES

Jail description: Doug Thorson, author interviews.

Harold McBride (pseudonym) background: author interviews with Harold McBride, March 30 and 31, 1996.

Arrests: interviews with Doug Thorson, Harold McBride, and Dick Burke; *The Sioux City Journal* and *The Le Mars Globe-Post*, September 8, 1955 and days following.

Pleas and sentences: Woodbury County district court criminal records, clerk's office, Sioux City, Iowa.

CHAPTER 10: MORALS CRUSADER

O'Brien background: *The Sioux City Journal*, October and November 1954.

O'Brien on "protecting young people": *The Sioux City Journal*, October 31, 1954.

O'Brien names assistants, assumes office: *The Sioux City*

Journal, December 17, 18, and 30, 1954, and January 4, 1955; confidential sources.

List of arrested men's hometowns and occupations: compiled from criminal records, Woodbury County district court.

Judge Prichard's reputation: author's personal interview with Donald O'Brien, September 13, 1996.

O'Brien view of Sioux City's predicament: Ibid.

Indictment pairings: criminal records, Woodbury County district court.

O'Brien reaction to indictment pairings: personal interview with O'Brien, July 21, 1995.

"Word Is Out": *The Des Moines Register*, November 25, 1955.

Gary Paul Marsh background and version of events: personal interview with Gary Paul Marsh (pseudonym), November 14, 1995.

Ralph Eckert (pseudonym) background: knowledgeable sources.

Maynard Post (pseudonym): Doug Thorson and Billy Ivers interviews; court documents, Woodbury County district court.

O'Brien campaign promise: *The Sioux City Journal*, November 4, 1956.

CHAPTER 11: THE ARRIVAL

Trip to Mount Pleasant: Doug Thorson interview.

Wards: author's personal interviews with Doug Thorson, Billy Ivers, Harold McBride, and Jackie Yamahiro.

"She wants to straighten him out": Mount Pleasant Mental Health Institute, admission note on Doug Thorson, September 29, 1955, courtesy of Doug Thorson.

Jackie and Roy Yamahiro background: author's phone interview with Jackie Yamahiro, February 10, 1996, and personal interviews, March 30 and 31, 1996.

Mount Pleasant background: Mount Pleasant Hospital records department.

Descriptions of the character of the institution: interview with Jackie Yamahiro and confidential interviews with a number of former employees of Mount Pleasant; telephone interview with Dr. Richard Gundersen, November 2, 1995.

CHAPTER 12: THE MEN IN THE PINK SHIRTS

Mount Pleasant town character and history: author's visit to Mount Pleasant, October 1995.

Roy and Jackie Yamahiro impressions: conversations with Jackie Yamahiro.

Mount Pleasant concerns: *Mt. Pleasant News*, August 20 and 23rd and September and October 1955; *The Des Moines Register*, August 24, 1955.

"Good people who just got carried away": author's interview with Tom Bell, October 5, 1995.

Pink shirts: phone conversation with Margaret Rehwolt, October 1995.

Dr. Brown's views: *The Des Moines Register*, November 25, 1955.

Gundersen impressions: Phone interview with Dr. Richard Gundersen, November 2, 1995.

CHAPTER 13: DANCING WITH GRETA GARBO

Photos: courtesy of Jackie Yamahiro.

Harold McBride's fears: personal interview.

Harold's moods: Mount Pleasant Mental Health Institute Psychology Department records, October 3, 1955 and November 3, 1955, courtesy of Harold McBride.

John Clemens phone call to Harold McBride: Harold McBride medical records, October 3, 1955.

O'Brien's apparent allusion to Harold's testimony: *The Des Moines Register*, November 25, 1955.

Mount Pleasant routines: interviews with Harold McBride, Doug Thorson, Billy Ivers, and Jackie Yamahiro.

Movies at Mount Pleasant: interview with Jackie Yamahiro.

Dances: interviews with Harold McBride, Doug Thorson, Billy Ivers, and Jackie Yamahiro.

Lloyd Madsen and patient orchestra: interview with Jackie Yamahiro; additional interviews of staff; author's interview with Lloyd Madsen (pseudonym).

Lloyd Madsen arrest and incarceration: *Fort Dodge Messenger*, August 16, 1955; Webster County district court records; confidential sources.

Billy Ivers background: interviews with Billy Ivers, 1996.

Billy Ivers arrest: Ibid; court documents, Woodbury County district court.

Visits, activities, anxieties: interviews with Jackie Yamahiro, Harold McBride, Doug Thorson, and Billy Ivers.

CHAPTER 14: THERAPY

Homosexuality viewed as mental illness: Miller, pp. 248-257.

Dr. Gundersen's views: phone interview with Gundersen.

Roy Yamahiro's views: interviews with Jackie Yamahiro; Roy Yamahiro notes on Harold McBride, November 3 and December 15, 1955, courtesy of Harold McBride.

Therapy group description: telephone interview with Gundersen; personal interviews of Doug Thorson.

Harold McBride psychotherapy: interview with Harold McBride; Roy Yamahiro's notes.

"Good Morning, Hotel Imperial!": Jackie Yamahiro interview.

CHAPTER 15: MATTERS OF THE HEART
Billy Ivers infatuation: Billy Ivers interviews.
Jackie as confidante: Jackie Yamahiro interview; Harold McBride interview.
Harold and Glenda's conjugal visit: Jackie Yamahiro interview.

CHAPTER 16: THE POWER AND THE GLORY
Mount Pleasant activities and caroling: *Mt. Pleasant News*, December 21, 1955.
Christmas pageant: personal interviews with Jackie Yamahiro, Harold McBride, and Doug Thorson.

CHAPTER 17: CHRISTMAS IN SIOUX CITY
Virgil Vance Wilson confession: *The Sioux City Journal*, December 12, 1955 and days following.
End-of-year survey: *The Sioux City Journal*, December 18, 1955.

CHAPTER 18: CURED
Harold McBride release: Mount Pleasant Mental Health Institute note, December 15, 1955; parole consideration note, December 27, 1955; Harold McBride release application, Woodbury County district court, December 26, 1955.
Journalistic scrutiny: *The Sioux City Journal*, November 17, 1955; *The Des Moines Register*, November 25, 1955.
Board of Control rethinks policy: *The Sioux City Journal*, December 10, 1955.
Doug Thorson release: Gundersen note, January 13, 1956; parole consideration note, January 25, 1956; staff note, January 31, 1956, all courtesy of Doug Thorson; personal interviews of Doug Thorson.
Other release applications and releases from Mount Pleasant:

Woodbury County district court records; Webster County district court records.

Duane Wheeler (psuedonym) release: phone conversation with his brother, winter 1996.

Cured certificates: Woodbury County district court records.

Harold McBride after release: personal interview.

Letter about friends' reactions: courtesy of Harold McBride.

Doug Thorson and Billy Ivers after release: personal interviews.

Leo Vandermeer (pseudonym) impressions: author's phone conversation, July 1995.

Thorson on Vandermeer: author's interview with Doug Thorson.

CHAPTER 19: CLOSING THE BOOKS

Reward fund: *The Sioux City Journal*, November 13, 1957.

Closed inquest: *The Sioux City Journal*, January 29, 1958.

CHAPTER 20: FIGHTING BACK

Pete Reynolds background and arrest: personal interviews with Pete Reynolds (pseudonym), September and December 1995, and January 1996; *The Sioux City Journal*, September 25, 1958.

J.B. Kuhler arrest and confession of embezzlement: interviews with Pete Reynolds and Dick Burke; confidential source.

Kuhler sentencing: *The Sioux City Journal*, October 1, 1958, and January 30, 1959.

List of occupations of those arrested in morals roundup: *The Sioux City Press-Dispatch*, October 2, 1958.

Press-Dispatch **editorial:** October 9, 1958.

Press-Dispatch **editorial cartoon:** October 30, 1958.

O'Brien cautionary statement: *The Sioux City Journal*, October 25, 1958.

O'Brien calls for national criminal sexual psychopath law: *The Sioux City Journal*, November 3, 1958.

Pete Reynolds as pariah in Sioux City: personal interview.
Complaints of lenient sentence: *The Sioux City Journal*,
October 5, 1958.
Pete changes his plea: author's interviews with Pete Reynolds;
court documents, Woodbury County district court.
Case of Dr. Knott: court documents for Peirce D. Knott and
Kurt Kistenmacher (pseudonym), Woodbury County district
court; *The Sioux City Journal*, October 1 and 2, November
16, December 16 and 19, 1958, and June 10, 1959; conver-
sation with Madeleine Burke; conversations with knowledge-
able sources.
Kistenmacher employment: *Polk's Sioux City* directories,
1950s and 1960s.
Pete Reynolds grand jury testimony and trial: Woodbury
County district court documents; district court minutes,
December 14–22, 1959; *The Sioux City Journal*, December
24, 1959 and January 19, 1961; personal conversations with
Pete Reynolds and Richard Rhinehart.
Judge Paradise background: *The Sioux City Journal*, February
16, 1956, April 12 and May 24, 1966, and July 11, 1970;
The Des Moines Register, August 27, 1939.
Reynolds after verdict and account of encounter with Schultz:
personal interview with Pete Reynolds.
Dick Burke "on crusade": author interview with Rhinehart.
O'Brien's version: author's interview with Don O'Brien,
September 13, 1996.

CHAPTER 21: CRIMES OF THE PAST 1
Triplett appeals: *The Sioux City Journal*, September 15,
1955, and November 14, 1956; *The Des Moines Register*,
May 1, 1958; *State v. Triplett, 79 North Western Reporter*,
2nd series, Iowa, pp. 391-398; Bartels, pp. 60-61; phone

conversation with William Abels, December 1995.

Triplett contacts Iowa School of Law: Bartels, pp. 53-59; phone conversation with Robert Bartels, 1996.

"Never drawed a sober breath": George Thomas's interview with Triplett in "Personal History," courtesy of George Thomas.

Bartels meets Triplett: Bartels, pp. 63-66.

Appeal of decision: author's conversations with Robert Bartels and Bill Sturges; Bartels, pp. 66-75; *The Des Moines Register*, October 15, 1972.

Sturges's conversation with Mike Dull and visit to former sheriff: personal interview with Bill Sturges.

Disintegration of case: Bartels, pp. 95-122; personal conversations with Bartels and Kay Dull, September 1995.

Mrs. Jensen (Bremmers) speaks out: *The Des Moines Register*, October 14, 1972.

Le Mars hearing and throwing out of Triplett's conviction: Bartels, pp. 130-137; *The Des Moines Register*, October 17, 1972; *The Sioux City Journal*, October 18, 1972; personal conversations with Bill Sturges.

Flood's reaction: *The Sioux City Journal*, October 18, 1972.

Mrs. Jensen's heart attack and death: author's interview with Karen Bremmers Hayden; *The Sioux City Journal*, February 26, 1975.

CHAPTER 22: CRIMES OF THE PAST 2

Don O'Brien's Kennedy connection: *The Sioux City Journal*, November 22, 1988.

O'Brien's inauspicious beginning as U.S. attorney: *The Sioux City Journal*, July 9, 1993.

O'Brien political background: *The Sioux City Journal*, September 30, 1968, and April 1, 1969.

McGovern's praise: *The Sioux City Journal*, July 9, 1993.
O'Brien's nomination and opposition to him: *The Des Moines Register*, December 4, 1977, and September 7 and 28, 1978; *The Des Moines Register*, October 4 and 5, 1978; American Bar Association press release, October 3, 1978; Statement of Thomas E. Deacy Jr. and Don H. Reuben before the Committee of the Judiciary, October 4, 1978; author's phone interviews with Thomas Deacy and Don Reuben.
O'Brien and the Triplett recording: Bartels, p. 114.
O'Brien's problem in defending himself: confidential source; guest opinion article by Don O'Brien, *The Des Moines Register*, November 4, 1977.
O'Brien before the Senate: *The Des Moines Register*, October 4, 5, and 7, 1978.
Sturges's view: author's interview with Bill Sturges, April 4, 1996.
Culver's harangue: Abourezk, *Advise & Dissent*; p. 158; *The Des Moines Register*, October 6 and 7, 1978.
ABA reaction to confirmation: author's telephone interviews with Don Reuben and Thomas Deacy, 1996.
O'Brien as decent person and competent lawyer: Abourezk, p. 157.
Abourezk's defense of O'Brien as champion of "little people": Ibid, p. 158.
"Just bullshit": author's interview with Thomas Deacy Jr.
O'Brien's decision in male-to-female transsexual case: *The Des Moines Register*, May 15, 1979; author's interview with O'Brien.

CHAPTER 23: SEX-CRIME PANIC
Conversations with Doug Thorson, Billy Ivers, Pete Reynolds, Gary Paul Marsh, and Harold McBride: author's interviews with them, 1995 and 1996.

Don O'Brien quotes: author's interviews with O'Brien, July 21, 1995 and September 13, 1996.

Wendell Pendleton statements: author's telephone interview with Pendleton, 1996.

Karen Bremmers Hayden comments: author's telephone interview with her, September 1996.

Robert Bartels comments: author's telephone interview.

Triplett and teenage boys: confidential source.

Law student's interview with Triplett: courtesy of George Thomas.